# Writing Revolution in Latin America

# Writing Revolution in Latin America

## From Martí to García Márquez to Bolaño

**Juan E. De Castro**

Vanderbilt University Press
Nashville

Library of Congress Cataloging-in-Publication Data
Names: De Castro, Juan E., 1959- author.
Title: Writing revolution in Latin America : from Marti to Garcia Marquez to
    Bolano / Juan De Castro.
Description: Nashville : Vanderbilt University Press, [2019] | Includes
    bibliographical references and index. |
Identifiers: LCCN 2019010305 (print) | LCCN 2019020238 (ebook) | ISBN
    9780826522603 (ebook) | ISBN 9780826522580 | ISBN
    9780826522580 (hardcover) | ISBN 9780826522597
    (paperback | ISBN 9780826522603 (ebook)
Subjects: LCSH: Latin American fiction--20th century--History and criticism.
    | Revolutionary literature, Latin American--History and criticism. |
    Revolutions in literature.
Classification: LCC PQ7082.N7 (ebook) | LCC PQ7082.N7 D4 2019 (print) | DDC
    863/.60998—dc23
LC record available at https://lccn.loc.gov/2019010305

*Para Magdalena*

# Contents

# Acknowledgments

This book has benefitted from the comments made by friends and colleagues in various stages of its composition. In particular, I must single out Nicholas Birns and Ignacio López-Calvo who generously read the manuscript. Additionally, Wilfrido H. Corral and James Fuerst made useful suggestions. Vanderbilt University Press's two anonymous readers made valuable comments. The book is infinitely better thanks to them. Obviously, all remaining flaws are my responsibility.

I am particularly grateful to the Vanderbilt University Press editors Zachary Gresham, for his enthusiasm for this project, and Joell Smith-Borne, for her work on the manuscript.

Mariano Siskind generously provided me with the text of the lecture he gave at the New School.

Earlier versions of sections of the fourth chapter, "Revolution after the Demise of Revolution: Roberto Bolaño and Carla Guelfenbein on Social Change," appeared in *Roberto Bolaño as World Literature* (Bloomsbury, 2017).

Like everything worthwhile I do, this book would not have been possible without the support of my wife Magdalena.

# Introduction

*Writing Revolution in Latin America: From Martí to García Márquez to Bolaño* studies the depiction of revolution in Latin American fiction. While the book begins by analyzing the first reactions to Marxist revolutionary ideas on the part of the region's radical intellectuals, it emphasizes novels written from the 1960s to the present by such major figures as Gabriel García Márquez, Carlos Fuentes, Mario Vargas Llosa, and Roberto Bolaño. These are the years when intense revolutionary enthusiasm, at least among the region's intelligentsia and students, progressively transformed into a generalized, though far from unanimous, belief in the free market as the solution for Latin America's social problems.[1]

From the Rio Grande to Patagonia, the ideological evolution from a revolutionary to a neoliberal mainstream was a consequence of, on the one hand, repression, dictatorships, and economic crises during the 1970s and beyond and, on the other, the political hardening of the Cuban Revolution beginning in the late 1960s and the implosion of "real existing socialism," which culminated with the fall of the Soviet bloc countries in 1989. The writers and works studied in this monograph are placed in dialogue with the political and historical evolution of the region, but not by means of a "vulgar" Marxist view of literature in which social changes are mechanically reflected in narrative. Through the analysis of several of the most important writers of the last fifty years, *Writing Revolution* provides a diachronic view of the political evolution of Latin America from the 1960s to the present. Despite once widely held clichéd views of the region as peopled by what essayist Carlos Rangel called "good revolutionaries," the evolution of the region is actually representative of global historical trends.[2] However, this study does not deny the tragic specificity of the region's history, nor the particularities of its social trajectory. This difference is, after all, one of the reasons that makes the study of Latin American culture of interest.

That said, unlike writers or, more generally, citizens in the United States or Western Europe, many Latin Americans saw the Cuban Revolution that once inspired so many to dream as an inherently local, even personal, event. Similarly, the Pinochet dictatorship in Chile, which served as the laboratory for many of the neoliberal policies that today seem commonsense to so many in the United States and Europe, was also seen as local.[3] Nor were the brutal military dictatorships in Argentina and Uruguay seen as foreign affairs. Given this generalized feeling of personal involvement on the part of the writers here studied, it makes sense that, as Diana Sorensen notes, "the Latin American difference is one of intensity, and that it is framed by the twin rhythms of euphoria and despair" (3). But the historical process that led from widely shared utopian expectations to neoliberal reaction was not exclusive to the region. Therefore, the study of these Latin American works and authors provides an angled view of the intellectual, cultural, and political processes that have changed the world as a whole.

Given the loose sense the word *revolution* often holds nowadays—it is used equally to describe political movements of reform, such as Ukraine's Orange Revolution; groups of isolated protests, such as Hong Kong's Umbrella revolution; or even televised wrestling events, such as WWE's New Year Revolution—it may be necessary to specify that in this study it means a radical reordering of society. As we will see, for the authors studied, revolution in this sense is generally associated with socialism.

Though using revolution to describe a wrestling match may be a typically twenty-first century issue, already in 1928 José Carlos Mariátegui commented on the polysemous meanings of the word in the Latin America of his time: "In this America of small revolutions, the same word Revolution frequently lends itself to misunderstanding. We have to reclaim it rigorously and intransigently. We have to restore its strict and exact meaning" ("Anniversary and Balance Sheet" 128). Underlying Mariátegui's complaint is the habit of calling military coups, or the coming to power of popular political leaders, "revolutions." While he describes, for instance, the wars of independence from Spain, as well as the French Revolution and its offshoots, as "the liberal revolution,"

Mariátegui, who is still writing under the spell of the 1917 Russian Revolution, insists on the need to reserve the contemporary use of the word for socialist movements.[4]

In his *Keywords*, Raymond Williams writes about the historical origins for this meaning of the word:

> The French Revolution made the modern sense of revolution decisive. The older sense of a restoration of lawful authority, though used in occasional justification, was overridden by the sense of necessary innovation of a new order, supported by the increasingly positive sense of progress. Of course, the sense of achievement of the original rights of man was also relevant. This sense of making a new *human* order was always as important as that of overthrowing an old order. (273)

For Williams, the French Revolution thus represents the main example of the term. However, like Mariátegui, he also notes the centrality of socialism in later definitions of the word:

> The sense of revolution as bringing about a wholly new social order was greatly strengthened by the socialist movement, and this led to some complexity in the distinction between revolutionary and *evolutionary* socialism. From one point of view the distinction was between violent overthrow of the old order and peaceful and constitutional change. From another point of view, which is at least equally valid, the distinction was between working for a wholly new social order (socialism as opposed to capitalism) and the more limited modification or reform of an existing order ("the pursuit of equality" within a "mixed economy" or "post-capitalist society"). (273)

As we will see, whether they support or oppose the idea of revolution, all the authors in this study respond to this maximalist definition as predicated on the "overthrow of the old order" and on "working for a wholly new social order."[5] Moreover, with the obvious exceptions of Martí and Mariátegui, who are, however, still reacting to this Marxist view of revolution, its meaning is primarily defined by Cuba's revolution.

While the Cuban Revolution—together with Vietnam's struggles for independence from France and then against neocolonial interference from the United States—fueled to a great degree the activism of the 1960s throughout the world, the impact of the political process led by Fidel Castro and the charismatic *barbudos* was understandably much greater and more direct in Latin America.[6] As Rafael Rojas notes, "For the young writers of the so-called 'boom of the Latin American novel' . . . who attempted to revolutionize the narrative of their countries, the coming to power of a groups of revolutionaries . . . of their own generation was enthralling" (*La polis literaria* ch. 3). But beyond this generational element, the coming to power of the Cuban guerrilla fighters seemed to prove that revolution, in the sense defined above, seen as synonymous with economic and social modernization, was possible in a region that had until then seemed tied to the anchor of neocolonial institutions and culture. The eloquent words of Mario Vargas Llosa in "Literature Is Fire," his acceptance speech for the Rómulo Gallegos Award for his novel *The Green House* (1967), illustrate the role played by Cuba in the radical imagination of the time:

> But within ten, twenty or fifty years, the hour of social justice will arrive in our countries, as it has in Cuba, and the whole of Latin America will have freed itself from the order that despoils it, from the castes that exploit it, from the forces that now insult and repress it. And I want this hour to arrive as soon as possible and for Latin America to enter, once and for all, a world of dignity and modernity, and for socialism to free us from our anachronism and our horror. (73)

Much could be said about "Literature Is Fire," one of Vargas Llosa's best-known nonfiction pieces, and I will return to it throughout the book. But what interests me now is the manner in which it reflects the centrality of Cuba for the radical imagination of the Latin American 1960s.

As we will study in the second chapter of the book, Cuba is a central obsession not only ideologically but personally for the four major Boom writers we consider. In addition to the common goal of modernizing the region's novel, it is their shared passion for the Cuban Revolution that brought them together. In fact, all to a greater or lesser degree participated in the cultural institutions of the Cuban Revolution and were seen by the revolutionary government as useful allies. Though García Márquez, Vargas Llosa, Fuentes, and Cortázar will continue writing for many years after the 1960s, the Boom qua group will fall apart toward the beginning of the 1970s, precisely over disagreements about how to respond to the Cuban government's growing repression of intellectuals.[7] Moreover, even those later writers who were not directly involved with the Cuban Revolution, such as Manuel Puig, Roberto Bolaño, and Carla Guelfenbein, are responding—directly or indirectly—to a vision of revolution shaped by Cuba.

The impact of the Cuban Revolution on the region's intelligentsia, its major writers, and its reading public was not, however, only due to the surprising success of the Cuban revolutionaries against overwhelming odds,[8] its generational appeal, or the attraction of utopian ideas during the decade. As Vargas Llosa noted in "Literature Is Fire," there were structural social and economic reasons why the status quo was completely unacceptable, and Cuba, for at least a decade, seemed to many to truly be "the first free territory of America," as the island's government liked to claim.[9]

Throughout the 1950s, Peru, Argentina, Paraguay, Nicaragua, Venezuela, Colombia, the Dominican Republic, Guatemala, Honduras, and Cuba itself were governed by repressive rightwing dictatorships. This growth in authoritarian leadership was partly the result of changes in US policy toward the region. In fact, the US government paradoxically saw its support of dictatorships not only as a bulwark against communism but also as a way to promote "development."[10] Starting in the 1950s, anti–North Americanism, anti-imperialism, and the struggle for freedom, no matter how we define the latter, were for many Latin Americans rightly seen as imbricated.[11]

———

This book offers a diachronic, even if unavoidably incomplete, view of the appearance, rise, and fall of the "structure of feeling" that believed in revolution as the answer to the region's problems and that after 1959 saw Cuba as its principal example.[12] The first chapter, "Revolution before Revolution," is divided into two sections, dedicated respectively to José Martí, the Cuban poet and patriot, and to José Carlos Mariátegui, often considered the "first Marxist" of Latin America. The study of these two central figures in the region's radical intellectual traditions helps set the background against which one can compare later representations and theorizations inspired by and responding to the Cuban Revolution.

Martí, who is the central figure in the Cuban national imagination, was also the first major Latin American writer to respond to the ideas of Karl Marx; he did so in an 1883 "Carta" (Letter), as his collaborations with the Argentine newspaper *La Nación* were called. In this text, Martí is extremely critical of the violence that the Cuban author identifies with Marxism and the labor movement that subscribed to its ideas. Instead, Martí embraces a reformism based on the optimistic perspective on US democracy he held at the time of writing. This first section also studies the tensions between Martí's explicitly antirevolutionary reformism and the appropriation of his work and figure by the Cuban Revolution.

The second section of the chapter highlights Mariátegui's vision of how to bring about a revolution in Peru and Latin America more generally. While, for him, the goal is always socialism and the way to achieve it is through revolution, Mariátegui proposes a cultural politics that, without rejecting the need for revolution, sees change in social mentalities as a necessary preamble. Moreover, in his political proposals, Mariátegui lays out a series of reformist measures he believed were necessary, such as establishing what today we would call a welfare state and implementing land reform. Mariátegui, in his cultural and political writings, fuses culture and politics and reform and revolution. Despite their profound differences, both authors attempt in their writings and actions to navigate the then-uncharted waters that separate reform from revolution in Latin America.

"Boom in the Revolution, Revolution in the Boom," the second chapter, analyzes how four major writers of the 1960s—Colombian Gabriel García Márquez and Peruvian Mario Vargas Llosa, both future Nobel laureates, as well as their close confrères Mexican Carlos Fuentes and Argentine Julio Cortázar—attempted to reconcile literature and revolution in their critical and narrative practices. This chapter also has two sections.

The first takes the participation of Vargas Llosa and Cortázar in a panel titled "The Intellectual and Politics" convened in April 1970 during the Amérique Latine Non-officielle series of cultural events in Paris, as the starting point for the analysis of the relationship between the Boom writers and the Cuban Revolution during the 1960s and beyond. Despite some differences, they all saw their novels as intrinsically revolutionary precisely because of their embrace of modernist literary techniques. However, though the Cuban government considered these authors to be key allies throughout the 1960s, toward the end of the decade the revolution's growing political and artistic rigidity led to a rift between the Castro regime and the Boom writers. This growing distance between literary and political revolution, manifested by the surprising aggression of the mainly leftist Amérique Latine Non-officielle audience toward Vargas Llosa and Cortázar, came to a head with the jailing of poet Heberto Padilla for supposedly antirevolutionary activities one year later. (Padilla would be freed after a self-incriminating confession.)

The second part of the chapter looks at two key novels of the 1960s—Fuentes's *The Death of Artemio Cruz* (1962) and García Márquez's *One Hundred Years of Solitude* (1967)—and examines how they depict putative revolutionary movements. While neither text deals primarily with Cuba or, for that matter, with socialist revolution, both offer surprisingly dark views on supposedly progressive political movements: Fuentes's novel presents a bitter portrayal of the Mexican revolution that is contrasted with an idealized version of the Spanish republic as a true revolutionary movement. García Márquez, on the other hand, depicts negatively the liberal side during the Colombian violence of the nineteenth and early twentieth century, which is surprising given his family's political background. Paradoxically, Boom writers actively supported the Cuban Revolution and revolution tout court while presenting pessimistic depictions of attempts at social change in their novels.

The third chapter, "The Fall of the Revolutionary and the Return of Liberal Democracy," examines two novels that reflect the growing obsolescence of the belief in revolution after the 1960s. This loss of faith in violent maximalist social change responded to the previously mentioned cultural hardening of the Cuban Revolution, the defeat of all guerrilla movements in the region, except in Central America and Colombia, and the coming to power of military dictatorships in the Southern Cone.

The first section studies Vargas Llosa's *The Real Life of Alejandro Mayta* (1984). This is the only novel written by a member of the core Boom group that represents the Latin American guerrilla movements, even if most of the novel's action is set in 1958.[13] However, by the time the book was written, Vargas Llosa was becoming a supporter and promoter of the reinvigorated free-market ideas proposed by Hernando de Soto and others in Peru. Moreover, he wrote the novel during the early days of the Shining Path insurgency, one of the last and bloodiest guerrilla movements in Latin America, which would lead to the death of nearly seventy thousand Peruvians. The novel reflects this biographical and historical evolution in its criticisms of the ultimate effects of Alejandro Mayta's guerrilla uprising. One of the most striking and—at the time of publication—polemical aspects of the novel is that it presents Mayta not only as a gay man but also as one who, at least conceptually, attempts to reconcile his Marxist beliefs with his sexual identity.

The chapter continues with the analysis of Argentine novelist Manuel Puig's *Kiss of the Spider Woman* (1976). While Puig's narrative as a whole is celebrated for its introduction of gay topics and sensibility, as well as for its interest in popular culture (film and Latin American popular music), *Kiss of the Spider Woman* most thoroughly explores the political options of the 1970s. It does so by depicting an Argentinian jail cell encounter between a gay window dresser (Molina) and a radical activist (Valentín).

The fourth and concluding chapter, "Revolution after the Demise of Revolution," is devoted to the novels and nonfiction writing of Roberto Bolaño, the most celebrated Latin American writer to come of age in the 1990s,[14] as well as to the writings of the also Chilean novelist Carla Guelfenbein, currently one of the country's best-selling authors and the winner of the prestigious Alfaguara Award in 2015 for her *In the Distance with You* (2015).

The first part of the chapter examines how Bolaño explicitly rejects the revolutionary politics of the 1960s. In particular, this section analyzes *Amulet* (1999), a novel that deals with the Mexican prodemocracy youth movement of the 1960s and its brutal repression by the country's government, and his "Caracas Address," given upon receiving the Rómulo Gallegos Award in 1998 for *The Savage Detectives* (1998), the novel that first brought him pan-Hispanic and then world fame. Both *Amulet* and the "Caracas Address" present a dire history of the region's Left as preying on the naive and idealistic Latin American youth during the 1960s.

The second part of the chapter analyzes Carla Guelfenbein's novel *Nadar desnudas* (To swim naked) (2012). *Nadar desnudas* is partly set during the final days of the Salvador Allende government and the early days of the repression unleashed by the Pinochet regime. In the novel's two halves, each marked by one of the tragic 9/11s—the date of both Chile's military coup and the terrorist attack on New York's twin towers—

Guelfenbein explores what she calls "the little history" of personal emotions, joys, and traumas in a style that borrows from the romance novel. While Guelfenbein is sympathetic to Allende's attempt to change Chilean society, *Nadar desnudas* paradoxically also reflects the turn toward commercial narrative styles that nowadays characterize much Latin American writing.

As this introduction details, in this study I provide an overview of the rise and fall of revolution in Latin America. It is my goal to do so without falling into the Scylla of nostalgia, which would imply that the social change these intellectuals and novelists wished was, given the actual social contexts, imminent. Not only was the Cuban Revolution far from the utopia many believed, but, as history would clearly show, the notion that socialism could be easily achieved through guerrilla uprisings was unfounded. But I aim also to avoid the Charybdis of euphoria that celebrates the demise of this desire for social change, as this implies not only that the belief in the imminent success of the revolutionary struggle was misguided, given its specific historical context, but also that the problems that gave rise to that desire for social change—neocolonial structures, injustice, inequality, racism, and the like—have been fully superseded or are in the process of being overcome, and that no comparable injustices have arisen in the last fifty years. That is far from being the case.

# 1

# Revolution before Revolution

## *José Martí and José Carlos Mariátegui*

The year 1959, when the Cuban Revolution came to power, must be placed next to the magical digits 1789 in any revision of Latin American history. After all, if the latter date represents the beginning of the belief in revolution for overcoming obsolete social structures throughout the Western World—and for some, even the birth of modernity itself—1959 marks the moment in the twentieth century when these utopian hopes seemed, for the first time since the heady days of the struggle for independence at the beginning of the nineteenth century, to be fully applicable to the region.

Of course, other events and the dates that represent them are significant in the region. One must mention 1776, when the first American colony began its successful fight for independence from a European power. In fact, the struggles for independence in Spanish America, which are conventionally seen as beginning in 1810, took place under the twin examples of the American and the French revolutions. The United States will be a shining light for the region's struggle against Spain up to and including Cuba. But as the writings of José Martí, the leader of Cuba's struggle for independence, illustrate, by the 1890s the luster of the United States had been dimmed by its imperialist attitudes and actions in the region.[1]

One must also keep in mind 1910, the year the Mexican Revolution began, the last and greatest peasant revolt that also provided one of the first intimations of a truly radical social revolution. The Russian Revolution of 1917—the ten days that shook the world and that seemed for more than a decade to prove that utopia was possible—must also be added to this list. Undeniably, the Mexican and Russian revolutions served as central intellectual and emotional touchstones for the activists and radicals who came of age in the 1920s, such as Peruvian politician Víctor Raúl Haya de la Torre and his compatriot, friend, and later enemy, José Carlos Mariátegui, the region's first major Marxist thinker, among many others.

However, the Mexican Revolution's inability to create a truly modern and egalitarian republic and its rapid ossification into a one-party system—famously described in 1990 as "the perfect dictatorship" by novelist Mario Vargas Llosa—meant that Mexico never fully achieved the role of political model.[2] Proof of the limited appeal of the Mexican Revolution can be found in its representation in literature: from Mariano Azuela's *The Underdogs* (1915), the novel that first portrays the revolution, to Carlos Fuentes's *The Death of Artemio Cruz* (1962), the stress has been on how the Mexican Revolution created an environment of violence and corruption rather than on any potential utopian dimension it may have had.

Likewise, Stalin's rise to power and his creation of a cult of personality and repressive political system destroyed whatever hopes could have been held for real existing socialism. This led to the Soviet Union's loss of allure outside the ideological ghettoes of the Latin American Communist parties. That the region's mass political movements of the first half of the twentieth century were, with the exception of Chile, mostly populist—from Haya's APRA to Peronism—underlines communism's inability to become a successful electoral or subversive movement in the region. Moreover, while nominally committed to promoting a socialist revolution, most Communist parties responded instrumentally to the Soviet Union's political interests. At best, the often small parties engaged in the struggle for civil and human rights, even for democratic processes, while also promoting labor organizing; at worst, they cynically supported whatever local policy or politician the Soviet Union felt was in their best interest. Given the social realities of the region, after the 1930s Communist parties were not interested in promoting socialist revolution—or any type of revolution, for that matter.[3]

It is tempting to add 1979 to this list of dates. This was the year when the Sandinistas toppled one of the oldest US-backed dictatorships, one that dated back to the 1930s. After all, the Sandinista revolution, the last success of the revolutionary Left in Latin America, helped rekindle the enthusiasm of progressive forces throughout the region and beyond. Moreover, it was characterized by a transformative progressive cultural policy that, following in the footsteps of José Vasconcelos's literacy and educational campaigns in 1920s Mexico, and the more successful attempt at promoting literacy in 1960s Cuba, not only advanced basic education, appreciation of literature, and knowledge of the Western classics but also stressed popular literary and artistic creation.[4] But despite this and other partial successes—for instance, in health care—the Sandinistas failed to gain the internal support that characterized the Cuban Revolution, at least during its first years. This may very well originate in the Sandinistas' coming to power as part of "a system of alliances that made possible their eventual victory in July 1979" (Hoyt 13). Furthermore, as Hoyt notes: "Until the signing of the Central American Peace Accord . . . in 1987, the United States funded and trained the contra [anti-Sandinista] army, carried out covert military operations against the Sandinista government, cut off all U.S. foreign aid to Nicaragua, stopped the multilateral lending agencies from lending money to Nicaragua, and from 1985 on, carried out a trade embargo against Nicaragua" (51). In 1990, Sandinista leader Daniel Ortega suffered electoral defeat at the hands of Violeta Chamorro, who, in addition to being the widow of Pedro Chamorro, who had been murdered by the Somoza regime, was a former member of the governmental junta and the director of the main Nicaraguan newspaper *La Prensa*. For these reasons, the lack of a "charismatic Fidel Castro . . . to ignite the passions of the Latin American masses" (Wright 166) and what historian Thomas C. Wright has called "the prevailing climate of reaction in the late 1970s and early 1980s," the Sandinista revolution "did not have an impact of the magnitude of the Cuban Revolution twenty years earlier" (166). The temporary success of the Sandinistas was unable to fully defuse the political skepticism generated by the failures of the Cuban Revolution and the triumph of the Southern Cone dictatorships beginning in 1973. Nor was it able to derail the growing embrace of the free market and liberal democracy by an ever-growing number of Latin Americans. It may not be a coincidence that the fall of Sandinista Nicaragua follows closely the fall of the Soviet bloc in 1989—even if the Nicaraguan Revolution did not imitate the Soviet model. Despite its falling out of power, Wright also notes that "the Nicaraguan Revolution clearly set the agenda for the politics of Central America for over a decade" (166).[5]

After the failure of independence, in which the democratic ideals of the French Revolution and the rationalism of the Enlightenment crashed against the shoals of the region's colonial social structures and conservative Catholic beliefs, after the ossification of both the Mexican and Soviet revolutions and of the political promises that many assigned to them, the Cuban Revolution renewed the promise of a modern egalitarian Latin America just around the corner, even if it lasted for only slightly more than a decade, after which the growing rigidity of the regime undermined its utopian promise.[6]

This brief historical presentation must end with 1989, the year when real existing socialism in Europe broke down, dimming the appeal of socialist ideas throughout the world, including Latin America, despite the ability of the Cuban regime to survive, even if barely.[7]

---

By looking at the writings of two iconic figures of Latin American radicalism—José Martí, the great nineteenth-century poet, essayist, and activist for Cuban independence, and José Carlos Mariátegui, who in the 1920s attempted to apply Marxist ideas to the understanding of Peruvian and Latin American societies and cultures—one can glean insight into the structures of feeling characteristic of the region before 1959, even among those most radical.

In the 1960s, both Martí and Mariátegui would become icons of the Left in their respective countries: Fidel Castro on many an occasion claimed Martí as the revolution's first and greatest influence, and in Peru, General Juan Velasco's left-leaning military government (1969–1975), the United Left of the 1980s, and even the murderous Shining Path celebrated Mariátegui's actions and writings. More importantly, Martí's ubiquity in Cuban revolutionary discourse led to a rediscovery or perhaps reimagining of the radical potential to be found in his classic essays, such as "Our America." The search for precedents for the resurgent Left in the region would transform Mariátegui from a historical footnote into "the first Marxist in America," to use the title of a well-known essay by Italian scholar Antonio Melis. Mariátegui may have been the region's first Marxist because of his creative adaptation of the ideas of the author of *Capital* rather than because of chronology, but forty years earlier, in one of his chronicles from New York City, Martí had written the first response to Karl Marx's actions and ideas by any major Latin American author.[8]

Despite the tendency in the region's scholarship and thought to classify both authors as belonging to a political, ideological, and intellectual continuum—for instance, by claiming Martí as a kind of Third World supplement to Marxism, if not a proto-Marxist, or by stressing the putative influence of the Cuban essayist on Mariátegui, despite a nearly complete lack of textual evidence—there are obvious and significant differences between them.[9] While both came into contact with the figure and ideas of Marx, their reactions were diametrically opposed. Nevertheless, despite their divergent relation to the notion of revolution, in the sense used in this study—that is, as a complete change in social structures leading to the establishment of socialism and modernity—both authors represent the attitudes of Latin Americans before 1959.

### *José Martí on Marx*

As the animator and martyr of the country's struggle for independence and the cornerstone of the country's literary tradition, Martí has loomed large in Cuban history and thought. As Enrico Mario Santí argues, "Cubans at home and abroad revere Martí as the very spirit of their national identity" (141). The appeal of the Cuban patriot helps explain, for instance, why the US would call its propaganda outlet aimed at Cuba Radio Televisión Martí. Not surprisingly, in a widely read interview with Ignacio Ramonet, Fidel Castro proudly stated: "I was first a Martí-an and then became a Martí-an, Marxist and Leninist" (157). By claiming Martí as one of the Cuban Revolution's intellectual progenitors, Castro implicitly presents the revolution as part of the island nation's cultural and political tradition, even as its fulfillment.[10] The proliferation of monuments and homages to the Cuban poet—for instance, the Havana airport is named after him—reflect Martí's centrality to national imaginings within the revolution.[11]

However, after Cuba was declared socialist in 1961, the figure of Martí had to be reconciled with that of Marx. One can identify a division of labor being established by the revolution and its intellectuals between both iconic figures. While Martí, who is generally seen as the quintessential Latin American anti-imperialist, was used to justify the revolution's foreign policy in its opposition to US actions and influence, Marx was presented as the inspiration for the economic changes set in place, even if both were described as mutually complementary intellectual figures.

But this linkage between Martí and Marx had to avoid the obvious hurdle of the German philosopher's absolute ignorance of the existence of the Cuban poet—unsurprising given that Marx died in 1883, twelve years before Martí's heroic death. More importantly, this forced connection had to overcome the Cuban hero's relative lack of interest in Marx: Martí referred directly to the author of *Capital* only on two occasions: in a personal letter and in a "Carta" (Letter)—as the Cuban poet called the chronicles he wrote in New York for the Argentine newspaper *La Nación*—written on 29 March 1883 and, given its length, published in two parts on 13 and 16 May. Not only are these mentions far from univocally positive, but, to add insult to injury, the piece originally published in *La Nación* consistently misspelled Marx as Max![12] Even though Martí's ideas were in flux throughout his life, one can identify certain constant concerns and attitudes. For instance, there is no reason to suppose that he ever changed his evaluation of Marx. This first part of this chapter will thus examine Martí's view of Marxist ideas and of the concept of revolution.

As Santí argues, "Martí's revolutionary nationalism, his aggressively native or indigenous imagination . . . makes him a natural precursor of the post-1959 regime. However, to attempt to demonstrate that Martí was a Marxist, or even a proto-Marxist, has been a more difficult task" (142). It is therefore not surprising that early Cuban Marxists, such as Julio Antonio Mella or Juan Marinello, presented a much more complicated view of Martí's relevance—or lack thereof—to revolutionary politics than did those writing after 1959.

For instance, Mella, in an essay in which he expresses his intense admiration for Martí as an ethical example for Cuban revolutionaries in the 1920s, concludes: "Even though José Martí was a patriot . . . he was . . . the representative of a democratic bourgeoisie [that was] still capable of achieving much, because it had not yet fulfilled its historical mission" (35). Thus, for Mella, Martí "was the interpreter of the need for social transformation in a specific social moment. Today, equally revolutionary, he would have become the interpreter of the social need of this moment" (32). In other words, Martí had been a revolutionary in the late nineteenth century because the island, in addition to still being a colony, had not yet experienced a bourgeois revolution. By the 1920s, after capitalism had been fully implemented, Martí, in order to be a true revolutionary, would have had to embrace socialism and its call for revolution.

Marinello's 1935 evaluation of Martí is much harsher—he even calls him "a great failure" (121). He also stresses the caducity of his ideas: "Martí's ideas, as all skillful political leaders know are by now 'defeated ideas.' The dominant political ideas are always the offspring of the dominant class. The bourgeoisie brought [to Cuba] liberalism, romanticism, and the mirage of democracy. Today the bourgeoisie is as a class as defeated as the ideas it imported" (122). But like Mella, he concludes: "If Martí were alive today . . . he would stand next to those who, following Lenin, put Marx's ideas into practice, know that the revolution is not a fortunate plot turn but rather the sharp and endless struggle for a humanity without oppressors or oppressed" (123). While Marinello seems to be putting the ideological cart before reality's horse—after all, he had no way of knowing there would be a revolution some twenty-five years in the future—he is also identifying Martí's actual ideas with the liberalism that in the late nineteenth century seemed to many to represent the best of social proposals (as it would again in the late twentieth and early twenty-first centuries).

Thus, for both Mella and Marinello, Martí's ideas are no longer relevant. There is, however, the intimation that, given his ethical exemplarity, if Martí were living in the 1920s or 1930s, he would be a Marxist activist and thinker. In fact, other, perhaps more radical, Marxists were outright critical of the Cuban hero as an obsolete bourgeois democrat and, therefore, necessarily opposed to working-class interests.[13] However, Mella's and Marinello's opinions are representative of Marxist interpretations of Martí before the Cuban Revolution: admiration for the man but emphasis on the limitations of the political thinker.

As we have seen, Castro claimed Martí as a central intellectual and political inspiration. Already in "History Will Absolve Me" (1953), the founding document of the Cuban revolutionary movement though clearly not a Marxist text, Castro states that "Martí was the inspiration for July 26" (52). While the Cuban Revolution "began with roots

firmly planted in the island's anti-Communist center-left political parties . . . In April 1961, just before the invasion of a CIA-trained exile
army at the Bay of Pigs, Castro declared the Cuban Revolution socialist;
by the end of the year he was calling it Marxist-Leninist" (Iber 117).
After 1961, if not earlier, the intellectual juggling that had characterized
earlier Marxist attempts to incorporate Martí as a symbolic precedent,
even as his ideas were rejected, was no longer possible. In an article
that describes Castro as "Martí's reader in chief," Rafael Saumell-Muñoz
argues that "Castro has placed Martí's texts in an even more privileged
place than the one they held before 1959. . . . They are—together with
those by Marx, Engels, and Lenin—the 'master narratives' (historical,
political, philosophical) that justify Castro's power" (101). It was thus
now necessary for the intellectuals aligned with the Cuban Revolution
to find in Martí the "intellectual author" of the socialist regime. Ethical
exemplarity could no longer stand in for political relevance.[14]

On occasion, and when responding to other ideological contexts,
Roberto Fernández Retamar, the best-known intellectual identified
with the Cuban Revolution, has proposed Martí as a supplement to
Marx. For instance, in an interview with Goffredo Diana and John Beverley, Fernández Retamar argues that one should see in Martí a kind
of precursor or, better said, an early proponent of postcolonialism, the
kind of social analysis associated with Edward Said, Gayatri Spivak, and
Homi Bhabha:

> With due respect to Fanon and others, to my mind the most
> important forerunner, if not the actual founder, of post- or, as I prefer,
> anticolonial thought is Martí, who unfortunately is still poorly known
> outside of Latin America. From the vantage point of New York City,
> with the consciousness of a colonized subject, combined with a global
> perspective and a commitment to "the poor of the earth," Martí was
> one of the initiators of a different reading of modernity, a reading of
> modernity from the point of view of its other. (422)

Implicit in the interview is the notion that Martí, as the founder of
"a reading of modernity from the point of view of its other," can supplement and correct the Eurocentrism still present in Marx, but not only
in Marx. Fernández Retamar's proposal of a postcolonial Martí, often

completely delinked from Cuba's political history, has met with notable success.[15]

But are these ideas compatible with what Martí actually wrote about Marx in his "Carta"? Given the variety of topics Martí writes about in the piece—the funerals of John Payne, the author of "Home Sweet Home," and of George Elliott, a bare-knuckle boxer; Columbia University's decision to found a college for women; and a costume ball at the Vanderbilt mansion—and the fact that many of these are of little immediate interest to current readers, the letter has never been translated in whole into English. Most versions understandably limit themselves to Martí's words about Marx included in his depiction of the Cooper Union Memorial Meeting on occasion of the German philosopher's death. Even in Spanish, it is best-known in abridged versions that concentrate on Martí's comments on Marx.[16] The circulation of the text in truncated versions has led to a distorted understanding of Martí's views about the author of *Capital*.

Esther Allen's translation of sections of Martí's "Carta," significantly titled "Tributes to Karl Marx Who Has Died," begins thus:

> Through gloomy taverns, boxing clubs, and dark streets, the youthful throng makes its way with broad shoulders and hands like clubs, which can drain the life from a man as if draining beer from a glass. But cities are like bodies; they have some noble viscera and some that are foul. The angry army of workingmen is full of other soldiers, as well. . . . Some of them have become fanatics out of love, others are fanatics out of hatred. All that can be seen of some is their teeth. Others—Justice's gentlemen—are handsome and well groomed and have unctuous voices. On these fields, the Frenchman does not hate the German nor the German the Russian, nor does the Italian abominate the Austrian, for all are united in a shared hatred. And this is the weakness of their institutions and the reason they inspire fear, for those that know that Justice bears no children—for love alone engenders them!—keep their distance from the battlefields of wrath.[17] ("Tributes" 130–31)

This version of Martí's "Carta" eliminates approximately two and half pages of text. In fact, the youthful throng with which this text begins is a clear reference to the masses who had raucously said goodbye to the dead boxer George—or Jorge, as Martí calls him—Elliott. This helps explain the mentions of taverns, boxing clubs, and "hands like clubs" in the passage. For Martí, boxing fans celebrated a brutal pastime, even death, rather than a noble sport. Only a few sentences earlier, Martí resorts to what has become one of the most pointed insults in Cuban culture in his description of Elliott's admirers: "He who has seen worms in Cuba can have an idea of what the multitude was like" ("Carta" 239).[18]

The comparison of cities to bodies and social groups to its organs is central in this passage. In the case of New York City, the topic of this and many other of Martí's "letters," it is clear that the "youthful throng" of boxing fans is one of the "foul" viscera. Among the noble organs one must count those who mourned the poet John Payne during a ceremony organized by the city of New York before the poet was transferred to Washington, DC, for burial: "The poet had less companions than the boxer, but the great procession is invisible. It is beautiful that a financial city honor a poet" ("Carta" 238). Ironically, in this text the great inspirer of the Cuban Revolution presents rich financiers much more favorably than the mostly poor boxing enthusiasts.

In Martí's "Carta," the working class resembles New York City. Both are composed of noble and foul parts. It is true, as the passage from Esther Allen's translation makes clear, that there are workers who, like the boxing enthusiasts, found their milieu in darkness and violence. One can thus list "negative" adjectives that Martí associates with some of the workers mourning Marx: they are described as being like animals in their glaring of teeth, others are fanatics, and so forth. But, there are "other soldiers" described as associated with love and justice, even if their actions are ultimately distorted by their having become "fanatics."

The working-class crowd attending the Cooper Union memorial is thus presented as motley. It includes beauty as well as ugliness. Martí's division of the working class into positive and negative elements overlaps with analogous related national, cultural, and even intellectual distinctions: "The Americans tend to resolve the concrete matter at hand while those from abroad raise it to an abstract plane. Good sense and the fact of having been born into a free cradle make the men of this place slow to wrath. The rage of those from abroad is roiling and explosive because the prolonged enslavement has repressed and concentrated it" ("Tributes" 131). Martí favors North American pragmatism over European radical theory, and North American reformism over European engagement in the class struggle. He sees North American virtues as originating in the "free cradle"—that is, democratic society and its institutions—in which the US working class has developed. These virtues are threatened by a European mentality trapped by the political and intellectual patterns developed in a struggle framed by the "Old World's" monarchical and totalitarian institutions.[19] However, Martí obviously sees a potential for positive social development in the American workers—and in "Justice's gentlemen" and the "fanatics out of love," if these belong to a different group.[20] It is the mostly European leaders who he finds troubling and in whom he identifies the potential of undermining working-class virtue: "But the rotten apple must not be allowed to spoil the whole healthy barrel—though it could!" ("Tributes" 131).

Given Martí's celebration of democracy and passionate opposition to anything smacking of the class struggle, it is not surprising that his description of Marx in the 1883 "Carta" is, like that of the working class that celebrates him, ambivalent. Already in the introductory paragraph to the complete version of the letter, Martí presents the author of *Capital* as "that German of silky soul and iron hand" ("Carta" 237). Moreover, in a frequently quoted passage, he notes:

> Karl Marx has died. He deserves to be honored for he placed himself on the side of the weak. But it is not the man who points out the harm and burns with generous eagerness to remedy it who does well—it is the man who advocates a mild remedy. To set men against men is an appalling task. The forced bestialization of some men for the profit of others stirs our indignation. But that indignation must be vented in such a way that the beast ceases to be, without escaping its bonds and causing fear. ("Tributes" 131).

While Marx is praised for having taken the side of the weak, in this context he is chastised for having argued for revolution as the solution to class exploitation. Again, reform and ameliorative measures are presented as the correct solution to social problems. Of course, Marx would have argued that he was not preaching violence. As Marx and Engels famously put it:

The history of all hitherto existing society is the history of class struggles.

Freeman and slave, patrician and plebeian, lord and serf, guild-master and journeyman, in a word, oppressor and oppressed, stood in constant opposition to one another, carried on an uninterrupted, now hidden, now open fight, a fight that each time ended, either in a revolutionary reconstitution of society at large, or in the common ruin of the contending classes.

In the earlier epochs of history, we find almost everywhere a complicated arrangement of society into various orders, a manifold gradation of social rank. In ancient Rome we have patricians, knights, plebeians, slaves; in the Middle Ages, feudal lords, vassals, guild-masters, journeymen, apprentices, serfs; in almost all of these classes, again, subordinate gradations.

The modern bourgeois society that has sprouted from the ruins of feudal society has not done away with class antagonisms. It has but established new classes, new conditions of oppression, new forms of struggle in place of the old ones. (34–35)

In other words, the class struggle and the violence it may create is inevitable given that all societies are built on the exploitation of one or more classes. The violence that Martí decries has its roots in the structure of capitalist society rather than in the ill will of foreign or local union leaders and militants.

Bruno Bosteels is thus correct when he argues that "Martí, then, can almost be said to want to take the class struggle out of Marxism" (33), if one erases "almost" from the sentence. As Bosteels also notes, for Martí, "Marx would have been the Apostle of the religion of hatred instead of love, of war instead of peace" (32). Against Marx's putative cult of violence, Martí would, like many after him, believe that all you need is love.[21] The ending of the section devoted to the memorial makes clear the Cuban poet's ultimate evaluation of Marx. He ends it by commenting on the music played in Marx's honor: "Music is heard and choirs ring out, but it is not the music of peace" ("Tributes" 133).

But while Martí's criticism of Marx is consistent with his stress (at least in 1883) on the peaceful resolution of social problems, the superficiality of his presentation of Marx's ideas lead one to ask whether he had actually read any of the latter's works.

In the "Carta," Martí acknowledges Marx's importance as an economic and social analyst. The Cuban patriot describes the German philosopher as a "profound seer into the causes of human misery and the destinies of men" and as having "studied the means of establishing the world on new bases" ("Tributes" 131–32), implying direct knowledge of his writing. However, in the "Carta" Martí makes no explicit reference to any of the German philosopher's works or characteristic concepts. While Martí criticizes Marx for what he takes to be the latter's role as an agitator who "set men against men," there is no explicit mention of the "class struggle," though there is an implicit rejection of the concept. Although the Cuban writer laments the "forced bestialization of some men for the profit of others," there is no reference to Marxian notions of surplus value or exploitation.

*Capital* only became available in Spanish in 1886 and in English in 1887. However, Martí could have read the French version by M. J. Roy, revised by Marx himself, which had been published serially between 1872 and 1875. Moreover, *The Communist Manifesto* had been translated into English in 1850 and reissued in New York in 1871, the same year in which the first Spanish-language edition of this seminal text by Marx and Engels was published. Since Martí wrote relatively long essays on figures he actually deemed important to his artistic and political development—such as Emerson, Whitman, and the heroes of Latin American independence José de San Martín and Simón Bolívar—this lack of textual and conceptual engagement by a notorious omnivore when it came to books can be interpreted as evidence of the Cuban poet's relative lack of interest in Marx.

Despite the absence of any mention of Marx's theoretical texts, Cathy Login Jrade sees in the letter proof of Martí's affinity with German philosophical idealism, a tradition within which she includes Marx. For Jrade, Martí fully shares the Hegelian/Marxian belief that "every conception of reality presupposes a way of thinking about the world and affects what the world is understood to be" (27). Jrade reads Martí's statement that "Marx studied the means of establishing the world on new bases; he woke the sleepers and showed them how to cast down the cracked pillars" ("Tributes" 131) as congruent with the Cuban patriot's "epistemological and political" "breaking down or breaking out" (Jrade 27). Despite this putative affinity with the German philosophical tradition, Jrade stops short of claiming the direct influence of Marx on

Martí: "Whether or not he was introduced to these ideas by German philosophers, such as Hegel or Marx, Martí demonstrates a receptivity to this 'new' way of thinking" (27). That said, Jrade sees the "Carta," together with other of Martí's writings, as proof of Martí's affinity with the German philosophical tradition's stress on the dialectical relationship between subject and object. However, she does not deal with Martí's criticisms of Marx, probably because she uses truncated versions of the letter.[22] Moreover, given Martí's lack of direct references to Marx's writings, his criticisms of the German socialist, and the pervasive influence of German idealism in the late nineteenth century, it is probable that Martí's acquaintance with this philosophical tradition came from other, perhaps indirect, sources.

As he introduces the many topics covered in the article, Martí describes Marx as "very famous" (*famosísimo*) ("Carta" 237). It is likely that Martí is implicitly referring to Marx's coverage in the press, due to the importance given to his death, as well as to his presence in newspapers and magazines before his demise.[23] In its obituary on 16 March, the *New York Sun*, a newspaper for which Martí had worked, described Marx in the most flattering of terms—"a vigorous and fruitful thinker"—and even concluded with the famous call for worker unity with which the *Communist Manifesto* ends ("A Vigorous and Fruitful Thinker" 66). But in addition to being frequently mentioned in working-class publications, such as *Voice of the People* or the US-based German-language publication *New Yorker Volkszeitung*, Marx had been occasionally featured in mainstream publications. For instance, both the *Chicago Tribune* (1879) and the *New York Sun* (1880) published interviews with him. Martí must have known of these interviews. Moreover, selections from Marx's writings, including *Capital*, were published in the workers' press. One can therefore assume that Martí had at least a superficial knowledge of Marx's basic ideas.

Bosteels correctly notes that despite the nods found in this letter toward Marx as an important social theorist, "Martí considers the true labor of the coauthor of *The Communist Manifesto* . . . his role as a political organizer" (30). As Martí writes, "The International was his work" (not *Capital* or *The Communist Manifesto*, one can add) ("Tributes" 131). Contradicting his references to the German philosopher's analytical abilities, Martí's evaluation is almost exclusively based on his impressions of Marx and his followers as labor organizers and agitators.

While one can convincingly argue that Marx's organizing efforts were, after all, a praxis informed by his theories, this praxis is precisely what is dismissed by the Cuban poet. For Martí, Marx's activity as an organizer of the working class promotes violence rather than dialogue, and frontal opposition rather than compromise.

Martí ends his 1883 "Carta" with a description of a costume ball held at the Vanderbilt mansion on Fifth Avenue. While the Cuban poet describes in rapturous terms the brilliance of the mansion, the party, and the elegance of the guests, his descriptions ultimately shine a light on the beautiful people's conspicuous consumption. Martí's stress on the many costumes that remind the reader of French and other royalty and courtiers highlights the relationship between the time of his writing and that of the French Revolution that destroyed the aristocratic and feudal world the Vanderbilts and their friends emulate and celebrate:

> The party has been taken amiss, and it is beginning to be said that such displays of excessive luxury and gracefulness of garment are ill suited to these times of wrath, revolt and ravenous and inflamed masses. The unfortunate do not understand them and the gravity of the times do not bear well with them; they are inappropriate to a republican country and are neither forgiven nor forgotten by the army that advances in darkness. . . . For the ball was given as a display of wealth and has been received as a slap in the face by the envious, miserable and discontented masses. The French Convention is still in session! But here, wisdom is seated at its side. ("Tributes" 138–39)

Despite Martí's dislike of violence, he believed that the world had changed in 1789, that the French Revolution had established a new epoch in which aristocracies, including those based on wealth or ability, could no longer exercise power autocratically. After all, as the passage states, "The French Convention is still in session." Martí thus returns to the topics mentioned in his description of the Marx memorial. However, Martí, who is now looking at US society as a whole, presents a much more optimistic conclusion than in his opinions on the memorial. Instead of being guided by the demands of the class struggle, the United States will tackle the tensions present between the wealthy and "the discontented masses" by embracing wisdom, that is, by means of reform. The goals of the French Convention—liberty, equality and solidarity—can be achieved by democratic means. At the end of the article, Martí reaffirms his optimism regarding reform in the United States based on his belief in the pragmatic nature of the US working class and in the functionality and solidity of its democracy. But as Martí's pre-1959 Marxist critics correctly noted, in no moment does Martí's reformism veer into full-fledged anticapitalism.

A little analyzed section of Martí's "Carta" strikes me as representative of the Cuban poet's politics, at least in 1883. I am referring to Martí's brief comments on Benjamin Franklin Butler, then governor of Massachusetts. In words reminiscent of Christian definitions of God, Martí writes: "Governor Butler is ubiquitous, insomniac, omnipresent, and alarming" ("Tributes" 133). Additionally, he is described as a political equivalent to the French Romantic movement: "He is a governmental romantic: he shakes the dust from the state as the young France of 1830 shook it from the academics" ("Tributes" 133). Butler, at the time one of the most radical politicians in the United States, is thus presented as a force for positive political change. By means of his godlike actions, he is shown as correcting institutions through legal and administrative measures. In the same way that Romanticism modernized French literature without destroying it, Martí sees Butler as bringing democratic institutions and laws up to date without abolishing them.

Martí's mention of Butler, though relatively brief, serves a key function in the "Carta." While in the "Carta" Martí expresses sympathy for the working men and women as a class, he decries their political actions because he sees their intransigence and violence as possibly undermining democratic institutions. Butler, as a public figure, exemplifies Martí's call for political change that respects democratic institutions and processes. As we have seen, Butler "shakes the dust from the state" rather than destroying or replacing it. Butler represents the kind of politics celebrated by Martí in the "Carta" and, arguably, beyond.

Examining the social context underlying Martí's obvious enthusiasm for US political life at the time, as described in the "Carta," provides additional insight. Martí describes Butler's actions as taking place in a society in which "Democrats and Republicans struggle to see who can reform the most and the fastest, so as not to be accused of lacking the spirit of reform" ("Tributes" 132).[24] Martí rejects revolution and any other violent means of achieving social change because he believes reforms are actually being implemented without subverting existing democratic institutions. His criticism of immigrant radical labor activism is framed by this belief in positive US social evolution.

However, Martí's rejection of revolution and class struggle, his embrace of social meliorism, and his stress on dialogue and collaboration as the keystone of union activity and politics, together with his optimistic view of reform in US society, takes place in 1883, well into the Gilded Age, a period synonymous with growing income inequality. Although he was aware of inequality—as evidenced by the juxtaposition in his "Carta" of the Marx memorial and the Vanderbilt ball, Martí saw class collaboration and growing democracy as ushering in a period of endless reform. However, in reality, inequality and exploitation were rapidly increasing.[25] In 1883, Martí saw 1789, that is the French Revolution, and 1776, that is the American Revolution, not only as compatible but as complementary.

According to many critics, Martí's optimism regarding the progressive nature of the United States' political institutions waned after the Haymarket Affair in 1886, which originated in an attack on the police with explosives during a labor demonstration on May 1, and especially after the quick and arbitrary trial that condemned seven workers to death and an eighth worker to fifteen years in prison.[26] (In the end, four were executed and one committed suicide before the incoming governor John Peter Altgeld pardoned the surviving accused.) As Christopher Conway notes,

> Martí read class conflict before 1887 through an idealist lens that sublimated social agents and their interaction through a universal system of correspondences in which unions, strikes, and scabs are analogically tied to elements in nature and the self. However, between May of 1886 and November of 1887, when the convicted Haymarket anarchists were executed, Martí shed some of the distance that had characterized his previous analysis of labor, and which had permitted him to criticize it as harshly as the moneyed class. In a significant breakthrough, Haymarket forced Martí to reassess his view of the U.S. as a classless society where democratic practices were a viable conduit for social change. (36)

For the mainstream of scholarship on Martí, he would have become critical of North American politics and society and, perhaps by consequence, more sympathetic to the working-class struggle after the Haymarket Affair ripped the meliorist mask off the country's face. His growing skepticism regarding US society and reform would lead to his birth as a progressive anti-imperialist.[27]

However, even the post-Haymarket Martí does not fully give in to the violent chords he heard during the Marx memorial. In fact, Martí's opinion on Marx did not change. In 1890, in his only other explicit mention of the German intellectual in all of his works, he states: "Each nation finds its own cure, in keeping with its nature, which either requires varying doses of the medicine, depending on whether this or that factor is present in the ailment—or requires a different medicine. Neither Saint-Simon, nor Karl Marx, nor Marlo, nor Bakunin. Instead the reforms that are best suited to our own bodies" (qtd. in the introduction to "Tributes to Karl Marx" 130). This passage contradicts avant la lettre any identification of the Cuban patriot's ideas with those of Marx. After all, one can argue that rather than privileging Marx, the brief passage dismisses him, together with the sui-generis utopian socialist Saint-Simon, the anarchist Bakunin, and the now mostly forgotten guild socialist Karl Marlo. Marx, instead of being the privileged interpreter of modernity, is just another theorist whose ideas should be studied, evaluated, mainly discarded, and modified according to Cuban needs and traditions. Martí's 1890 take on Marx is also compatible with the ideas expressed in his earlier "Carta." In both texts, the Cuban hero embraces reform rather than revolution. If in the "Carta" he celebrates US political mores, it was not because he thought the country's political system perfect but rather because he believed in its perfectibility. Butler is the one unequivocally positive political actor in the "Carta" precisely because he is seen as the incarnation of a reformist wave that, according to the Cuban hero, was propagating throughout the country. And the relative praise of Marx in this text, so often used by critics to establish an imaginary relation between the Cuban poet and the German thinker, is hedged by the overall celebration of reform over revolution.[28]

## José Carlos Mariátegui

If Martí's "Carta" marks the first, albeit superficial, encounter between Latin American thinkers and Marx, José Carlos Mariátegui's writings are often acknowledged to be the first full, even if heterodox, attempt to apply the ideas of the author of *Capital* to the interpretation of the region's society and history. However, like Martí, but with a different set of political and social values and goals, Mariátegui believed in the adaptation of European ideas to the reality of the region and, more specifically, of his native Peru, as the title of his masterwork *Seven Interpretive Essays on Peruvian Reality* (1928) insinuates.[29] As he famously stated in one of the editorials published in *Amauta*, the cultural and political journal he founded in 1926, "We certainly do not want socialism in Latin America to be a copy or imitation. It should be heroic creation. We have to give life to Indo-American socialism with our own reality, in our own language" ("Anniversary and Balance Sheet" 130). Given that there were then, as now, living indigenous cultures in the Peruvian Andes, Mariátegui's translational view of Marxism gains added significance. As he notes in the same seminal text published in 1928: "Socialism, finally, is in the American tradition. The most advanced primitive communist organization that history records is that of the Incas" (129–30). Needless to say, these ideas were incompatible with the rapidly hardening Soviet Communism that saw its interpretation of Marx's ideas as a one-size-fits-all solution.[30]

Mariátegui died in 1930, before the effects of Stalin's full control of Soviet institutions had become widely known in Latin America. Thus, his writing and activism—one must remember he founded the Peruvian Socialist Party and the first national labor union, the Confederación General de Trabajadores (General Workers Federation)—still responded to the hopes and expectations of 1917. However, Mariátegui, unlike Martí, rejected capitalism and embraced socialism as the only means to solve Peru's and Latin America's inequalities. Whereas the Cuban poet, at least in 1883, believed in the ability of liberal democracy and capitalism to ultimately solve all problems, Mariátegui in 1928 embraced the need for revolution. In the same text, he writes, "Capitalism or Socialism. This is the problem of our epoch. We do not anticipate the syntheses, the transactions that can only operate through history. We think and feel like Gobetti that history is reformist on the condition that the revolutionaries act as such. Marx, Sorel, Lenin, these are the men who make history" (130). In this passage, beguiled by the music of Marx and his fellow band members, the Peruvian socialist seems to embrace revolution and reject reform.

"Anniversary and Balance Sheet" had been published in response to the news that his friend and till-then collaborator Víctor Raúl Haya de la Torre had proclaimed his candidacy for the presidency of Peru from Mexico, where he lived in forced exile.[31] The Peruvian Left had been united through much of the 1920s in their rejection of neocolonial hacienda land tenancy, the exploitation of indigenous peasants, structural anti-indigenous racism, and the growing presence of US corporations (primarily in mining and agriculture), together with support for a loosely defined "socialism." This Left was splintered by Haya's candidacy and his transformation of the Alianza Popular Revolucionaria Americana (APRA, Popular American Revolutionary Alliance) from an alliance of anti-imperialist activists into a political party, as well as by the intensity with which these actions were rejected by Mariátegui and other radicals.[32] Although Haya, like Mariátegui, had claimed to be a Marxist, the diverse electoral documents published during the run up to the elections did not include any explicit reference to socialism.[33]

While Haya's candidacy would ultimately flame out—despite all the political ballyhoo, he did not fulfill the constitutional age requirement—the split between those who agglutinated around Haya's candidacy and party (the direct forerunner of the later Aprista Party) and the more radical sectors, whether Communist or independent, would be permanent.[34]

Earlier that same year, in May 1928, Haya had responded to Mariátegui's complaints about the lack of reference to socialism in the political literature produced by the would-be electoral campaign: "You ask for the word socialism . . . Words, words, and words!" (Mariátegui, *José Carlos Mariátegui. Correspondencia* 379). And: "We will make the revolution without mentioning the word socialism, but redistributing lands and fighting against imperialism" (379). For Haya, Mariátegui would be trapped by words, by ideology, while what really mattered were the concrete measures the new political party proposed, which the leader of the APRA saw correctly as among the main goals that, until then, had united the Peruvian Left.

Against this backdrop of a newly redefined APRA, which includes the word "revolutionary" in its name, Mariátegui, in "Anniversary and Balance Sheet," attempts to provide his own definition of what a revolution truly was:

In this America of small revolutions, the same word Revolution frequently lends itself to misunderstanding. . . . We have to restore its strict and exact meaning. The Latin American Revolution will be nothing more and nothing less than a stage, a phase of the world revolution. It will simply and clearly be the socialist revolution. Add all the adjectives you want to this word according to a particular case: "anti-imperialist," "agrarian," "national revolutionary." Socialism supposes, precedes, and includes all of them. (128)

Mariátegui, here still in thrall of 1917, believes that the world is moving in the direction of socialism, as defined by the experience of the Russian Revolution. Moreover, he argues that all meaningful social change will necessarily be associated with this expanding socialist revolution.

Nevertheless, Mariátegui is still making an important point. For him, land reform, or, better said, the promise of land reform, and anti-imperialist rhetoric, even action, were not necessarily revolutionary by the 1920s. While today many would see this as an extreme position, land reform in itself is not a socialist measure, as Mariátegui often pointed out, and anti-imperialism can often camouflage the desires of local bourgeoisies.[35] A true revolution that would reshape Peru's economy and that would imply a full accounting and supersession of neocolonial institutions and ideas was, for the author of *Seven Interpretive Essays*, only possible through socialism. This linkage between revolution, socialism, and successful social change became central to the political and cultural ideas of the 1960s. But the political horizon of the Boom authors and their contemporaries is constituted not by the world revolution, or at least not primarily by that revolution, but by that of Latin America. The privileged utopian example is no longer the Soviet Union, by then thoroughly discredited, but Cuba, which was seen as a socialist tropical exception. Of course, in the cases of both the Soviet Union and the Cuban Revolution, it would take only a few years for evidence to surface that these hopes had been misplaced.

The passage from "Anniversary and Balance Sheet" quoted at the start of this chapter signals the heterodoxy that, beyond the caricature of Mariátegui as a stalwart Leninist, even Stalinist, is the main characteristic of the Peruvian socialist's thought and action.[36] After all, Piero Gobetti was a radical liberal who believed that Italy had experienced an incomplete liberal revolution but who, at the same time, gave priority to the struggle against fascism.[37] Along these lines, French syndicalist Georges Sorel's celebration of the "myth"—that is, the need for irrational belief as a guide for political action—had long been rejected by official communism. In fact, Lenin himself had described Sorel as "a notorious muddlehead" (249).[38] The recurring presence of Sorel and Gobetti in his writings serves to demonstrate how Mariátegui's brand of Marxism differed from the version that the Stalinist Third International (Comintern) had begun to impose in Latin America. While insisting on the need for revolutionaries to be revolutionaries, Mariátegui surprisingly accepts the non-Leninist idea that history itself may be reformist.[39] Paradoxically, for the Peruvian Marxist being a revolutionary was potentially the ultimate way of being a reformist.

The tensions present in Mariátegui's view of revolution are also found in his explicit objections to Haya's candidacy. While one could argue that he, like many a Marxist, was skeptical about the actual possibility of elections ever serving as the framework for significant political change—a position that could have reflected the influence of Sorel, who disdained representative democracy—the Peruvian socialist's criticism of Haya's candidacy was not directly based on the defense of bullets over ballots.[40] One of the key aspects of his response to APRA's transformation was his concern about the hierarchical character of the Partido Nacionalista Libertador (aka Partido Nacionalista Peruano).

Mariátegui's criticisms were, in fact, on target. In "Esquema del plan de México," the political platform of the new party, Haya is presented as the "supreme leader" and the members of the Mexico "committee," that is, Delmar, Portal and others, as next in line (290). Moreover, the party is described as a "revolutionary political military organism" (290). For Haya and his confreres, the party that represented the new generation was to mimic the military in its structure.

Mariátegui would propose two alternative, though not necessarily incompatible, explanations for the turn of sections of the "new generation" to a hierarchical and personalist political model that sees its leader as "supreme" and therefore as the ultimate arbiter of policy and politics. The first of these explanations looked to Latin American history for precedents for the kind of politics that Haya's new party seemed to present. In a letter from December 1928, Mariátegui states, "Haya suffers too deeply the demon of *caudillismo* and personalism" (*José Carlos Mariátegui. Correspondencia* 490). And:

> I know *caudillismo* can still be useful, but only on the condition that it be totally subordinated to a doctrine and a group. If one has to adapt to the [Peruvian cultural] environment, we have no reason to criticize the old politics. . . . Haya does not care about language; I do. And not due to a literary consideration but because of ideology and morality. If we do not, at least, distinguish ourselves from the past, I fear that in the end, for the same reasons of adaptation and mimicry, we will end up different [from this political past] only in the names of the personalities. (491)

Thus, for Mariátegui, the APRA turned political party could be seen as a return to an earlier (and alas, unbeknownst to him, also future) Latin American politics in which loyalty is given not to specific policies or causes but instead to charismatic individuals (the *caudillo*) who, perhaps fittingly, often had a military background. Moreover, these charismatic individuals often provided rhetorical solutions to social problems rather than implementing actual measures to solve those same problems.

Mariátegui thus places a surprising stress on means rather than on ends and, therefore, on the rhetoric used in the political arena. Instead of the emotional oratory of nineteenth- and early twentieth-century politicians, of which Haya's speeches would become one of the outstanding examples, a new analytical transparency was to be the key to a new politics.[41] Moreover, this transparent speech opened the possibility of new interpellations that would, in turn, lead to revolutionary ways of looking at the world. For Mariátegui, not only did style reflect the woman or man, but it also shaped how she or he understood reality.

It is worth noting the symmetry as well as the differences between the criticisms Haya and Mariátegui leveled at each other when it comes to the discourse they believed should characterize radical politics. According to Mariátegui, Haya had an instrumental view of language: the goal of political discourse is exclusively to further political results, including the new party's policy goals, which, one must note, were still compatible with the proposals that the APRA had put forth before its transformation into an electoral movement. For instance, the "Esquema del plan de México" clearly stressed the need for radical land reform.[42]

However, for Haya, success in politics was based on manipulating language, on making words mean whatever was useful for achieving political goals.

Mariátegui, on the other hand, saw this instrumental view of language as the key characteristic of the Latin American caudillos, who often became political chameleons in their struggles to attain and hold onto power. Instead Mariátegui insisted on the necessary correspondence between political actions and political discourse. Means—political rhetoric, as well as tactics—necessarily had to correspond with ends—the actual political goals to be implemented. This is why he rejected Haya's rhetorical manipulation of nationalist emotions.

One can easily see in Mariátegui's criticisms of Haya's electoral turn one of the first, albeit nontheoretical, responses to what would become one of the political trademarks of the region: populism.[43] But the leader worship, rhetorical manipulation, and top-down hierarchical political structure criticized by Mariátegui are not exclusive to populism; better said, populist traits will continue even in regimes that appear distant from it, such as during the Cuban Revolution. As no less a figure than Ernesto "Che" Guevara noted about Fidel Castro's purported ability to know the needs and desires of the Cuban people:

> In this Fidel is a master. His own special way of fusing himself with the people can be appreciated only by seeing him in action. At the great public mass meetings one can observe something like the dialogue of two tuning forks whose vibrations interact, producing new sounds. Fidel and the mass begin to vibrate together in a dialogue of growing intensity until they reach the climax in an abrupt conclusion crowned by our cry of struggle and victory. The difficult thing to understand for someone not living through the experience of the revolution is this close dialectical unity between the individual and the mass, in which both are interrelated and, at the same time, in which the mass, as an aggregate of individuals, interacts with its leaders.[44] ("Socialism and Man in Cuba" 214)

While one cannot know whether Mariátegui, had he lived, would have seen Fidel's caudillismo as "useful," there is little doubt that Che's text bears no proof of Castro's subordination to any group. In fact, Che's description of Fidel can be seen as an extreme example of the populist leader as "the voice of the people, which means as both political outsiders and authentic representatives of the common people" (Mudde and Kaltwasser 63).

Mariátegui's second interpretation of the embryonic APRA party saw in it a repetition, in a Peruvian key, of the political evolution that led to the birth of fascism in Italy. Alluding to the leftist background of Haya and his close supporters, Mariátegui notes:

> Who constituted the first fascists? Almost all these elements had a deeper revolutionary background and history than we do. They were extreme radical leftists, like Mussolini, a protagonist of the red week in Bologna; heroic revolutionary unionists, like Carridoni, a formidable worker organizer; anarchists who were great intellectuals and philosophers, like Massimo Rocca. . . . All these people were or felt revolutionary, anticlerical, republican, "beyond communism," according to Marinetti's phrase. . . . Tactics forced them to attack the revolutionary bureaucracy, break with the socialist party, destroy the workers' organization. . . . Socialism, the proletariat, were, despite all its bureaucratic deadweight, the revolution. Fascism had necessarily to be a reactionary force. (*José Carlos Mariátegui. Correspondencia* 372–73)

Mariátegui, who had been in Italy during Mussolini's March on Rome, believed that Haya and his collaborators were, through their claims to be both revolutionaries and nonsocialists, bound to repeat the evolution of Italian fascism. Mariátegui also notes the often-made connection between fascism and populism. For instance, Federico Finchelstein has pointed out that Peronism, which he considers to be the paradigmatic example of populism, "was a sui generis radical reformulation of fascism" (*Transatlantic Fascism* 165). However, Mariátegui witnessed *aprismo* and populism at only the earliest stages and was unable to go beyond noting certain key similarities between the new politics being developed by Haya and what the Peruvian socialist had seen in Europe between 1922 and 1924.[45]

That said, Mariátegui was apparently unaware that the positions he so strenuously rejected had not been developed by the APRA leader by means of studying Mussolini's actions, but rather by analyzing Lenin and the Russian Revolution. As Haya put it in a 1926 letter to, of all people, Peruvian émigré Eudocio Ravines, who was, unbeknownst to Haya, an agent of the Comintern, "This is why my main concern is to form action cadres as quickly as possible. What is necessary this moment is to create proletarian cadres, in other words, to constitute the red army; to organize the masses and agitate the masses intensely and extensively, to attempt the greatest possible revolutionary agitation" (qtd. In Flores Galindo, "Un viejo debate" 73).[46] And: "Reject as reactionary, friend Ravines, any reformist, evolutionist, or lazy view of our revolution. . . . The waiting time [for revolution] is not too long and that is why we must hurry to understand and make reality Lenin's maxim: The key question of every revolution is undoubtedly the question of power" (qtd. Flores Galindo, "Un viejo debate" 79). But by 1928 Lenin was no longer mentioned in Haya's speeches and writings.

These three different explanations for the type of party dreamt by Haya de la Torre—a mass hierarchical party led by a supreme leader—are not necessarily incompatible. One could argue that it is a clear example of overdetermination, as the caudillo tradition, the new fascist mass politics and charismatic leadership, and the Leninist transformation of Russian social democracy into a hierarchical and hypostatized party all served to reinforce these personalist and anti-democratic traits. In what could seem a contradiction, however, in the late 1920s the early populist Haya, rather than the first Marxist of America Mariátegui, was closer to Leninist politics, which stressed party discipline and underground activism.

Mariátegui thus represents a view on how to achieve maximalist, revolutionary, social change that contradicts Haya's belief in achieving power, for him the sine qua non of politics, by any means necessary: electoral politics, military action, or popular uprising. In fact, as Mariátegui wrote to the group of APRA leaders in Mexico who supported Haya's impossible electoral foray: "I believe that our movement should not base its success on decoys or tricks. Truth is its strength, its only strength, its best strength. I don't believe with you that in order to win you must use 'all *criollo* methods.' Tactics, praxis, are in themselves more than just forms and systems. The means, even in the cases of well indoctrinated movements, end up substituting for the ends" (*José Carlos Mariátegui. Correspondencia* 372). Though contemporary Latin American intellectuals often present political action and ethical criticism as incompatible, Mariátegui dreamed about an ethical politics of truth in which the means were as important as the ends. But Mariátegui was much more than a critic and intellectual; he was also an activist and practical politician. Therefore, it is necessary to look at his political actions—that is, at the means he developed to help bring about the desired end: a socialist Peru.

Mariátegui's first response to the APRA's electoral turn was the creation of a new Partido Socialista (Socialist Party), aligned with the Comintern. Given Mariátegui's belief in internal party democracy, it is impossible to see this socialist party as a full expression of the Peruvian Marxist's personal ideas.[47] Instead, it is a compromise not only with the other founding members, but also with the Comintern itself. However, one can see in the politics it practiced and prescribed an outline of what revolutionary politics meant for Mariátegui.

The name of the party already signals Mariátegui's distance from Haya and his group. Instead of nationalism, socialism is boldly blazoned in its title. In fact, its "Programmatic Principles" begin with an implicit rejection of closed nationalism by noting "the international character of the contemporary economy" (238). While Mariátegui is most often recognized as the proponent of a Marxism that, as in the title of his best-known work, is based on the interpretation of Peruvian reality, he is far from an uncritical defender of nationalism. If Haya in his letter had commanded him "to get back to reality and attempt to follow the discipline not of revolutionary Europe but instead revolutionary America" (*José Carlos Mariátegui. Correspondencia* 379), for Mariátegui the dichotomy presented by the leader of the APRA was incomprehensible. In the same way that all local and national capitalisms participated within global capitalism—his *Seven Interpretive Essays on Peruvian Reality* can easily be seen as reflections on locality inserted within a world economic system beginning with the country's conquest—he also presents national and regional socialist movements as necessarily connected to global socialist struggles, but without losing their specificity. As he also notes in the first of the "Programmatic Principles": "The Socialist Party adapts its practice to the country's specific circumstances, but it follows a broad class vision and its national context is subordinated to the rhythm of world history" (237). If capitalism had become fully globalized, the struggle against it needed to have a similar global range, but, in order to be successful, it also had also to take into account local reality.

Precisely because Mariátegui believed that only a global socialism could oppose a global capitalism, the "Programmatic Principles" necessarily had to consider the Comintern and its requirements. However, Mariátegui's decision to name the party socialist, while a rebuke to the APRA group, also contradicted the requirements of the Communist International established in 1919 that clearly stated:

> Every party that wishes to belong to the Communist International must bear the name Communist Party of this or that country (Section of the Communist International). The question of the name is not formal, but a highly political question of great importance. The Communist International has declared war on the whole bourgeois world and on all yellow social-democratic parties. The difference between the communist parties and the old official "social democratic" or "socialist" parties that have betrayed the banner of the working class must be clear to every simple toiler. ("Minutes of the Second Congress of the Communist International")

Thus the new party's name reflects not only Mariátegui and his group's desire to fully identify their politics and, in this manner, respond to the Aprista refusal to name theirs as socialist but, at the same, implies a surprising disregard for one of the principal requirements for participation in the institution that claimed to represent what the "Programmatic Principles" call "the global anti-imperialist struggle" (239).

The "Programmatic Principles" note that Peruvian radical politics needed to reckon with international political and social tendencies of the time, such as globalization, imperialism, the existence of a world socialist movement, and so on. Of course, political activism must also respond to a "Peruvian reality" characterized by the concentration of land tenancy, the presence of indigenous communes, neocolonial institutions, and the like. Thus, the "Immediate Demands" of the "Programmatic Principles" propose concrete measures—a minimum wage, the transfer of land from the haciendas to the indigenous agrarian communities, free basic and higher education, the creation of a social security system, what today we would call a welfare state, and so forth—that deal with injustices that these local realities generate. But missing is any discussion of party structure. The clear implication is that for Mariátegui what truly would define the Peruvian Socialist Party were its political proposals. Instead of emphasizing caudillismo, the "Programmatic Principles" ultimately prioritize analysis and the concrete measures that derive from it.

Furthermore, and in a gesture that seems to point toward reform rather than revolution, there is a stress on working within existing legal frameworks:

> We will immediately fight for these main demands of the Socialist Party. All are urgent demands for the material and intellectual emancipation of the masses. All demands have to be actively supported by the proletariat and by conscious elements of the middle class. The very act of the public establishment of this group lays claim to the rights of the freedom for the Party to act lawfully and openly under the Constitution and to claim the guarantees it grants citizens to access press freedoms without restrictions and to hold congresses and debates. ("Programmatic Principles" 242)

In its emphasis on participation in open democratic processes, which, one must admit, does not foreclose the possibility of other types of subversive political activities if required, in its surprising appeal to the middle classes, in addition to the proletariat and peasantry, and in the party's name and structure, Mariátegui seems distant from both Leninist politics and from the cult of the leader that was developing in the APRA turned party.

Alberto Flores Galindo has noted that, at the time, the Comintern proposed a policy "of class against class, of the bourgeoisie against the proletariat" (100). He adds: "Against that argument, Mariátegui's position is not very clear. Before the rupture with Haya, in the same way he had valued the revolutionary effects of nationalism, he also exalted the radical role of the middle classes, and, by means of [the magazine] *Amauta*, the support of intellectuals. After the break-up with the APRA all these ideas were revised" (100). However, the "Programmatic Principles" clearly show that while Mariátegui was skeptical of nationalism as an organizing political principle, he continued to believe in a potential radical role for the middle classes. Furthermore, the importance he gave to naming the party as socialist is consistent with his belief in the need for an agglutinative radical socialism capable of including all working-class groups—and beyond—and interests.

Rather than seeing socialist politics as consisting of "class against [clearly defined] class," Mariátegui always saw it as based on alliances and fronts, though without denying the ultimate goal of achieving a true socialist revolution. An example of how these political values continued even after his split with the APRA is found in the Confederación General de Trabajadores del Perú (CGTP, General Confederation of Peruvian Workers), which he helped create in 1929.

The Comintern required that "every organisation that wishes to affiliate to the Communist International must regularly and methodically remove reformists and centrists from every responsible post in the labour movement (party organisations, editorial boards, trades unions, parliamentary factions, co-operatives, local government" ("Minutes of Second Congress"). Mariátegui, instead, argues in the "Manifesto of the General Confederation of Peruvian Workers to the Peruvian Working Class" that the aim was to "fight for the creation of a united labor front without any distinction as to political tendencies in a United Proletariat Central" (346). Although now clearly focused on the development of working-class identity, Mariátegui is attempting to radicalize united front policies within a Peruvian political reality fractured by the constitution of the Partido Nacionalista Libertador and against the Comintern's hierarchical democratic centralism and policy of subordination to party and Soviet dictates.

This requirement to "remove reformists and centrists," part of the famous "eleven points" for admission to the Comintern developed in 1920, had been established during the leadership of Lenin himself and is consistent with the Russian Bolshevik's earlier writings and ideas. As early as 1902, in *What Is to Be Done*, Lenin writes: "We must take upon ourselves the task of organising an all-round political struggle under the leadership of our Party in such a manner as to make it possible for all oppositional strata to render their fullest support to the struggle and to our Party" (52). For Lenin, alliances between workers belonging to different factions is inconceivable. Instead, political and ideological homogeneity was the prerequisite for any successful political action. Mariátegui, on the other hand, is more concerned with unity in goals. Whereas for the Russian leader, a common set of political beliefs was necessary to achieve political change, for Mariátegui, shared objectives, rather than ideology, were the main requisite for radical political action. Even if the socialist party claimed Marxism-Leninism as the necessary method, Mariátegui, as a labor organizer, rejected any explicit ideological restrictions. Revolutionary consciousness was possible among workers of any political stripe.

Mariátegui's belief in the need for alliances across groups and even classes does not necessarily mean that he had renounced revolution as a concept or practice. In fact, the "Programmatic Principles" use the word "revolution" or "revolutionary" eleven times, though this includes one reference each to "independence revolution," "liberal revolution," "bourgeois-democratic revolution," and "revolutionary pedagogy," examples that do not reflect the politics he proposed, with the possible exception of the last one.

Mariátegui's politics combine reformism—working for concrete policies attainable without completely overturning economic structures, such as free education, minimum wage, and so on—within a revolutionary framework that channels the progressive movement toward truly radical social change. This attempt at developing support for revolution while working for concrete social goals is reflected in the creation of a socialist party that, unlike Haya's nationalist party or, later, his APRA party, had no immediate electoral or insurrectional goals; the founding of a national labor union, particularly active among Andean miners; and finally the continuing publication of the magazine *Amauta* that, while boycotted by most supporters of Haya after the break between the two leaders, featured topics far from the Communist mainstream, such as the symbolist poetry of José María Eguren, and included among its contributors Aprista philosopher Antenor Orrego and the future Aprista leader and literary critic Luis Alberto Sánchez.

Mariátegui did not reject the need for revolution but saw it as the ultimate result of a long and arduous process of political activism and intellectual discussion. This is precisely why words mattered so much for the Peruvian socialist. Only by keeping in mind that the end goal is not the mere taking of power or even the achievement of specific measures, no matter how worthy, can politics avoid compromising with existing political and social structures, institutions, and groups. This is also an example of a heroic creation—that is, of adapting socialist goals and ideas to the specific realities of a peripheral, mostly agrarian, culturally and linguistically heterogeneous society.

Mariátegui's afterlife was even more complex than that of Martí, who became the historical figure that helped define what it means to be Cuban, even if widely divergent interpretations were taken up by different political sectors. After Mariátegui's death in 1930, Eudocio Ravines helped change the socialist party Mariátegui had founded into a cookie-cutter Peruvian Communist Party. Ironically, one of the first measures that the new party took was to rid itself of the influence of Mariátegui and instead follow uncritically all the measures proposed by the Soviet-led Communist international. In an anonymous editorial titled "Bajo la bandera de Lenin" (Under Lenin's flag), published at the end of 1933, the Communist Party leadership made clear its evaluation of the man they still considered its founder: "*Mariateguismo* is a confusion of ideas. . . . He had not only theoretical but practical errors. There are, in reality, few points of contact between Leninism and *mariateguismo*. . . . *Mariateguismo* confuses the national problem with the indigenous problem; attributes to imperialism and capitalism a progressive function in Peru; [and] substitutes debate and discussion, etc. for revolutionary tactic and strategy" (21). Mariátegui will only begin to be rediscovered in 1950, when his adult children began republishing his works. Later, when the Cuban Revolution led scholars and activists to look for possible antecedents to what then seemed an original version of socialism, Mariátegui's works seemed for some to offer a precedent.

However, even though Mariátegui would be rediscovered during the 1960s, his proposals were distant from the politics of that revolutionary decade. In fact, there is nothing further from Mariátegui, who envisioned socialism as the end result of a long-term program of political debate, punctual policy action, and collaboration among diverse progressive sectors (even if this praxis is ultimately framed by the belief that 1917 signaled the beginning of a world movement toward socialism), than Che Guevara's *foco*, with its belief that armed action by a small guerrilla group in the countryside could start a revolution if the circumstances were right.[48] It is true that Mariátegui would have agreed with Che's criticism of those "who sit down to wait until some mechanical way all necessary objective and subjective conditions are given without working to accelerate them" (*Guerrilla Warfare* 50). Nevertheless, the basic political methodologies proposed by the two Marxists are significantly different.

Ironically, and for different reasons, Martí and Mariátegui can be seen as far from the revolutionary politics inaugurated in 1959, even if both still saw social change on the horizon. At least in 1883, the author of "Our America" believed that through reform the needed social changes could be achieved, and the Peruvian Marxist argued that true revolutionary, rather than putschist, politics could only be the result of long, patient ideological and political labor.

Contradicting the politics of both Martí and Mariátegui, the promise of the Cuban Revolution was that revolutionary change required only the will to make it, given the always potentially revolutionary conditions of Latin America. Diana Sorensen's description of the structures of feeling of the 1960s is accurate: "Imminence as possibility is entwined with the spirit of utopia" (2). This "imminence as possibility" is one of the central effects of the Cuban Revolution and found its practical and theoretical expression in Guevara's (and his disciple Regis Debray's) notion of the *foco*. This belief in the imminence of revolution reflected a significant change in the structures of feeling of the region and in how Latin American writers related to radical politics. For a whole generation of writers, socialism was no longer a theoretical possibility, not even a goal to work progressively toward; rather, it was seen as the means with which to modernize Latin America and create more just societies. However, as we will see, the impact of 1959 on literature led to much more than a simple celebration of imminent revolutions or charismatic revolutionaries.

# 2

## Boom in the Revolution, Revolution in the Boom

### What Is Revolutionary about the Latin American Novel of the 1960s?

#### *Theory*

In April 1970, Mario Vargas Llosa and Julio Cortázar, two of the region's literary superstars, participated in a panel, "The Intellectual and Politics," that also included the Argentine painter Julio Le Parc; Roberto Schwarz, who would in future decades acquire an international reputation as a scholar of Brazilian literature; and the Paraguayan writer Rubén Bareiro Saguier. The panel took place in Paris as part of a series of cultural events titled Amérique Latine Non-officielle (Unofficial Latin America).[1] However, as Cortázar notes, "visual elements predominated," which is not surprising since most of the organizers were "plastic artists from our countries" ("La América Latina no oficial" 10). In fact, the core of the event was an art installation that attempted to "demystify the official [political] versions that practically all Latin American countries disseminate in Europe" (10).[2] In addition to the main exhibition, panels, and roundtables, the event showed Latin American films "almost all unknown in France" (10), including Octavio Getino and Fernando Solanas's now-classic agitprop *The Hour of the Furnaces*, which was then a relative novelty, having had only sporadic showings since its completion in 1968. Amérique Latine Non-officielle was therefore an attempt, through art and cultural activities, to inform Latin Americans residing in Paris and a wider audience of Parisian radicals—as evidenced by the panels being held in French—about the negative social realities of the region, as well as its political and social possibilities.[3]

The topic of the panel—"The Intellectual and Politics"—seemed unusually appropriate for the two Latin American novelists, even if during their presentations Vargas Llosa and Cortázar attempted to "establish a difference between the intellectual and the writer" (Vargas Llosa, "El escritor y la política" 34). During the 1960s, writers and especially novelists were seen as the intellectuals par excellence, capable of opining not only on literary or cultural topics, but also on political ones.[4] Moreover, in addition to participating in public discussions on cultural and political issues, Vargas Llosa and Cortázar, as two core members of the Boom—that is, the group of novelists who gained regional and international celebrity during the 1960s—were at the very apex of the region's literary and cultural hierarchy.[5]

Though they diverged in their degree of commitment to leftist political activity, the central Boom writers—a group that also included Gabriel García Márquez and Carlos Fuentes[6]—were united in promoting radical and progressive movements and, at least in principle, in defending the Cuban Revolution, a position that was during this radical decade practically a condition for being considered an intellectual.[7] It is difficult to overstate the importance of the Cuban Revolution not only for the culture and politics of the 1960s, but also for the constitution of the Boom writers as a group.[8] While Cortázar, Vargas Llosa, Fuentes, and García Márquez had disagreed publicly—and privately—with specific measures and proposals of the Cuban government, only with the "Padilla affair" in 1971 did their joint public support for the island's revolution fracture.[9] José Donoso, the Chilean novelist and self-appointed historian of the Boom, points out, "I think that this faith and political unanimity—or near unanimity—was then and continued to be until the Padilla case exploded in 1971, one of the major factors in the internationalization of the Latin American novel" (49). The Cuban Revolution was, as Donoso notes, the key unifying factor of the Boom and, given the international curiosity raised by the political changes taking place in the island, also one of the underlying reasons for the worldwide interest in the region's new novel.[10] Moreover, as the reference to the

Padilla affair—the brief jailing of poet Heberto Padilla for antirevolutionary activities, his public confession of guilt, and his liberation—makes clear, the identity of these writers as a coherent group would break down precisely when it became more difficult to support Fidel Castro's regime. However, in 1970, those days were still in the future, even if only by a few months.[11]

But the processes that would lead to the jailing of Padilla and to the concomitant breakup of the Boom were already in place. The subject of the panel "The Intellectual and Politics"—the latter understood as revolutionary politics—had been discussed among leftist political groups, particularly in Cuba, since the death of Ernesto "Che" Guevara in 1967. As early as 1968, the "general resolution" of El Congreso Cultural de La Habana had proclaimed that "in an underdeveloped country the cultural event par excellence is the revolution" (qtd. in Gilman 207). Claudia Gilman traces the links of this (literal) anti-intellectualism to the political changes on the island. According to Gilman: "The end of 1968 found Cuba more threatened than ever, in a defensive position, and in a state of disquiet, due to counterrevolutionary sabotage, the North American blockade, and the economic restrictions" (219). As a result, the revolution had progressively grown to depend on the army and, perhaps more relevantly, on the cadres of the Cuban Communist Party, both of which espoused hard-line Stalinist cultural positions. Thus, the revolution and its supporters became prey to the devaluation of intellectual pursuits, which had, until then, been prized for their supposedly intrinsically radical potential. Even established Cuban intellectuals, such as Ambrosio Fornet, argued that among the "intellectuals from an underdeveloped country in revolution, participating in literacy campaigns, learning how to handle fire arms, cutting sugar cane, were part of our basic obligations" (qtd. in Gilman 217).

Although, as Gilman notes, there was resistance to these new views, for instance, among the group behind the Casa de las Américas—the main Cuban literary institution that had been the venue for the participation of both Cortázar and Vargas Llosa in Cuban culture—many on the island and elsewhere embraced this rejection of letters.[12] This is the backdrop to Vargas Llosa's and Cortázar's participation at Amérique Latine Non-officielle. The positive view of literature as intrinsically subversive was being replaced among the more political by an anti-intellectualism that saw revolutionary action as the only activity of value. As Gilman argues, "It is the lack itself of a role for literature that anti-intellectualism proposes, given that it understands as the exclusive role the revolutionary role" (179). In their presentations, both Boom writers were not only responding to the audience present during the panel presentations, but also addressing a perspective regarding culture and letters that was in the process of rapidly becoming hegemonic, at least among the Latin American and international Left.

---

None of the Boom writers had been more identified with revolutionary politics than Vargas Llosa. After all, his Rómulo Gallegos Speech "Literature Is Fire" was, in Efraín Kristal's words, "arguably the most widely disseminated statement in support of committed literature in Latin America of the 1960s" (*Temptation of the Word* 7). In fact, such well-known commentators as Ángel Rama, the most eminent Latin American critic at the time, and the poet and novelist Mario Benedetti had even argued that there was a "very close affinity between the novels of Vargas Llosa"—*Time of the Hero* (1963), *The Green House* (1969), and *Conversation in The Cathedral* (1969)—"and the revolutionary process in Latin America" (Kristal, "La política y la crítica literaria" 343). As Kristal notes, the Peruvian novelist "was . . . gratified by the official recognition he had received from the Cuban government. He participated in editorial boards, on juries for literary prizes, and in other activities sponsored by the cultural organizations of the Cuban Revolution. He was proud that many considered him to be an intellectual spokesman for the Cuban Revolution ever since he denounced the Bay of Pigs Invasion" (*Temptation of the Word* 23).[13] But, by the time of the panel, Vargas Llosa had already begun to publicly criticize specific decisions of the Cuban government. In particular, he had chastised Fidel Castro for his support for the Soviet invasion of Czechoslovakia in 1968.[14] However, he still defended the Cuban Revolution as a whole and would continue doing so even after his public denunciation of the regime's behavior during the Padilla affair, though now with ever-growing caveats.[15]

While Vargas Llosa was seen as the most radical of the Boom masters—perhaps ironically given his later defense of the free market—Cortázar had arguably been the least politically active of the group. Despite his public support for the Cuban Revolution, his best-known literary works—the novels *The Winners* (1960), *Hopscotch* (1963), and *62: A Model Kit* (1968)—hinted at an indifference toward political action by stressing metafictional play over social commentary. Sometimes this position was explicit—for instance, when Horacio Oliveira, *Hopscotch*'s protagonist, argued against activism in favor of the Algerian struggle: "False action is almost always the most spectacular. . . . So it was better to sin through omission than commission" (418). For many, these and other statements reflected a belief in the need to keep politics and literature apart. Vargas Llosa himself described Cortázar as living (until 1968) an apolitical life when he describes the Argentine author's books as "poles of a spiritual autobiography. . . . [T]hey seem to mark a continuity in his life and work, in his manner of conceiving and practicing literature as a permanent impudence, a jocular irreverence" ("The Trumpet of Deyá" 32).[16] Despite his actual enthusiasm regarding the Cuban Revolution, Cortázar in the early 1960s seemed to share in the prioritization of the aesthetics proposed by the protagonist of his best-known novel.

Cortázar would state that "what woke me up to Latin America's reality was Cuba" (Orloff 1),[17] thus dating the beginning of his politicization to his visit to the island in 1963, after having finished *Hopscotch*.[18] In fact, the cultural openness of the first years of the Cuban Revolution is evidenced by a writer of apolitical texts being welcomed with open arms by the island's cultural functionaries and institutions. One must remember that Castro in his speech "Words to Intellectuals" (1961) had famously stated: "What are the rights of writers and artists, revolutionary or non-revolutionary? Within the revolution everything; against the revolution, there are no rights" (220–21). With hindsight, one can discern a not-so-veiled threat that would become real toward the end of the decade.[19] However, at the time Castro's speech seemed to signal the Cuban Revolution's rejection of Soviet political strictures and its prescription of socialist realism as the only acceptable style. Thus, by not being antirevolutionary a writer like Cortázar could have a place in the Cuban cultural banquet, despite his high-modernist aesthetics.

Donoso describes the Argentine writer's evolution regarding the Cuban and other revolutions as progressing throughout the decade, as "from a passive sympathizer [he] came to be a very active one" (49). Vargas Llosa adds to his comment about Cortázar's apparent lack of interest in politics: "But we are also dealing with a mirage because, at the end of the sixties, Cortázar underwent one of those transformations that, as he would say, 'occur only in literature.' . . . Cortázar's change . . . took place, according to the official version—which he himself consecrated—in France of May 1968. He was seen in those tumultuous days on the barricades of Paris, distributing pamphlets of his own invention, mixing with the students who wanted to elevate 'imagination to power.' He was fifty-four years old" ("The Trumpet of Deyá" 33). Be that as it may, by 1970, when Cortázar participated in the panel, he was a fully politically committed individual and novelist.[20]

Although they must have been aware of the growing anti-intellectualism of the Latin American Left, given their celebrity and their identification with the region's leftist movements, neither Cortázar nor Vargas Llosa could have fully expected the negative reception that they got at the Amérique Latine Non-officielle event. The Argentine novelist would later describe the audience as characterized by "a disposition . . . to monotonously reiterate a 'functional' idea of literature as an activity merely in the service of a cause. . . . One cannot, therefore, be surprised that someone asked Vargas Llosa whether he believed that his novels 'clarified' Peru's situation better than did armed struggle" ("Viaje alrededor de una mesa" 12).[21] The clear implication is that it would have been better for Vargas Llosa to drop the pen, take up a rifle, and join a Peruvian guerrilla movement, which, one must note, was nonexistent in 1970.[22] For the left-wing audience in Paris, literature was politically irrelevant, regardless of the writer's explicit ideological position or activity.

Even if one is appalled at the closed-mindedness of the audience and at the political underpinnings of their anti-intellectualism, their reaction highlights the question about the relationship between the Boom novelists, their works, and the politics of the time. I will for heuristic reasons use Cortázar's and Vargas Llosa's participation in Amérique Non-officielle, and especially their comments regarding the relationship between literature and revolution, as a springboard to investigate this topic in their essays and fiction, as well as in the writing of the other Boom novelists. Of the Boom authors, the Argentine and the Peruvian novelists were the ones to best attempt to reconcile *theoretically* their professional and artistic lives with their passionate belief in the radical revolutionary politics of their day.

Their statements at the panel must be seen as part of a series of debates in which these writers participated in print and in person between 1967, when Vargas Llosa read his legendary "Literature Is Fire" at the first Rómulo Gallegos Award presentation, and 1971, when the Padilla affair finally broke up what had once been their close comradery. Among these debates are the public dialogue between García Márquez and Vargas Llosa in 1967 in Lima, the written argument between Cortázar and the Peruvian *indigenista* writer José María Arguedas between 1967 and 1969 (it was cut short by Arguedas's suicide), and the well-known exchange of essays by Cortázar and Vargas Llosa with critic Óscar Collazos, who presents a more sophisticated version of the Parisian audience's demand for a directly political literature, first published in the Uruguayan magazine *Marcha* between 1969 and early 1970.[23]

Despite obvious differences in context and individual perspective, both Vargas Llosa and Cortázar consistently defend the autonomy of literature vis-à-vis the political demands of the time. Moreover, as we will see, the ideas these writers present are compatible with those put forward by García Márquez and Fuentes. Furthermore, in the second section of this chapter I explore the manner in which the Boom novels written during the 1960s—when these writers constituted a tightly knit group—represent political and, arguably, revolutionary action. I aim to explore the question of whether the theory and practice of the Boom was fire, to put it in Vargas Llosian terms.

Cortázar's participation at Amérique Latine Non-officielle stressed the intrinsic value of literature by positing writing and art as revolutionary interventions on their own. He thus plays up the role of literary and cultural innovation within the revolutionary process he believed Latin America and the world were experiencing. For him, form was, in its own way, a political intervention. He even expressed dismay at the panel format used for the discussion: "It seems absurd that surrounded by heart-wrenching or exultant testimonies of a Latin American reality—both prerevolutionary and post-revolutionary—we will be entering again into this rigid, ordered, regulated, conventional ceremony called a round table" ("Viaje alrededor de una mesa" 10).[24] Obviously, Cortázar does not limit himself to discussing the potential political value of presentation formats. He notes about literature and other arts: "Any creation that exceeds a certain level goes beyond the present in which it is received. It is precisely in this manner that the more audacious creations become revolutionary acts and, by definition, go beyond the present and toward the new man. There are books, like there are gestures and sacrifices, that contribute to invent *the present to come*. They are already this future that covers the present in order to penetrate and fertilize it" ("Viaje alrededor de una mesa" 12). Cortázar here takes the well-known modernist and avant-garde notion that literature and art could create new ways of seeing and understanding the world—one of the ideas that is parodied as it animates the plot of *Hopscotch*—and gives it a political spin. Moreover, he is implicitly addressing and rejecting the emergent notion that only explicitly political interventions have revolutionary consequences.

This statement assigns a radical political value to works of art and literature that could easily be seen as apolitical—Cortázar mentions Schoenberg, Van Gogh, and Joyce—and, in this manner, retroactively assigns a hitherto unsuspected political revolutionary value to his earlier novels.[25] But by delinking the revolutionary worth of a work of art from the explicit politics of the author, he implicitly ascribes this revolutionary effect even to works made by authors distant from any version of left-wing politics. In the Latin American context, the main exemplar of an innovative modernist author who was politically conservative would be Jorge Luis Borges. In fact, we know that Cortázar correctly considered *Ficciones* and *The Aleph* as precisely "creation that exceeds a certain level" ("Viaje alrededor de una mesa" 12).[26] While the author of *Hopscotch* stresses the ethical importance of being "responsible"—that is, actively supporting the Cuban and other revolutions—he clearly differentiates between revolution in politics and revolution in literature, precisely as he stresses the political value of the latter. Thus, an author like Borges could, despite his political conservatism, create a work that, against the explicit intention of the author, could contribute to creating a truly revolutionary way of seeing the world. Moreover, the reference to the "new man" in the above quotation should be seen as a clear nod to Ernesto "Che" Guevara and, in particular, to his well-known essay "Socialism and Man in Cuba"—a text that had by 1970 acquired a central position not only in discussions about revolutionary politics but also in those regarding culture and literature. For Guevara, the revolution in power acts as a school that helps reshape men and women, leading them away from their individualist, bourgeois intellectual and emotional tendencies: "Individuals continually feel the impact of the new social power and perceive that they do not entirely measure up to its standards. Under the pressure of indirect education, they try to adjust themselves to a situation that they feel is right and that their own lack of development had prevented them from reaching previously. They educate themselves" ("Socialism and Man in Cuba" 218). And: "In this period of the building of socialism we can see the new man and woman being born. The image is not yet completely finished—it never will be, since the process goes forward hand in hand with the development of new economic forms" (218). By presenting literature and more generally the arts as, paraphrasing the quotation from "Viaje alrededor de una mesa," "going toward the new man," Cortázar necessarily assigns the aesthetic a political and revolutionary role. For the author of *Hopscotch*, the birth of the new man and woman would be ushered in not only by revolution, by its educational effect, or even by the creation of socialist modes of production, but also by a new literature and a new art.

One could argue that, in 1970, Cortázar is explicitly more faithful to the fusion of politics and aesthetics characteristic of surrealism—one of his acknowledged artistic sources—than he had been in his classic novels. (As mentioned above, in *Hopscotch* explicit political action is presented in negative terms.) After all, in 1938, Breton, together with no less a figure than the exiled Trotsky, had written:[27]

> True art, which is not content to play variations on ready-made models but rather insists on expressing the inner needs of man and mankind in its time—true art is unable not to be revolutionary, not to aspire to a complete and radical reconstruction of society. This it must do, were it only to deliver intellectual creation from the chains which bind it, and to allow all mankind to raise itself to those heights which only isolated geniuses have achieved in the past. (484)

However, as the conclusion to his presentation makes clear, Cortázar is now linking this earlier radical avant-garde view of the political value of literature to the specific political realities of Latin America in the 1960s:

> In Latin America, the revolutionary intellectual is not revolutionary enough. . . . We have to go much further in the search, in the experiences, in the adventures, in the combat with language and

narrative structures. Because our revolutionary language in speeches, press, as well as literature, is not revolutionary enough in the precise sense I have just given to the notion of creation. . . . We need to create the language of the revolution, we have to battle against linguistic and aesthetic forms that do not let the new generation appreciate this global attempt to create an entirely new Latin America from its roots to its last page in its total force and beauty. I have said we are still missing the Che Guevaras of literature. Yes, we need to create four, five, ten, Vietnams in the citadel of the intelligentsia.[28] ("Viaje alrededor de una mesa" 12)

Cortázar seems to find in literature an activity analogous to revolution itself. After all, the reference to Che Guevara concludes with Cortázar paraphrasing the Argentine revolutionary's well-known remark found in his "Message to the Tricontinental" about the need for more Vietnams, except now the revolution is being held in the field of knowledge.[29] Without denying the need for political action, Cortázar, perhaps goaded by the Parisian audience's indifference toward the aesthetic and more generally by the growing anti-intellectualism among leftists, proclaims the unavoidable political value of literature when, as Trotsky and Breton would say, it becomes "true art."

In his "Literatura en la revolución," written in December 1969, Cortázar also links writers with revolutionaries, though in this case much more explicitly: "Few doubt my conviction that Fidel Castro or Che Guevara have established the guidelines for our true Latin American destiny; but under no circumstance am I willing to admit that [César Vallejo's] *Human Poems* or *One Hundred Years of Solitude* are inferior answers in the cultural field to these political proposals" (44). In this essay, however, he still maintains a degree of separation between politics and aesthetics, while in the text presented at Amérique Latine Non-officielle, Cortázar emphasizes the political dimension to be found in any aesthetic product. The new man and woman, in fact the new Latin America, can only be achieved if a new language is created.

In one of the texts he added to the published version of the presentation, Cortázar stresses that, for him, writers are the ultimate arbiters of the value of literature, whether aesthetic or political. This, again, can be interpreted as a response to the audience's insistence that they are able to judge whether a work of art is politically progressive or not "based on the 'content' of a literature considered merely as a cause for revolution" ("Viaje alrededor de una mesa" 13). Given the difficulties faced in judging the political value of modernist innovation, Cortázar concludes that this process should be left to those with knowledge and experience as writers:

> No one would dare to discuss a physician's diagnosis or how a typographer sets a text without belonging to their respective professions, but . . . any teenager who has read three novels or written a couple of poems thinks she is able to judge a literary creation. . . . I'll say it again . . . in this there is no sense of privilege. The pilot of a plane does not have a sense of privilege when she forbids the entry of amateurs into the cabin; it is merely a question of competence and of security, without arrogance or pretention. ("Viaje alrededor de una mesa" 13)

Cortázar thus emphasizes the need for hierarchies in the evaluation of literature, with the modernist writer at the top.

But, not all writers belong to this aesthetic vanguard. As mentioned earlier, another of the major debates held by Cortázar during the heyday of the Boom brought him into conflict with José María Arguedas, arguably the major *indigenista* writer (a nonindigenous author who attempted to represent indigenous cultures and populations). While a full analysis of the back and forth between the two writers exceeds the purpose of this chapter, a brief reference to the opening salvo of the debate, Cortázar's 1967 "Acerca de la situación del intelectual latinoamericano" (Regarding the situation of the Latin American intellectual) is relevant to fully understand how the Argentine novelist understood the actual "vanguard" in the republic of letters.[30] In this text, Cortázar argued about his own work: "I am astonished that it is sometimes not acknowledged that the degree of influence of my books in Latin America originates in that they propose a literature in which the national and regional roots are maximized thanks to a more open and complex experience, in which each evocation or recreation of what was originally mine reaches its extreme tension thanks to that opening to and from a world that surpasses and, in conclusion, selects and perfects it" (276). The Argentine writer, obviously responding to a criticism in principle similar to that faced in Paris, here argues for his cosmopolitan location, for his being "a Latin American writer in France" (276), as the necessary condition for his literary achievement. As Mabel Moraña perceptively writes, "The inscription of the intellectual at the center of the great Western cultural system would guarantee the supersession of contingent values by means of a transcendental humanism that vindicates for itself an ethical and aesthetic universalism that includes and surpasses the circumstantiality of the local" (145). Paradoxically, Cortázar's location in Paris, the capital of modernity and the "Greenwich Meridian" of the republic of letters, makes him into a more representative Latin American author than those who remained in the region.

Cortázar explicitly disparages any literature based on local or regional cultural resources: "Regionalism [*telurismo*] . . . is foreign to me because it is narrow, parochial, and even small town. . . . [I]t seems to me to foreshadow the worse advances of a negative nationalism when it becomes the credo of writers who, almost always due to cultural lack, insist in praising the values of the homeland against value in itself, the country against the world, the race against other races (because this is where it ends. . . . And then we know what happens, what happened in 1945, what could happen again)" ("Acerca de la situación" 270). Cortázar thus not only rejects realism, in its socialist realist version, but also in its *indigenista* and other regionalist versions. And, in what can only be considered a rhetorical low blow, tars local writers with Nazi feathers.

Not surprisingly, Arguedas took umbrage with Cortázar's disparaging of any literature that did not look at local reality from what the Argentine avant-gardist claims to be "a more open and complex experience" (276). However, what matters for this chapter is that for Cortázar, writers like Arguedas were barred from the cockpit of literature's plane. Looking at the debate from the perspective of the Amérique Latine Non-officielle roundtable, it is clear that for the author of *Hopscotch* only sophisticated and cosmopolitan modernist writers, at home with the latest European and world trends in literary fashion, were qualified to judge whether a work was revolutionary or not.

Cortázar's ideas run into a political and aesthetic quandary. After all, if conservative authors can create revolutionary works, should they not also be qualified to evaluate the political qualities of these and other modernist texts?

Vargas Llosa followed Cortázar's presentation at Amérique Latine Non-officielle with what, for him, was an unusually subdued performance. It lacks the passionate oratory found, for instance, in his classic "Literature Is Fire." Moreover, while he begins his presentation by claiming that he "had little to add to what Julio Cortázar has said" ("El escritor y la política" 34), the author of *The Cubs* exhibits a general lack of interest in the key argument made by his Boom colleague: the centrality of modernist literature in the creation of the new man and woman. Instead, he brings to the forefront an issue that had been only in the background of Cortázar's presentation: the disassociation between conscious intention and literary production. Thus, the writer as a citizen must "do everything he can . . . in favor of the revolution, of progress, while as a writer must follow with no distrust, with all freedom—simultaneously with his ideas and convictions—his obsessions, his intuitions, his demons" (35). In this manner, Vargas Llosa rejects the growing belief in the necessity of a programmatic socialist literature by claiming the impossibility of willing into being a truly political literature.

Instead, for Vargas Llosa, the "demons"—"all those dark and irrational aspects of the personality"—are what "have inspired . . . more memorable literary works (in other words more useful socially) than strict political ideas" (35).[31] However, since true literature is ultimately the product of a writer's unconscious, it is impossible to predict whether the ultimate result will be politically progressive. That said, Vargas Llosa implies that if literature is truly literature, rather than an act of pandering to market demands, it will express widely shared needs and desires, in addition to being true to the author's demons.

In this text, Vargas Llosa does not deny the importance of political ideas on their own, in addition to serving as guides to behavior. However, for Vargas Llosa, the political value is ultimately determined independently from the author's ideology or intention. He agrees with Cortázar's assertion that reactionary writers can create revolutionary works: "The French have the most important example of this kind of [ideological] divorce: Balzac" (34). In a better-known essay, "Luzbel, Europa y otras conspiraciones," published in April 1970, the same month as the Amérique Latine Non-officielle panel, Vargas Llosa reiterates the same core ideas, while further developing his view of the role played by the "demons" in literary creation:

A writer is not "responsible" for her subject matter, just as an individual is not "responsible" for her dreams or nightmares, because she does not choose it freely and rationally. However, she has complete responsibility in the domain of writing and structure, because [in these] she can choose, select, search and reject, with freedom and rationality. . . . It is to this duplicity characteristic of human beings, not only writers, to which we owe cases like that of Balzac, supporter of the absolute monarchy, anti-Semite, and conformist, and the creator of novelistic summa that strikes us as major example of a critical realist literature. (83)

One can question whether "writing and structure" are as rational as the Peruvian novelist argues, or whether one can so easily separate "subject matter" from other components of a literary work. That said, Vargas Llosa consistently stresses the disassociation between an author's political ideas and the effect of the text. But equally importantly, as the example of Balzac illustrates, Vargas Llosa does not share Cortázar's embrace of literary and artistic modernism as the only intrinsically progressive literary style. Moreover, nowhere in the presentation does the future Nobel Prize laureate explain who determines whether a work is revolutionary. Based on his arguments, one could conclude that, as in the case of Balzac, readers, or perhaps the posterity of readers, determine the political value of a work of literature.[32]

However, in "Novela primitiva y novela de creación en América Latina," published in 1969, Vargas Llosa establishes a hierarchy of novelistic practice that resembles that proposed by Cortázar.[33] In that article and in its revised English version "The Latin American Novel Today," Vargas Llosa presents three types of novels that correspond to three clearly delineated stages in the development of the form in the region: imitative novels that with minor exceptions produced only pale copies of European literature; primitive novels, characterized by "an aggressive provincialism" (7), that, however, "are valid geographical testimonials, important documentaries," even though of limited literary value (8); and "creative novels," which exhibit "a thematic shift in the axis of Latin American fiction from nature to man" (8).[34] Although Balzac is not mentioned in either "Novela primitiva y novela de creación en América Latina" or "The Latin American Novel Today," one can notice an obvious connection, despite Balzac's realism, between the French master, a writer concerned with human interaction, and the creative novels. However, as Vargas Llosa makes clear in both essays, the novels of the Boom are all seen as exemplary creative novels.

The connection between Vargas Llosa's creative novels and Cortázar's more explicitly avant-garde canon is evidenced by the lists of "creative" narrators the Peruvian novelist provides: "Writers such as Borges, Onetti, Fuentes, Carpentier, Guimarães Rosa, Cortázar, García Márquez, have not only put our novel, bluntly speaking, on an equal footing with even the best of other countries; they have in addition made the narration of the twenties and thirties [primitive novel] appear in comparison to be as anachronistic as that of the nineteenth century" ("The Latin American Novel Today" 8). Vargas Llosa implies that the true predecessors of the creative novels are not the "primitive" novelists "Mariano Azuela, Alcides Arguedas, Eustasio Rivera, Ricardo Güiraldes, Rómulo Gallegos, and Ciro Alegría" (7), but instead "Joyce, Proust, Kafka, Faulkner" (8). Even if he does so with less ferocity than Cortázar, Vargas Llosa also excludes the primitive novelists and those who anachronistically continue writing primitive "documentaries" from the high-end neighborhoods of the republic of letters.[35]

As mentioned earlier, Vargas Llosa had previously written about the political value of literature. In his best-known statement about the subject, his Rómulo Gallegos reception speech of 1968, Vargas Llosa argued: "Literature is fire. . . . [I]t means non-conformity and rebellion, that the *raison d'être* of the writer is protest, disagreement and criticism. . . . The literary vocation is born out of the disagreement between a man and the world, out of his intuition of the deficiencies, disparities and misery that surround him. Literature is a form of permanent insurrection" ("Literature Is Fire" 72). As I have noted elsewhere, the little-known context of this speech was the beginning of Vargas Llosa's disillusionment with the Cuban Revolution, which is reflected in his stress that socialism, though presented as the solution for "our anachronism and our horror," did not mean an end to writers "saying no, rebelling, demanding recognition for our right to dissent" (73), and it may also explain the Trotskyite echoes in "Literature Is Fire."[36]

As he would do in the Paris panel, Vargas Llosa in "Literature Is Fire" stresses the role of the demons—that is, the unconscious elements that goad creation. However, in his Rómulo Gallegos Speech, the conscious and unconscious aspects of writing are seen as imbricated, though perhaps too facilely. Again writing about the need for a "permanent insurrection" even after the revolution, he notes: "Within the new society, and along, the road that our personal ghosts and demons drive us, we will continue as before, as now, saying no, rebelling, demanding for our right to dissent, showing in this living and magical way, as only literature can, that dogma, censorship, and arbitrary acts are also mortal enemies of progress and human dignity" (73). Though later, during the Amérique Latine Non-officielle panel, in a manner consistent with much academic literary criticism at the time, Vargas Llosa detached intent from the effect and affect of the literary text, in "Literature Is Fire" he argues for a direct connection between the writer's dissatisfaction with existing society and the radical and radicalizing output in the text.[37] But in no moment does he even attempt to explain what constitutes subversion in a text.

Despite their lacunae, Vargas Llosa's ideas and, to a lesser degree Cortázar's, can be seen as representative of the views held by the Boom writers as a whole regarding the relationship between literature and politics.

Though it may very well have been a result of logistical problems, the absence of both Carlos Fuentes and García Márquez from any of the Amérique Latine Non-officielle events can be taken as representing their distance from revolutionary politics at the time. While both remained steadfast in their public support of the Cuban Revolution, especially when it came to the US embargo and other aggressions, by 1970 they were seen by many on the left as less politically committed than either Vargas Llosa or Cortázar.

Despite having been among those who welcomed Castro into Havana when the revolution came to power, Fuentes fell out of the Cuban government's favor when he visited the United States as part of the PEN International Congress in 1967.[38] Because of the agitation against him—and against Pablo Neruda, who also participated in the congress—by Cuba's revolutionary intelligentsia, Fuentes, as Maarten van Delden and Yvon Grenier explain, "never returned to the island and became increasingly critical of the Castro regime" (153). Even before the "Padilla affair," one finds in Fuentes's *La nueva novela hispanoamericana* (1969) the name of Padilla among a list of writers who have "suffered violent attacks, censorship, or jail" (85). Vargas Llosa and Cortázar were problematic figures for (some) in the Amérique Latine Non-officielle audience, but Fuentes was by now persona non grata, though he still, in principle, supported the Cuban Revolution.[39]

The case of García Márquez was somewhat different. On the one hand, unlike his other Boom confreres, García Márquez was adverse to theorizing literature, including his own praxis. In 1967, as part of a public conversation held between the two future Nobel Prize winners in Lima, García Márquez bluntly told Vargas Llosa: "In reality I rarely theorize" (*Diálogo sobre la novela latinoamericana* 22).[40] But his absence at the panel could also be seen as responding to the fact that García Márquez, who had been a supporter of Fidel Castro before he came to power, had by this time recused himself (temporarily) from political statement or agitation. García Márquez's distance from active politics was such then, that, according to his friend Beatriz de Moura, one of the founders of the publishing house Tusquets, "Gabo was completely apolitical" (qtd. in Martin, *Gabriel García Márquez: A Life* 338). However, both Fuentes and García Márquez, on the few occasions that he dealt with literary topics, proposed views compatible with those proposed by Cortázar and especially Vargas Llosa.

García Márquez spoke about the relationship between literature and revolution during the public conversation with Vargas Llosa in Lima in 1967, shortly after the latter received the Rómulo Gallegos Award, the occasion when they began their passionate nine-year bromance. Perhaps because of Vargas Llosa's role as host, perhaps as a response to the growing acclaim received by *One Hundred Years of Solitude*, the Colombian author's recently published novel, the Peruvian novelist mostly fulfilled the role of interviewer. As part of his response to the question "What do you think is the usefulness of your being a writer?" García Márquez stated:

> Fortunately or unfortunately I believe that it is a subversive role . . . in the sense that I know of no literature that serves to exalt established values, what is already hegemonic, and to contribute to create new ways of live, new societies; in conclusion, to improve the life of men [and women]. . . . [I]f the writer has a solid ideological position, this ideological position will be reflected in her story, in other words, it will nourish her story, and it is in that moment that that story attains the subversive force I mentioned. I don't believe it [the subversive force]

is deliberate, but I believe it is unavoidable. (*Diálogo sobre la novela latinoamericana* 22)

García Márquez's brief answer seems to be a version of Vargas Llosa's ideas described above. However, García Márquez ultimately posits a direct relationship between the writer and her text. Revolutionary writers will necessarily create revolutionary literature, even if the connection between ideas and literary product seems to bypass intention and reason. But the counterexamples of authors like Balzac—reactionaries who create revolutionary works—become even more difficult to explain in García Márquez's revision of Vargas Llosa's ideas.

For his part, Fuentes sketches a position regarding literature that resembles both Cortázar's and Vargas Llosa's. In his *La nueva novela hispanoamericana*, the Mexican novelist describes literature as "the enemy word: the word that does not entertain or advert, but perhaps converts. This is the word that in our current world would be impossible, or, if it attempts to make itself possible, would be repressed" (85). As is the case for Vargas Llosa, "the enemy word," which is nothing but another name for literature, is fire and in permanent insurrection. In a way that perhaps clarifies Vargas Llosa's parallel reflections regarding literature, the reason literature is subversive and often repressed is, according to Fuentes, that it "shows us the real: what consecrated reality obscures: the totality hidden or mutilated by conventional logic" (85). (One must note, however, that Vargas Llosa was working on the relationship between the novel and totality at about the same time as Fuentes.[41])

Fuentes sees Europe and the United States as having become nearly seamless consumer societies—only African Americans seem to have resisted full incorporation into this "system" (one must remember he is writing not long after the murders of Martin Luther King Jr. and Malcolm X). This is a version of capitalism ultimately based on the control of discourse: "Words are the reality of a consumer society: a whole system is built on the use of language" (*La nueva novela* 89). But, for him, Latin America has not achieved the same level of homogeneity or, for that matter, development. This does not mean that the region's discourse is any less deceptive, since it has the purpose of hiding class and other divisions in society. Fuentes notes: "The corruption of Latin American language is such that any true act of language is in itself revolutionary" (94). Moreover, he establishes a genealogy of writers who have "adumbrated" "our true language": "Darío and Neruda, Reyes and Paz, Borges and Huidobro, Vallejo and Lezama Lima, Cortázar and Carpentier" (94). Like Cortázar, Fuentes here links conservative writers (Borges), centrists (Reyes, Paz, Huidobro), leftists (Cortázar, Neruda, Carpentier, Vallejo), and apparently apolitical writers (Darío, Lezama Lima).

In summary, for Fuentes, literature, as the "enemy word," can be contrasted with political discourse—whether in Europe, the United States, or Latin America—advertising, and mainstream literature. Like Cortázar and to a lesser degree Vargas Llosa, Fuentes sees Latin America's subversive literature as mostly avant-garde. In a manner similar to that of Vargas Llosa but more theoretically developed, true literature is seen as undermining capitalist liberal democracy. Fuentes differs from both of his fellow writers in his fear that the subversive possibilities of literature are doomed if—and this is a big if—Latin American heterogeneity disappears in "a fascist populism" (*La nueva novela* 96), in a poverty that would transform the region into "the India of the Western hemisphere" (97), or by following "the North American model" (97). Fuentes contemplates the possibility of "even our language becoming disposable; Spanish [then] would not be language of this 'progress'; before it, our language is only a mountain of trash on the side of the highway, a cemetery of useless cars" (97). This fear is obviously the flip side of his optimistic belief in the transformative power of literature.

At least up to the Padilla affair, the Boom writers in 1970 present a common defense of literature as an activity with political implications and value against the rising tide of revolutionary anti-intellectualism. They not only saw their writing as compatible with revolutionary ways of thinking but even, on occasion, as a revolutionary act on its own. The next section of this chapter looks at two key Boom novels, how they represent revolutionary action, and in what way, if any, they claim to contribute to the possibility of radical politics.

### Practice

Toward the end of "Literature Is Fire," Vargas Llosa states, "Within the new society, and along the road that our personal ghosts and demons drive us, we will continue as before, as now, saying no, rebelling, demanding recognition for our right to dissent. . . . As yesterday, as today, if we love our vocation, we will have to continue fighting the thirty-two wars of Colonel Aureliano Buendía even though, like him, we lose them all" (73). Given his stress on the individuality of the author, Vargas Llosa here refers to the writing profession in terms that are as compatible with liberalism as with the socialism "Literature Is Fire" supposedly defends. Nevertheless, with García Márquez in the audience, Vargas Llosa presents Colonel Aureliano Buendía, one of the characters of *One Hundred Years of Solitude*, as an exemplary radical, implicitly as a role model for revolutionary writers and perhaps also for political revolutionaries.[42] With great eloquence, the Peruvian novelist presents literature not only as an intrinsic element in any true revolutionary transformation, but as a revolutionary act in itself, even if revolution has become transmuted into the right to dissent. In this manner, he is arguing that García Márquez's novel is revolutionary not only at the level of "form"—which was the argument proposed by Cortázar during the Amérique Latine Non-officielle panel—but also at the level of plot, content, and ideology.

In addition to examining *One Hundred Years of Solitude*, this section also analyzes Fuentes's *The Death of Artemio Cruz*, the Boom novel of the 1960s that deals most explicitly with the question of revolution. Here I ask the somewhat naive but still important question of whether García Márquez's *One Hundred Years of Solitude* and Fuentes's *The Death of Artemio Cruz* present a positive vision of revolution or, alternatively, imply a socialist solution to the problems represented in the texts.

The contrast between Vargas Llosa's description of Colonel Aureliano Buendía as a revolutionary paragon and his portrayal in *One Hundred Years of Solitude* is enormous.[43] In part, this is due to the obvious fact that the idea of socialism as a concept, and perhaps even as an idea, is completely absent from the novel.[44] Despite García Márquez's leftist sympathies, this omission is far from surprising. After all, the plot of the novel, which details the imbricated birth and death of the Buendía dynasty and Macondo, the town they founded, apparently concludes by the early 1930s, a couple of decades before the Cuban Revolution brought the issues of revolution and socialism to the forefront of regional discussion.[45] While Colonel Aureliano Buendía is described as "Commander in Chief of the revolutionary forces," and his followers are described more than once as "revolutionaries," the term is used in reference to what the iconic Latin American Marxist José Carlos Mariátegui once called "small revolutions" (Mariátegui, "Anniversary and Balance Sheet" 128). For Mariátegui, these "small revolutions," nothing more than political uprisings that have as their exclusive goal a change in the party in power, not a change in the economic and social structure, had to be distinguished from "the socialist revolution" (128).[46] Nevertheless, one would perhaps have expected García Márquez to sympathize with the *liberales*, if only from a sense of personal loyalty to his grandfather Colonel Nicolás Márquez, the model for the fictional Colonel Aureliano Buendía, who was, as one would have expected, "a veteran of the bitter Thousand Day War . . . a lifelong stalwart of the Colombian Liberal Party" (Martin, *Gabriel García Márquez* 1) Or, alternatively, he might have sympathized with them because of a somewhat vulgar Marxist perspective that could find the *liberales* to be representatives of a bourgeois and democratic capitalist modernity that would, in principle, be socially, economically, and politically superior to the anachronistic, semifeudal society, values, and policies defended by the *conservadores*. But the novel's portrayal of the nineteenth-century political rivalry is much more complex, even if *One Hundred Years of Solitude* presents Aureliano Buendía's embrace of liberalism as a rightful reaction against conservative electoral manipulations.

The novel exhibits a skeptical view regarding the value of the struggles between *liberales* and *conservadores* that marked Colombia and much of Latin America during the nineteenth and twentieth centuries.[47] It is true that one should dismiss as biased (and ironical) the following description of the differences between the political factions of Macondo:

> The Liberals . . . were Freemasons, bad people, wanting to hang priests, to institute civil marriage and divorce, to recognize the rights of illegitimate children as equal to those of legitimate ones, and to cut the country up into a federal system that would take power away from the supreme authority. The Conservatives, on the other hand, who had received their power directly from God, proposed the establishment of public order and family morality. They were the defenders of the faith of Christ, of the principle of authority, and were not prepared to permit the country to be broken down into autonomous entities. (95)

As readers of the novel know, this description is provided by Apolinar Moscote, who in addition to being Macondo's conservative magistrate was Aureliano's former father-in-law. He is immediately afterward shown stuffing the town's ballot boxes. Although presented as self-serving, the description of *liberales* and *conservadores* is only an exaggeration, even if grotesque, of the actual political proposals that characterized the political tendencies. The opposition between *conservadores* and *liberales* in nineteenth-century Colombia has been described as leading the former to "agitate the religious flag as a mobilizing factor for the general masses against the measures proposing the secularization of the state proposed by the *liberales*" (Suárez Fernández et al. 114).

In a turn of the screw, the novel even finds the apparently progressive measures proposed by the *liberales* to be completely disassociated from the actual beliefs and desires of the masses of an unnamed but clearly identifiable Colombia. After he, having been transformed into the leader of the liberal cause, returned to Macondo,

> Colonel Aureliano Buendía . . . listened in silence to the brief
> proposals of the emissaries. They asked first that he renounce the
> revision of property titles in order to get back the support of the
> Liberal landowners. They asked, secondly, that he renounce the fight
> against clerical influence in order to obtain the support of the Catholic
> masses. They asked, finally, that he renounce the aim of equal rights for
> natural and illegitimate children in order to preserve the integrity of
> the home. (167–68)

Aureliano, and through him the novel, comes to a surprising conclusion: "If these changes are good, it means that the Conservative regime is good. If we succeed in broadening the popular base of the war with them, as you people say, it means that the regime has a broad popular base. It means, in short, that for almost twenty years we've been fighting against the sentiments of the nation" (168).

But in addition to presenting *conservadurismo* as the de facto ideology of the Colombian people, *One Hundred Years of Solitude* delineates a positive portrayal of at least some *conservadores*, such as General José Raquel Moncada: "He wore civilian clothes, replaced the soldiers with unarmed policemen, enforced the amnesty laws, and helped a few families of Liberals who had been killed in the war. He succeeded in having

Macondo raised to the status of a municipality and he was therefore its first mayor, and he created an atmosphere of confidence that made people think of the war as an absurd nightmare of the past" (146). As part of her effort to have Aureliano reverse his decision to execute Moncada, Úrsula, the colonel's mother and matriarch of the Buendía clan, declares: "His government was the best we've ever had in Macondo" (157). She fails, and this failure signals the moral downfall of Colonel Aureliano Buendía.

It would be a mistake, however, to see the novel as sympathetic to the *conservadores*. For instance, it is during a *conservador* administration that the massacre of the workers of the banana company takes place. The presence of the "solemn lawyers dressed in black who in different times had followed Colonel Aureliano Buendía everywhere" now fluttering around the US executives of the banana company shows that the ideological differences between *conservadores* and *liberales* are ultimately undermined by significant political sectors who benefit regardless of the party in power (226).

The actual portrayal of Colonel Aureliano Buendía in the novel is thus ambiguous at best. Though his taking up arms may seem to have been justified given conservative tampering with the vote, the novel stresses the negative moral and affective impact of his political and military activity. This ethical declension is evidenced by García Márquez's narrativization of metaphors that illustrate Aureliano Buendía's loss of morality as he acquires political power: "The same night that his authority was recognized by all the rebel commands, he woke up in a fright, calling for a blanket. An inner coldness which shattered his bones and tortured him even in the heat of the sun would not let him sleep for several months, until it became a habit" (166). Around the time of the execution of Moncada, "he decided that no human being, not even Úrsula, could come closer to him than ten feet. In the center of the chalk circle that his aides would draw wherever he stopped, and which only he could enter, he would decide with brief orders that had no appeal the fate of the world" (155). The novel contradicts Vargas Llosa's description in "Literature Is Fire" of Colonel Aureliano Buendía as a kind of literary analogue for a Che Guevara seen in the most favorable light.

In *One Hundred Years of Solitude*, one finds a brief mention of the fictional revolutionary named in the title of Carlos Fuentes's *The Death of Artemio Cruz* (1962).[48] As part of García Márquez's description of the jailing of the union leaders who were struggling against the abuses of the (US American) banana company, the novel notes: "Taken among them were José Arcadio Segundo and Lorenzo Gavilán, a colonel in the Mexican revolution, exiled in Macondo, who said that he had been witness to the heroism of his comrade Artemio Cruz" (300). This reference to Artemio Cruz by García Márquez contrasts with Fuentes's depiction of the character. In Fuentes's novel, Artemio Cruz may be bold in pursuit of personal gain, but he is capable of cowardice in actual battle. However, this mistaken evaluation of Artemio Cruz's behavior and character accurately reflects the perspective of a certain Major, later Colonel, Gavilán in *The Death of Artemio Cruz*.[49]

According to Fuentes's novel, Cruz had actually abandoned a wounded soldier, then was lightly wounded when trying to save himself because of his desire to return alive to his lover Regina:

> His love for Regina would compensate for the guilt of abandoning the soldier. That's the way it should be. He lowered his head and thought that for the first time in his life he was experiencing shame. Shame: it wasn't shame that showed in Major Gavilán's clear, direct eyes. The officer rubbed his fuzzy blond beard with his free hand crusted with dust and sun.
>
> "We owe our lives to you and your men, Lieutenant. You halted the enemy's advance. The general will welcome you like a hero . . . Artemio." (73)

Unlike the reader of the novel, who is privy to all of Artemio's secret deeds, thoughts, and motivations, Gavilán, apparently in both novels, is fooled by Cruz's deceitful facade.

The connections between the two key Boom texts go beyond sharing the character of Gavilán or the brief reference in *One Hundred Years of Solitude* to the protagonist of *The Death of Artemio Cruz*. In fact, both share a similar view of presocialist "revolutions."

Written as the deathbed confession of a minor participant of the Mexican Revolution who eventually becomes an industrial and media mogul, *The Death of Artemio Cruz* presents in a fractured high-modernist style—chapters have first-, second-, and third-person narrators—a retrospective evaluation of Mexico's defining social event.

While the Mexican Revolution cannot be described as one of Mariáte-gui's "small revolutions" given its multitudinous social participation, the radical values and measures some of its leaders proposed, the level of social upheaval it created, and the violence that accompanied it, the brief description above indicates how the novel sketches the revolution's failure. The Mexican Revolution is depicted as making possible the rise to power and wealth of a lucky and dishonest few. Its results, in the end, are not that different from those of the "small revolutions." An epigraph indicates that Fuentes's novel was partly written in Havana (1960) and finished in Mexico City (1961). Given the dates and locations of writing, it is not surprising that the novel has the Cuban Revolution in mind.[50]

Perhaps in a nod to Beckett, the dying Artemio Cruz has his assistant play him the recordings of their conversation during the previous day, and in it one finds the following exchange:[51]

> "Say, the old boy at the Embassy wants to make a speech comparing this Cuban mess with the old-time Mexican Revolution. Why don't you lay the groundwork with an editorial . . ."
> "Yes, yes. We'll do it. How about twenty thousand pesos?"
> "Seems fair enough. Any ideas?"
> "Sure. Tell him to show the sharp differences between an anarchic, bloody movement that destroys private property and human rights and an orderly, peaceful, legal revolution like Mexico's, a revolution led by a middle class that found its inspiration in Jefferson. After all, people have bad memories. Tell him to praise Mexico." (193)

The immorality of Cruz, who as a former colonel in the revolution is fully aware that it had been a chaotic and violent movement led by leaders far from Jeffersonian or middle class, is in full display here. The novel has him acknowledge his cynicism. Cruz, who among other business interests owns newspapers, believes he will get away with his bold-faced lie because "people have bad memories." Moreover, regardless of one's view, the words used by Artemio Cruz to describe the Cuban Revolution—anarchic, bloody—better fit the Mexican Revolution. More than a million died in this bloodiest of all *jacqueries*, led by peasants and even bandits, such as Emiliano Zapata and Pancho Villa, respectively, in addition to bourgeois leaders such as Francisco Madero and Venustiano Carranza.

Further contradicting Cruz's deceitful description, Zapata and Villa best represented the unfulfilled political promises of the Mexican Revolution. Indeed, Cruz is at first presented as fighting for an unnamed general whose policies are reminiscent of Pancho Villa's:

> In every town they passed through, the general would investigate working conditions, reduce the workday to eight hours by public decree, and distribute land to the peasants. If there was a hacienda in the area, he would have the company store burned to the ground. If there were loan sharks—and there were always loan sharks, unless they'd fled with the federales—he would rescind all loans. The bad part was that the bulk of the population was under arms and almost all were peasants, so there was no one to enforce the general's decrees. Thus, it was better for them instantly to appropriate the wealth of the rich who remained in each town, and hope the Revolution would triumph, so the land reforms and the eight-hour day would be legalized. (64)

The promise of the revolution—redistribution of land, better working conditions, elimination of punitive loans—is ultimately undermined by its inability to fully implement and codify its brief achievements.

But the radical potential of the Mexican Revolution was not only compromised by the chaotic nature of the revolt, which explains why its best leaders, like Pancho Villa, meted out justice only to have their reforms subverted, if not turned back, after their armies moved to new towns, regions, and battles. According to *The Death of Artemio Cruz*, rather than a complete upturning of the country's social hierarchies, the Mexican Revolution ultimately led to the renewal of the social classes and social structures that had characterized prerevolutionary Mexico. By detailing its titular character's journey from revolutionary rags to capitalist riches, Fuentes's novel presents the net result of the revolution as at best the replacement of one class by another, rather than, as is the goal of socialism, the elimination of all class structures and the class exploitation on which they are based.

Gamaliel, the previous owner of Cruz's hacienda, makes explicit the failure of the revolution to create a truly new social order:

Artemio Cruz. So that was the name of the new world rising out of the
civil war; that was the name of those who had come to take his place.
Unfortunate land—the old man said, as he returned, slowly once
again, to the library and that undesired but fascinating presence—
unfortunate land that has to destroy its old possessors with each new
generation and put in their place new owners just as rapacious and
ambitious as the old ones. (44)

Gamaliel's view is reflected in the novel. Rather than abolishing structures of social oppression, the Mexican Revolution is presented as the
replacement of one group—those who benefited from Benito Juárez's
liberal reforms—by the triumphant revolutionaries, who, despite their
mestizo or even indigenous origins, will exploit the peasants and other
subaltern groups with the same brutality and rapacity.

But even this already dark view of the Mexican Revolution may
ironically be too optimistic, if that is the right word. As, again, Gamaliel
notes: "This man can save us. And that's all that matters" (46). After all,
while Gamaliel may have been replaced by Cruz, Artemio also marries
his daughter Catalina, despite the deep hatred she feels for the inter-
loper. What seems to be the substitution of one class for another is, at
the same time, the manner in which Gamaliel's "peculiarly Creole civilization, a civilization of enlightened despots" (44) manages to survive,
as it disappears, in postrevolutionary times.

As Doris Sommer notes, it is tempting to see in Artemio's relationship with Catalina the socially foundational promise that characterized
national romances, those nineteenth-century novels "that provided a
figure for apparently nonviolent consolidation, during internecine con-
flicts" (6). However, as she argues, "The pair seems perfect: a beautiful
aristocratic girl and a resourceful boy from the provinces with heroic
credentials. . . . But if she had given in, would Artemio have become
more honest or admirable in reconstructing Mexico on a popular base?
Or would he merely have seemed more genuine while reproducing the
class structure that equally shameless exploiters bequeathed to Catalina's more elegant father" (29). The novel, as Sommer implies, not only
presents postrevolutionary Mexico as a renewed version of precisely
the class structure that had benefitted *liberal* creole reformers, among
whom one can include Gamaliel, but does so in a way that repeats as it
undermines the romantic tropes of nineteenth-century "foundational

fictions." Fuentes's novel thus illustrates the manner in which earlier dominant classes manage to reproduce themselves under new political and social circumstances. After all, in addition to being a poor mestizo boy from the provinces, Artemio is also the illegitimate son of Atanasio Menchaca, whose father had been friend and companion of Antonio López de Santa Anna, the caudillo who governed Mexico during its first decades of independence. In fact, through biological, though not economic, inheritance, Artemio can be seen as a direct descendant of the first Mexican creole oligarchy that had been deposed by Gamaliel and his Juarista comrades.[52] Breaking free from Artemio's perspective, the novel includes his grandmother Ludovinia Menchaca's interior monologue: "As if I couldn't sense that there is flesh of my flesh prowling out there, an extension of Ireneo and Atanasio, another Menchaca, another man like them, out there, listen to me. . . . Of course he's mine, even though you haven't sought him. . . . Blood answers blood without having to come near" (253). Mexican history is, from this perspective, nothing but a repeating cycle of structural class exploitation and its renewal through violence and the intermarriage of the different dominant groups. Instead of promising, even if only rhetorically, the overcoming of class and racial division, the foundational couple of Artemio and Catalina constitutes the renewal and continuation of oppression. Their personal strife—Artemio and Catalina both love and hate each other— is nothing but an index of the social violence within the creole oligarchy that makes their long-term hegemony possible.

While Cuba is mentioned only briefly, an earlier and frustrated attempt at a full social revolution occupies a central place in Fuentes's novel: the Spanish Republic (1931–1939). Perhaps its contradictions make it difficult for us today to see the Second Spanish Republic as resembling utopia. As we know, the Republic was constituted by an uncomfortable alliance of divergent political groups—anarchists who attempted to directly destroy the existing religious, cultural, and political order; socialists; Communists who blindly followed Soviet dictates; and liberals—that on numerous occasions broke down into violence among themselves.[53] However, General Francisco Franco's right-wing military uprising against the Republic was seen by many as one of the Fascist waves that, starting with Benito Mussolini's March on Rome in 1922 and continuing with Adolf Hitler's coming to power in Germany in 1933, threatened to drown European democracy. Therefore, despite its many contradictions, the fight for the Republic was often seen as an opportunity, perhaps the last, to stop fascism from overtaking Europe. But the organized support from the Italian and German militaries ultimately guaranteed the triumph of Francisco Franco's Nationalists.

The Spanish Republic is presented *The Death of Artemio Cruz* as a genuine even if ultimately defeated revolution. In other words, the struggle for the Republic during the Civil War is presented as a movement that strived to create a free, inclusive, and egalitarian society. This ethical and revolutionary appeal is made evident as Lorenzo, Artemio's son, joins the fight for the Republic precisely as it is becoming a lost cause. Lorenzo himself states it, even if unclearly: "As soon as we cross the border, this late arrival to the international brigades calls it quits and begins a new life. I'll never forget this one, Papa, because I learned everything I know here. It's simple. I'll tell you everything when I get back. Just now I can't think of the right words" (231).

While what this "everything" actually means is never explained, it clearly refers to a transformative political experience. In the novel, the Spanish Republic is a true revolution because it permits Lorenzo Cruz the experience of utopia.[54] Lorenzo's statements and Fuentes's description of the Spanish Civil War brings to mind a comment made by Slavoj Žižek:

> In a proper revolutionary breakthrough, the utopian future is neither simply fully realized in the present nor simply evoked as a distant promise which justifies present violence—it is rather as if, in a unique suspension of temporality, in the short-circuit between the present and the future, we are—as if by Grace—for a brief time allowed to act as if the utopian future is (not yet fully here, but) already at hand, just there to be grabbed. Revolution is not experienced as a present hardship we have to endure for the happiness and freedom of the future generations, but as the present hardship over which this future happiness and freedom already cast their shadow—in it, we are already free while fighting for freedom, we are already happy while fighting for happiness, no matter how difficult the circumstances. Revolution is not a Merleau-Pontyan wager, an act suspended in the *futur antérieur*, to be legitimized or delegitimized by the long term outcome of the present acts; it is as it were its own ontological proof, an immediate index of its own truth. ("From Revolutionary to Catastrophic Utopia" 247)

Lorenzo lacks the words to describe the utopian "everything" he has learned because, as a true revolution, Spain exceeds all of his previous experiences and the language he has till now used to describe them. Ironically, Lorenzo will never be able to attempt this potentially impossible linguistic task. He will be killed by German planes before making it to safety. His last words both state the experience of utopia—understood here as liberty, fraternity and sorority, and equality—and the impossibility of putting this lived freedom and happiness into words.

As a "proper revolutionary breakthrough," Spain serves as a counterpoint to the Mexican Revolution and also as measuring stick with which to evaluate it. In a similar manner, Lorenzo's life and experience permits us to understand the limits of Artemio Cruz as a revolutionary. In one of his many moments of lucidity, as he remembers Lorenzo's brief life, the dying Cruz addresses his son: "Oh, thank you for showing me what my life could be. Oh, thank you for living that day for me" (235). Van Delden argues, "Lorenzo is perhaps the most important person in Artemio's life, for it is through his son that Artemio hopes to achieve a form of redemption from his own injured life" (*Carlos Fuentes* 60). But Lorenzo can redeem Artemio because the son is able to achieve the insight, generosity, and solidarity that the father lacked. And this is possible because, for Fuentes, the Spanish Civil War, unlike the Mexican Revolution, was an index of its own utopian truth.

We have already mentioned the moment that is echoed in Lorenzo's death: when Artemio abandons the wounded soldier and, ironically, gets credit for the military success of the fighters he had in reality deserted. The first and perhaps understandable act of selfishness—after all, he is trying to preserve himself out of love for Regina—becomes the first link in the chain of self-interest that characterizes Artemio's life.

One would assume that self-interest would contradict the goals of any true revolution. For instance, the French Revolution proudly proclaimed liberty, fraternity, and equality as its utopian goals. However, Artemio Cruz's revolutionary ideals were shaped by his "teacher Sebastián," whose values seem distant from the goals of the French Revolution or, for that matter, from those of any socialist revolution. Artemio thus reminisces on his deathbed,

You sat at his knee, learning those simple things with which you must begin in order to be a free man, not a slave of commandments written without your even being consulted. Oh, how happy those apprenticeship days were, learning the tasks which he taught you so you could earn a living: days at the forge with the hammers, when your teacher Sebastián would return tired but begin classes only for you, so that you could be something in life and make your own rules, you the rebel, you free, you unique and new. . . . He ordered you, you went to the Revolution. (117–18)

Sebastian's emphasis on the need to develop one's own sense of morality independently from social constraints and his stress on the individual rather than the community summarize some of Nietzsche's key lessons.[55] Despite the idyllic nature of these memories, the moral declension of Artemio, who went from idealism to greed, is already implicit in this passage, as is the root of this ethical fall. After all, Sebastián's apparently Nietzschean lessons—"be a free man, not a slave of commandments," "make your own rules," "you the rebel, you unique and new"—had in them the worm of the individualism that would, in later years, lead Artemio to become a ruthless capitalist.[56]

Lorenzo understands the meaning of revolutionary action differently. Referring to the opinions of his Spanish revolutionary friend Miguel, which he clearly shares, he notes: "He said his greatest sorrow, the one he'd carry to his grave, was that all the workers of the world had not taken up arms to defend Spain, because if Spain lost, it was as if all of them lost" (229). In other words, unlike the Nietzschean roots of Artemio's rebellion, which, when push came to shove, contributed to his lack of concern for the social consequences of his actions, Lorenzo understands the revolution as based on solidarity. A loss for one is a loss for all.

Despite their obvious differences, both *The Death of Artemio Cruz*, the first novel produced in the 1960s by a member of the Boom, and *One Hundred Years of Solitude*, the novel which for many brings the Boom to fruition, have one major trait in common: they implicitly reject any view of linear historical progress.

As we have seen, Fuentes presents the history of Mexico as characterized by reformist or revolutionary upheavals that ultimately lead to a new ruling class, but one that maintains the basic oppressive structures of the country. The title of the novel may imply that the political and social system represented by the titular character is coming to its end along with the cyclical structure of which he is the latest beneficiary. However, the novel in no moment presents the classes or groups that would replace those set in power by the Mexican Revolution. In fact, several readers, Lanin A. Gyurko among them, have pointed out "the cyclical time patterning that characterizes the work" (84).

García Márquez's novel has also been seen as presenting a cyclical view of history. For instance, Gene Bell-Villada argues that "*One Hundred Years of Solitude* conveys a sense of time that is circular, cyclical and looped, rather than forward, sequential, or linear" (7). This circularity is made explicit in the novel during the description of the strike against the banana company: "The atmosphere of the following months was so tense that even Úrsula perceived it in her dark corner, and she had the impression that once more she was living through the dangerous times when her son Aureliano carried the homeopathic pills of subversion in his pocket. She tried to speak to José Arcadio Segundo, to let him know about that precedent, but Aureliano Segundo told her that since the night of the attempt on his life no one knew his whereabouts." Úrsula then adds: "Just like Aureliano. . . . It's as if the world were repeating itself" (298).

However, this cyclicality is embedded within a linear narrative. After all, *One Hundred Years of Solitude* also presents a history of humanity and of Macondo from genesis—when "the world was so new that many things lacked names" (1)—to apocalypse—"Macondo was already a fearful whirlwind of dust and rubble being spun about by the wrath of the biblical hurricane" (416). The novel ends as the last Buendía and Macondian reads the manuscript that details the apocalypse he is experiencing: "It was foreseen that the city of mirrors (or mirages) would be wiped out by the wind and exiled from the memory of men at the precise moment when Aureliano Babilonia would finish deciphering the parchments, and that everything written on them was unrepeatable since time immemorial and forever more, because races condemned to one hundred years of solitude did not have a second opportunity on earth" (417). It is difficult to exaggerate the darkness of this ending. Who are these condemned "races"? Are they Colombians? Are they the dwellers of the Caribbean? Are they Latin Americans? Are they the peoples of the Global South? Nor can one exaggerate the bleakness of its denial of a "second chance" to all of those allegorized by Macondo.

How, then, could *The Death of Artemio Cruz, One Hundred Years of Solitude*, and, by extension, the other Boom novels be seen as revolutionary texts? Neither Fuentes nor García Márquez present in their texts a way out from the prison house of history. Unlike socialist realism, which idealized working-class rebellions, these Boom novels present history as a nightmare from which no waking is possible. As we saw when analyzing the Amérique Latine Non-officielle panel, by 1970 many of the more politically committed readers had begun to criticize the Boom novels precisely on these terms. One part of the answer lies in the Cuban Revolution.

For instance, Maarten van Delden notes that *The Death of Artemio Cruz* must be read within a framework that sees the Cuban Revolution as an example of how to exit the historical vicious circle described in the novel:

> The Cuban Revolution is a strong presence in Fuentes's novel, for if the Lorenzo episode [Spanish Civil War] harks back to the Mexican Revolution, it also looks forward to the Cuban Revolution. Fuentes sketches a narrative in Artemio Cruz in which the revolutionary ideal, betrayed in Mexico, and defeated in Spain, now experiences a new dawn in Cuba. . . . [T]he Mexican Revolution and the Spanish Civil War are presented in Artemio Cruz as stages in a historical development that culminates for now in the Cuban Revolution. It is wrong, therefore, to compare the Mexican Revolution and the Spanish Civil War as if they were discrete episodes, rather than part of a larger narrative that encompasses them both. (*Carlos Fuentes* 60)

Van Delden is probably interpreting the novel from a perspective close to that held by Fuentes at the time of writing. After all, Fuentes did not need to stress the virtues of the Cuban Revolution in his text because for him, as for many of his readers, it served as the background to their retrospective evaluation of the Mexican Revolution. Van Delden's interpretation of *The Death of Artemio Cruz* reflects his study of the Mexican novelist's journalism during the early 1960s: "These articles reveal a strong element of utopianism in Fuentes's political views, a utopianism that takes the form of a fervent belief in the concept of revolution, and receives its most significant inspiration from the example of the Cuban revolution" (41).

Another example of Fuentes's belief at the time in the Cuban Revolution is provided by José Donoso in *The Boom in Spanish American Literature* when he writes about his first meeting with Fuentes in 1962:

The most important thing that Carlos Fuentes told me during the trip to Concepción was that after the Cuban Revolution he agreed to speak publicly only of politics, never of literature; that in Latin America the two were inseparable and that now Latin America could only look toward Cuba. His enthusiasm for the figure of Fidel Castro in that period and his faith in the revolution excited the entire Congress of Intellectuals. (49)

Nevertheless, this passion for the Cuban Revolution is not directly expressed in the text of *The Death of Artemio Cruz*, except, perhaps, in his criticism of the Mexican Revolution.

In a similar vein, Gerald Martin has pointed out the need to take the Cuban Revolution into account in any attempt at understanding the political dimension of García Márquez's masterpiece.[57] For the (future) official biographer of García Márquez, "The apocalypse of the Buendías is not—how could it be?—the end of Latin America but the end of primitive neocolonialism, its conscious or unconscious collaborators, and an epoch of illusions" (*Journeys through the Labyrinth* 233). Even though he acknowledges that "the novel does not actually say this" (233), he comes to the conclusion: "For the New Novelists of the 1960s the two key signs of the impending transformation of Latin America were, as we have seen, the Cuban Revolution and the 'boom' of the Latin American novel itself" (233). Literary and, more importantly, political and social modernization were just around the corner. This is why, according to Martin, the ending of *One Hundred Years of Solitude* is characterized by a "sense of euphoria" (233). For García Márquez, as well as for many Latin American readers at the time, the apocalypse would paradoxically be soon followed by the creation of a modern socialist society in which solidarity would finally replace solitude. The problem with both van Delden's and Martin's readings is that they are necessarily bound to the original context of writing and reception. Without Fuentes or García Márquez having had to change one word, the meaning of their works evolved and migrated throughout the years. While some, perhaps many, readers of the 1960s could see the Cuban Revolution as a solution to all of Latin America's problems, this position is much more difficult to hold fifty or more years later. Today we read these and other Boom novels as the ruins of the Cuban Revolution seem to crumble before our eyes. The pessimism of *The Death of Artemio Cruz* and *One Hundred Years of Solitude* now have no countervailing social context, even if the literary achievements of these novels can still thrill the reader.[58]

These novels, however, display an additional political dimension independent of the ups and downs of the Cuban Revolution. The following statement by Subcomandante Marcos, perhaps the best-known "comandante" since Che and Fidel, made during an interview conducted by García Márquez and Álvaro Pombo, can serve as an example:

My parents introduced us to García Márquez, Carlos Fuentes, Monsiváis, Vargas Llosa (regardless of his ideas), to mention only a few. They set us to reading them. *A Hundred Years of Solitude* to explain what the provinces were like at the time. *The Death of Artemio Cruz* to show what had happened to the Mexican Revolution. *Días de guardar* to describe what was happening in the middle classes. As for *La ciudad y los perros* [*The Time of the Hero*], it was in a way a portrait of us, but in the nude. All these things were there. We went out into the world in the same way that we went out into literature. I think this marked us. We didn't look out at the world through a news-wire but through a novel, an essay or a poem. ("Subcomandante Marcos" 77–78)

Afterward, Marcos adds, "But the Latin American boom came first, then Cervantes, then García Lorca, and then came a phase of poetry. So in a way you [looking at GGM] are an accessory to all this" (78). And the "this" implicit in Marcos's statement is precisely his political activity, that is, his helping organize the peaceful uprising of the indigenous communities in Chiapas. In order to better understand the influence of the Boom novels on Marcos, it may be useful to remember that *One Hundred Years of Solitude*, *The Death of Artemio Cruz*, and *The Time of the Hero* are all paradigmatic "total novels." While the term was popularized by Vargas Llosa, whose narrative of the 1960s can be described under this rubric, all the novels mentioned by Marcos can be described as "total novels."[59]

In "The Latin American Novel Today," one of the first essays in which the Peruvian Nobel Prize winner uses the term, Vargas Llosa writes of the "total novels" "as wishing to recapture with fantasy and words the total image of the world, of seeking to write novels that express this total reality not only qualitatively, but also quantitatively" (11). In addition to *The Human Comedy*, *The Man without Qualities*, and *Ulysses*, he lists *The Lost Steps*, *Hopscotch*, and *One Hundred Years of Solitude* among these total novels. The absence of any 1960s English-language novels is not an accident. As Vargas Llosa notes: "The European or North American novelist in our day rarely attempts to write a 'total novel'" (11).

Vargas Llosa's definition of the "total novel" here and in other texts is somewhat vague. In fact, he never explains how these total novels reconcile fantasy and reality.[60] However, one could very well argue that the novels of the Boom, in particular *One Hundred Years of Solitude*, became the conduit through which the goal of expressing total reality of a specific society or social group—for instance, African Americans in Toni Morrison's *Song of Solomon* or Indians in Salman Rushdie's *Midnight's Children*—was reintroduced into the Anglophone novel.

Thus, despite the tensions in Vargas Llosa's definition, the political value of *The Death of Artemio Cruz*, *One Hundred Years of Solitude*, and *The Time of the Hero* resides in their ability to inform the reader of social reality. As Mark Anderson notes, this happens because "the total novel models its broad array of characters, settings, and plots on real life, but it also encompasses subjective aspects of human experience" (206). Nicholas Birns adds that, in the case of the total novel, "a work of fiction was expected to sum up history, society, culture and imagination" (*Contemporary Australian Literature* 68).[61] Another way of defining the total novel that clarifies Vargas Llosa's definition is to say that it presents a "cognitive map" of specific Latin American countries and through them of the region. Fredric Jameson, who coined the term, writes about cognitive maps as "enabl[ing] a situational representation on the part of the individual subject to that vaster and properly unrepresentable totality which is the ensemble of society's structures as a whole" (51). These novels' popularity, as well as their political value—or, better said, their value for political readings—originates in their ability to "cognitively map our individual social relationship to local, national, and international class realities" (51). The fact that *One Hundred Years of Solitude* has often been assigned in courses dealing with Latin American society acknowledges its status as a cognitive map.

Let us return, then, to Marcos's statement on the political value of literature. The reason these three novels—*The Death of Artemio Cruz*, *The Time of the Hero*, and *One Hundred Years of Solitude*—are valued by the Zapatista leader is because they provide, as he says, descriptions that help explain the Mexican Revolution, the "nude"—hidden? uncensored? subconscious?—aspects of Latin America, and life in the region's hinterlands in the (not so) recent past, respectively.[62] In other words, Marcos is claiming that these novels, as well as the "literary" chronicles of Monsiváis and Cervantes's *Don Quixote*, a novel that Vargas Llosa has described as "a pristine example of the total novel" ("Four Centuries of *Don Quixote* 21), constitute "cognitive maps" of Mexico, Latin America, and the Hispanic world that he finds more useful for understanding the region, and therefore for planning his political action, than the information found in nonliterary texts.[63]

———

While the "Padilla affair" led to the breakdown of the Boom, Vargas Llosa and Cortázar first tried to recapture their political unity by founding a new magazine, *Libre* (Free). (The links between *Libre* and the Padilla affair are evidenced by the first issue of the journal, which reproduced several of the key documents related to the case.) In hindsight, one cannot but be amazed at the journal's ambition and inclusiveness. Not only did *Libre*'s editorial board include Vargas Llosa and Cortázar, but, as Gilman notes, "it was composed by many of the intellectuals who had protested against Padilla's arrest and auto-criticism" (281). Among these were some who had maintained their distance from the Cuban regime, such as the future Nobel Prize–winning Mexican poet Octavio Paz, the Cuban exiles Severo Sarduy and Carlos Franqui, Donoso, some of the central figures of new Spanish literature, including those then living in exile, such as Jorge Semprún and Juan Goytisolo, and up-and-coming luminaries living under the Franco regime, such as Manuel Vásquez Montalbán. Moreover, Carlos Fuentes, who had been marginalized by the Cuban Revolution because of his close contacts with the US cultural establishment, would become a major presence in the journal. (According to Gilman, the Cuban cultural establishment attributed "a fundamental role" in the direction of the magazine to "Carlos Fuentes, Juan Goytisolo, and Vargas Llosa" [284].) Even García Márquez collaborated with the magazine: the second issue included an interview with him.

What seems more surprising is how all of these diverse figures—there was even talk of including Guillermo Cabrera Infante, the most notorious anti-Castro writer-in-exile—were able to come together under the banner of what today we would call "democratic socialism," even if the politics of *Libre* were more radical than what now goes by that name.[64] (The second issue of the journal, edited by Jorge Semprún, was dedicated to the topic of "Freedom and Socialism.") Moreover, that a journal with the title "Free" could be aligned with a leftist position shows how different the political environment of 1971 was from ours. Today we would immediately associate a journal with that title with a neoliberal or even libertarian position. However, the potentially antisocialist connotations of the journal's title were already highlighted by the *Revista Casa de las Américas* in 1971 in an editorial significantly titled "Ellos escogieron la libertad" (They chose freedom): "Such a beautiful name does not avoid being often manipulated, and is, overall, the hobbyhorse of capitalist ideologues. . . . Only with difficulty could they have found a name more revealing than this, [those] defenders of the intellectual free enterprise that comfortably settled in the free world get together to give a lesson on revolution to the little and poor underdeveloped" (qtd. in Gilman 292). Even if the title was meant as a riposte to the Cuban Revolution's subordination of art to political expediency, the ambiguity remained relevant given the political evolution of Vargas Llosa and the region as a whole. However, the tenuous unity of such a heterogeneous group—from the anticommunist progressive Octavio Paz, to budding critics of the Cuban Revolution, to Cuban exiles—was bound to break when Castro gave the regions' writers an ultimatum.

Fidel Castro's notorious closing address at the Education Congress on 1 May 1971 only deepened the differences between the Boom writers— and other progressive intellectuals—and the Cuban Revolution. In this speech, the Cuban leader directly addressed the Boom writers and their criticisms of the growing curtailment of freedoms of speech and of thought in the island and, in particular, of the treatment of Padilla and his collaborators. With his inimitable passion and eloquence, Castro stated:

> They are at war against a country having a position such as Cuba's— only 90 miles from the United States—and which has never made a single concession or made the slightest hint of submission, and which is a part of a world of hundreds of millions who will not be able to serve as pretext for the brazen pseudo-leftists who want to win laurels—these living in Paris, London, and Rome. They are really

brazen Latin Americans, who instead of being here in the trenches live in the bourgeois salons 10,000 miles from the problems and enjoy some of the renown that they won when they were initially able to express something of the Latin American problems. ("Speech by Cuban Prime Minister").

Given this attack from the undisputed leader of the Cuban Revolution and, implicitly, of the Latin American Left, the Boom writers were forced to either capitulate to Castro and the Cuban Revolution or to break with it. The Padilla affair and its aftermath thus put an end to the apparent ideological unity of the Boom. While the four writers would continue to maintain friendly relations—at least until 1976, when Vargas Llosa, for reasons still not fully known, punched García Márquez outside a Mexican cinema—their politics began to diverge significantly.[65]

On the one hand, both Fuentes, who had begun to distance himself from the revolution since 1967, a process that obviously accelerated after 1971, and Vargas Llosa became critics of the Cuban government, but their political evolution was very different. Fuentes remained committed to leftist and liberal causes, while Vargas Llosa moved ideologically rightward, having become by the mid-1980s the region's best-known paladin of what would later be known as neoliberalism.[66] Nevertheless, at least in principle he has held onto the beliefs about the subversive nature of literature expressed in "Literature Is Fire." In fact, in 2016, while receiving an honorary doctorate from De La Salle University in Manila, he declared: "Good books develop in us a kind of natural criticism of the world as it is, and the longing for a better world, better societies, better institutions, values that would be able to create opportunities open to all the citizens, societies, in which inequalities will be diminished, in which there would be opportunities for everybody to materialize their dreams" (qtd. in Cayabyab). But now subversion seems to be linked to all good literature qua good literature rather than to a specifically radical group of texts.

On the other hand, Cortázar and, at first less stridently, García Márquez took the side of the island's government. For instance, the author of *Hopscotch* published a political poem, "Policrítica en la hora de los chacales" (Policriticism during the time of the jackals), in the July–August 1971 issue of *Revista Casa de las Américas* (and subsquently widely reprinted throughout Latin America). The poem, written in direct response to Castro's speech, included these verses:

You are right Fidel: only within the struggle is there a
    right to be discontent
Only from inside must criticism arise, the search for better
    formulas
But within is so outside sometimes.
And today I distance myself permanently from the dilettante
    liberal, who
signs those virtuous texts (34)[67]

Cortázar would continue supporting radical causes throughout the remainder of his life, in particular that of Sandinista Nicaragua, but as that country's novelist and then vice president Sergio Ramírez points out: "Cortazar's political proposals developed first regarding Cuba, then Nicaragua, but they were almost never expressed in his books, not even in *A Manual for Manuel,* but instead were to be found in his civic behavior" (28). Nevertheless, there is little doubt, at least to my mind, that Cortázar's "policriticism" must be read as a capitulation of his critical independence when it came to politics.

A similar case can be made regarding García Márquez, whose progressive rapprochement with the Cuban government accelerated after the Chilean coup in 1973. According to Martin, "Cuba, though also problematical, was more progressive than the USSR and had to be supported by all serious anti-imperialist Latin Americans, who should nonetheless do what they could to moderate any repressive, undemocratic or dictatorial aspects of the regime" (*Gabriel García Márquez* 376). Despite supposedly becoming Fidel Castro's "best friend," García Márquez would use his influence to "moderate" the Cuban regime by working for measures he believed were necessary. For instance, he played a central role in convincing the Cuban government to allow Padilla and his wife to emigrate to the United States in 1979.[68]

Even more importantly, the end of the 1960s marked, for all practical purposes, the demise of the total novel, in particular those that attempted to portray specific national and regional societies and histories. Not only did younger writers stop writing total novels, but key aspects of the genre would be abandoned by the Boom writers themselves. For instance, Martin describes García Márquez's *The Autumn of the Patriarch* as "barely penetrable" and having "almost no significant Colombian dimension, not least because Colombia never had the sort of patriarch it portrays" (*Gabriel García Márquez* 544, 383). Something similar could be said of Fuentes's *Terra Nostra* (1975), which attempts to encompass the whole of the Hispanic world and its history from the sixteenth century to the present while also presenting a mash-up of historical characters—Philip II, Cervantes, and so forth—with those from literature—Pierre Menard (from Borges's short story "Pierre Menard, Author of the Quixote"), Horacio Oliveira (protagonist of *Hopscotch*), and Zavalita (protagonist of Vargas Llosa's *Conversation in the Cathedral*), among others. While these novels maintain and expand the intellectual inclusiveness that characterized the total novel, they ultimately abandon the attempt at national or regional cognitive mapping that had been one of its central traits.

Nevertheless, some described Vargas Llosa's *War of the End of the World* (1981), set in late nineteenth-century Brazil, and *Feast of the Goat* (2000), which describes the Dominican Republic under dictator Rafael Trujillo, as total novels. However, as Jeff Browitt points out, unlike Vargas Llosa's masterpieces of the 1960s, the most ambitious attempts at creating cognitive maps in Latin American literature, these later novels can be read as "parables of corruption" or even as "thinly disguised pedagogical instruction on ideology and fanaticism" (93). Moreover, his most characteristic texts of the 1970s—*Captain Pantoja and the Special Service* (1973) and *Aunt Julia and the Scriptwriter* (1977)—exemplify what Raymond L. Williams has called "the discovery of humor" (*Mario Vargas Llosa* 93). In fact, one could even see *Aunt Julia and the Scriptwriter*, which narrates Vargas Llosa's real-life romance and marriage to his aunt-in-law, as a precedent and influence on autofiction or the nonfiction novel, a genre that is currently surging in popularity in Peru and Latin America, and that, given its stress on individual experience over the representation of national or local society, rarely attempts to create cognitive maps. In the case of Peru, where Vargas Llosa's influence is strongest, three of the most acclaimed and widely read recent novels can be described as nonfiction or autofiction: Jeremías Gamboa's *Contarlo todo* (2013), Renato Cisneros's *La distancia que nos separa* (2015), and José Carlos Yrigoyen's *Absolutamente sólo* (2016).[69]

The Boom novelists did not idealize revolutionaries in their fiction, even if they often did so in their public statements during the 1960s. Moreover, they rejected any concession to the demands of the region's leftists for edifying socialist propaganda. Instead, in the 1960s, they saw literature as a way of understanding Latin American social reality and, therefore, as a political intervention. It is thus no accident that in 2001 Subcomandante Marcos, the Zapatista leader, mentioned three classic novels of the period as among the texts that helped guide his actions. Although Latin American literature has not been bereft of major novels after the Boom—some of them will be studied in the next chapters— the cognitive social mapping that helped Marcos, the so-called post-modern revolutionary, understand the social structures of Mexico and Latin America is longer a dominant trait of the region's writing.

# 3

# The Fall of the Revolutionary and the Return of Liberal Democracy

*Vargas Llosa's* The Real Life of Alejandro Mayta *(1984) and* Manuel Puig's Kiss of the Spider Woman *(1976)*

It may surprise those who do not follow Latin American literature closely to discover that none of the four major Boom writers wrote a novel about the guerrilla movements in the region as they were happening in the 1960s. Perhaps this omission is a result of these authors' need to achieve novelistic objectivity in order to portray a historical event that, at least temporarily, seemed to augur the birth of a new Latin America. Unlike previous "small" and not-so-small revolutions, which García Márquez satirized in *One Hundred Years of Solitude* and Fuentes rued in *The Death of Artemio Cruz*, the Boom writers believed that the Cuban Revolution and other radical movements of the time represented an attempt to achieve, in Mario Vargas Llosa's words, "a Latin America with dignity and modernity, and for socialism to free us from our anachronism and our horror" ("Literature Is Fire" 73). Furthermore, they saw themselves and their literature as participating in this process of change. It is therefore understandable that the first novel by one of the Boom authors to deal with the insurgency of the 1960s—even if the attempt at starting an insurrection is set in 1958—would be published only in 1984, when the revolutionary wave had mostly waned. I am referring here to Vargas Llosa's *The Real Life of Alejandro Mayta*. But, perhaps reflecting the progressive loss of belief in the centrality of revolutionary action, Vargas Llosa does not limit himself to exploring the life of a fictional revolutionary who is gay and also a Trotskyist, but he also investigates the process of writing such a novel.

However, as mentioned in the previous chapter, Vargas Llosa had traveled far from the ideological positions he had passionately defended during the heady revolutionary days of the 1960s, or even from those expressed during the Amérique Latine Non-officielle panel. By the 1980s, he was rapidly becoming the best-known promoter in the region of the renewed free-market ideas that were beginning to be known as neoliberalism. Vargas Llosa's newfound beliefs, into which, as is his wont, he put all his considerable energy and intellectual ability, have long raised questions about whether *The Real Life of Alejandro Mayta* should be read as a fictional exploration of the Latin American guerrilla movements or as an attack, even a diatribe, on the Left of the 1960s and what remained of it into the 1980s. This chapter looks at Vargas Llosa's novel and attempts to separate the ideological chaff from the fictional wheat, to the degree that this may be possible.

The second section of the chapter looks at an earlier novel that also includes a member of an armed revolutionary group as one of its central characters, though, as befits the country in which it is set and in which it was partly written, he belongs to an urban guerrilla group. I am referring to Manuel Puig's *The Kiss of the Spider Woman* (1976). While Puig's novels could be seen as late contributions to the Boom—his first novel *Betrayed by Rita Hayworth* (1968) was published only one year after *One Hundred Years of Solitude*—his work can more rightly be ranked among the first attempts at developing a post-Boom aesthetic that, as Jean Franco notes, "has explored the potentiality of mass modern culture" and "draw[s] on Hollywood film, boleros and tangos" (*Spanish-American Literature since Independence* 340). In many ways, Puig can be seen as a forerunner to current Spanish American novels that often embrace mass culture, even if today that culture is no longer as varied in its national or regional provenance as was the case in Puig's work.[1] Now it is rock, rather than Argentine tango or Mexican and Cuban boleros, that imprints Latin American narrative.[2]

*Kiss of the Spider Woman* also wallows in films as Luis Alberto Molina, a gay window dresser, recounts these to Valentín Arregui, a leftist activist and urban guerrilla with whom he shares a jail cell. These include real films, as in the case of Jacques Tourneur's *Cat People* (1942) and *I Walked with a Zombie* (1943), and made-up ones, as in the supposedly UFA Nazi and the Mexican *cabaretera* movies. As one would expect, popular music, in particular boleros, such as Mario Clavel's "La carta" (The letter), also serves as counterpoint to the story of the deepening relationship between the two inmates. Thus, in addition to embracing popular and mass culture, the Argentine writer explores the problematic relationship between gay and lesbian identities and revolution, between drag queen and guerrilla fighter, and between sexual identity and social change. By linking sexuality and revolution, Puig moves beyond the parameters that had characterized cultural and political discourse in the 1960s. But he also presents an alternative narrative model to that proposed by the Boom: instead of so-called total novels, the maps of Mexican or Peruvian history, culture, and mores written by Fuentes and Vargas Llosa in the 1960s, Puig concentrates on how politics and history impact individual characters within specific personal circumstances.

As the title of this chapter indicates, I trace here the auratic loss of the revolutionary and the rise of new political issues, social figures, and modes of political activity. However, by rejecting maximalist revolution—that is, the creation of a whole new social system—these new movements unavoidably end up accepting liberal democracy as the framework for political activity. Vargas Llosa's *The Real Life of Alejandro Mayta* and Puig's *Kiss of the Spider Woman* reflect this waning of the cult of revolution and its replacement by questions of identity, gender, and sexuality, among other options.

In "Boom in the Revolution," we saw that by the late 1960s, "culture"—that is, literature and all the arts—had for many among the more radical circles of the Left become subordinated to politics. In fact, not long after Ernesto Guevara's death, the Cuban writer Miguel Barnet, in a poem significantly (and redundantly) titled "Poema," also known as "Che," addressed the revolutionary leader: "It's not that I want to give you / quill for gun / but the poet is you" (29). Barnet thus elevated Ernesto "Che" Guevara into a major, perhaps the central, cultural figure of the region.[3] In different manners and from different ideological positions, Puig and Vargas Llosa put into question this earlier celebration of the guerrilla fighter that, even if rapidly becoming residual by 1976 and surely so by 1984, was still present among some radical sectors of Latin American culture.

This questioning of violent revolution, perhaps revolution tout court, responds in both novels to the tragic political changes that had taken place in the early 1970s, and, in the case of Vargas Llosa, to the region's evolution into the early 1980s. These changes dashed the political hopes that had animated many throughout Latin America in the 1960s.

As we saw, the Cuban Revolution had experienced a process of cultural hardening throughout the 1960s that only gained international exposure with the Padilla affair. However, the diminishment of individual and creative freedoms continued and perhaps intensified into the early 1970s, to the point that the period between 1971 and 1975 became known as "el quinquenio gris" (the gray five years). According to Ambrosio Fornet, who coined the term, "I would say that in '71, the relative equilibrium [between bureaucrats and artists] that had till then favored us broke, and with it, the consensus on which cultural politics had been based . . . to a period in which everything was consulted and discussed . . . followed one of ukases: a cultural politics imposed by decree" ("El quinquenio gris" 12). Pace Fornet, even if the Padilla affair marked the beginning of a period of growing intolerance, the end of the "gray five years" did not mean the end of restrictions to artistic and individual liberties.

However, the key political events of the early 1970s were the election of leftist Salvador Allende to the presidency of Chile in 1970 with a plurality of the vote and then the toppling of this unique socialist and democratic experiment by the military on 11 September 1973 in a military coup led by General Augusto Pinochet, and supported and aided by the US political and military establishment. Allende had been elected as the candidate for the Unidad Popular (Popular Unity), a front that included the Socialist Party, to which Allende belonged, the Communist Party, and other assorted left-leaning political groups. As Joan Garcés notes, "The government of the Unidad Popular between 1970 and 1973 was one of the most developed instances of economic and social democracy till then practiced within a pluralist and representative political system, of a socialist orientation" (9). In many ways, the Unidad Popular represented the politics desired by the many collaborators of *Libre*.[4] As Rafael Rojas points out, "The major Latin American narrators identified with Chilean democratic socialism and, to a greater or lesser degree, they celebrated the contrast that this [Chilean] political project established with the evolution of the Cuban political system toward the Soviet model" (*La polis literaria*).

As one would expect, this socialist experiment faced the rabid opposition of the United States. According to Gerald Martin: "The CIA had been working against Allende even before his election: the United States, beleaguered in its Vietnamese quagmire and already obsessed with Cuba, was desperate that there should be no further anti-capitalist regimes in the Western hemisphere" (*Gabriel García Márquez* 376).

The coup in Chile was part of a series of military interventions in the Southern Cone during the 1970s with the purpose of forestalling any possible repetition of Cuba. These include coups in Uruguay in 1973, which predated Chile by a couple of months, and in Argentina in 1976. In fact, the brutality of the Pinochet regime, which murdered at least three thousand and tortured tens of thousands, was exceeded by the Argentine military dictatorship, which organized a genocidal orgy that killed, according to human rights organizations, thirty thousand people.[5] Of course, these Southern Cone military coups had an important precedent, perhaps even a trial run on the part of US agencies, in Brazil, when in 1964 the military overthrew the government of João Goulart. As Idelber Avelar notes, in all of these cases, "the dictatorships' raison d'être was the physical and symbolic elimination of all resistance of market logic" (1). This implied the elimination of revolutionary politics not only as a physical reality—something that all of these dictatorships achieved by killing or jailing thousands—but also as a theoretical or, as Avelar calls it, symbolic possibility. This series of coups seemed to debunk any and all belief in the feasibility of revolutionary change in Latin America.

However, only in Chile was a socialist government deposed. This is why, as Martin perceptively notes, "the savage destruction of the Chilean experiment, before the eyes of the entire world, would have something of the effect on leftists that the defeat of the Republicans in the Spanish Civil War had exerted almost forty years before" (*Gabriel García Márquez* 376). While the Padilla affair and the "gray five years" had undermined the belief in the Cuban regime and violent revolution, the coup in Chile seemed to prove the impossibility of achieving socialism within democracy, even if here the blame was primarily placed on the Chilean military, the country's upper classes, and the US government that supported and promoted the coup, rather than on Allende or his government.

Vargas Llosa's *The Real Life of Alejandro Mayta* responded not only to the dashing of revolutionary hopes in the early 1970s but also to two key events in the two regions where, after the Southern Cone coups, revolutionary movements would remain on the offensive for the next decade: Central America, where radical guerrilla movements aimed to take power, and did so in Nicaragua in 1979; and Peru, where the Maoist (though, in reality, sui generis) Shining Path uprising, which began timidly in 1980, ultimately unleashed an unprecedented wave of violence. The novel's connections with these residual examples of the 1960s guerrilla fervor is evidenced not only by the fact that the Shining Path provides an extratextual frame through which readers often understand the novel, but also by the cameo Ernesto Cardenal, poet and then minister in the leftist Sandinista government, makes.

## Vargas Llosa and The Real Life of Alejandro Mayta

As we have seen, by 1984 Vargas Llosa had long ceased being a man of the Left. His political drift began publicly with his participation as a critic of the Cuban government during the Padilla affair. It reached a milestone with his reevaluation of Camus in "Albert Camus and the Morality of Limits" (1974). In this essay, he embraces the liberal political virtues of the author of *The Plague* over the violent political praxis associated with the revolutionary Left, including Ernesto "Che" Guevara: "It is possible that this voice of Camus, the voice of reason and moderation, of tolerance and prudence but also of courage, freedom, beauty and pleasure, might be less stimulating and attractive for young people than the voices of those prophets of violent adventure and apocalyptic denial, like Che Guevara or Frantz Fanon, which move and inspire them to such a degree. I consider that this is unjust" (115). Here, for the first time in his work, moderation overrides claims for justice. By 1979, in another essay dealing with the existentialists, this time with his former hero Jean-Paul Sartre, he would embrace a political position that has much in common with the then surging neoliberal and libertarian positions: "We must mistrust utopias; they usually end in holocausts. . . . We cannot abolish governments but we can, on the other hand, weaken them, restrain them, counterbalance them, so that they cause as little damage as possible" ("Sartre, Fierabrás, and Utopia" 130).[6] At this time, he was also actively collaborating with Hernando de Soto and the group of Peruvian intellectuals who, inspired by Friedrich von Hayek, Karl Popper, and Milton Friedman, founded the think tank Instituto Libertad y Democracia.[7] In fact, his fame as a paladin of the free market led to his being the lone Latin American writer invited by Margaret Thatcher to her notorious dinner at Downing Street in 1982, together with such luminaries as Tom Stoppard, V. S. Naipaul, and Vargas Llosa's hero Isaiah Berlin, even if he was strangely "described by one guest as 'some Panamanian novelist'" (Farndale). By the publication of *The Real Life of Alejandro Mayta*, Vargas Llosa was rapidly becoming a luminary of the free-market Right and the bête noir of the region's Left.[8]

Despite his political transformation, Vargas Llosa would claim in his "Transforming a Lie into Truth: A Metaphor of the Novelist's Task" (1990), an article published in William F. Buckley's influential conservative journal *National Review*, that he did not intend to write *The Real Life of Alejandro Mayta* "as a novel against revolution, as an indictment of Marxism in Latin America" (70). In fact, Efraín Kristal in *The Temptation of the Word*—a study that, in addition to being the best introduction to the Peruvian's novelist work has the imprimatur of Vargas Llosa himself—argues that *The Real Life of Alejandro Mayta* is a study of "Mayta's stubborn fanaticism in all of its pathetic tenacity" (150).[9] But fanaticism is not criticized in the abstract but through the depiction of a left-wing revolutionary.

Clumsily translated as *The Real Life of Alejandro Mayta*, the novel's original title *Historia de Mayta* played with the double meaning of the word *historia* in Spanish as either history or story—in other words, fact or fiction. While the novel recounts the life of a fictional (would-be) guerrilla fighter, Alejandro Mayta, it does so by depicting the "novelist's" investigation into the character's frustrated attempt at starting an uprising in the Andes. With justification, Michel Rybalka has compared the novel with Orson Welles's masterpiece *Citizen Kane*, a film structured around a journalist's reportage on the life of a mogul, media master, and politician.[10] However, while Welles, the archetypal film modernist, ultimately provides a reason and explanation for Charles Foster Kane's rootless and ruthless life—a nostalgia for his idyllic childhood represented in the film by, of all things, a sled—the equivalent gesture in Vargas Llosa's novel, when the narrator meets the "real-life" Mayta, raises more questions than answers.

For critics like Jean O'Bryan-Knight, this novel "is the work of a creator who is caught in what can best be described as the postmodern predicament" (*The Story of the Storyteller* 112).[11] Rather than writing a search for truth as Welles did—the complexity of *Kane* is an expression of the earnestness of Welles's filmic attempt at uncovering reality, perhaps even the real, through art—in *The Real Life of Alejandro Mayta*, Vargas Llosa pens, at least in part, metafiction: writing about the act of writing a novel. As he notes in the *National Review* article, *The Real Life of Alejandro Mayta* was primarily a novel about "two kinds of fiction, ideological fiction and literary fiction" ("Transforming a Lie" 70). Moreover, according to Vargas Llosa: "My idea was to have the novel flow on two levels. First, there was the story of the narrator, someone who would have my name (but only in order to misguide the reader), collecting material to write a novel about Mayta. This would be the so-called fake objective level. Then, there would be an *imaginary* level in which the reader would follow the process of building a fiction" (69–70; italics in the original). The novel is, therefore, as much a reconstruction of Mayta's life as of the research that supposedly went into the novel one is reading.

Given the nature of the narrator's collection of information and the difficulties he faces constructing a coherent representation of Mayta, critics have argued that the metafictional aspects of the novel imply a reflection on the possibilities or impossibilities of historical discourse. As Deborah Cohn explains, "The narrator's reflections on the difficulties of reconstructing the past change history's presumption of objectivity, unmediated referentiality and truth value, all of which supposedly distinguish it from fiction: by interweaving historical subject matter and self-conscious aesthetic discourse, 'fact' and fiction, his meditations foreground the discursivity of the object depicted even as they that art is a part of and participates in the writing of history" (90). Despite his well-known aversion toward deconstruction, Vargas Llosa comes surprisingly close in this novel to the position of Paul de Man, for whom "the bases for historical knowledge are not empirical facts but written texts" (403).[12] For Cohn, among other things, *The Real Life of Alejandro Mayta* reflects the impossibility of historical truth, perhaps truth itself.

*The Real Life of Alejandro Mayta* is inspired by a little-known attempt at starting a guerrilla movement in Jauja, the first city founded by the Spanish in the Peruvian Andes. According to the novel, Alejandro Mayta, a forty-something Trotskyist agitator, and Vallejos, a young lieutenant in the Republican Guard, a branch of the police responsible for guarding official buildings, start the uprising in 1958.[13] Vargas Llosa situates the would-be guerrilla movement after Fidel Castro's start of the Sierra Maestra campaign in Cuba but before the triumph of the revolution on 1 January 1959, perhaps in order to stress the independent nature of Peruvian socialism.[14] That is why Mayta describes Vallejos in terms critical of the Cuban Revolution: "He's an ideological virgin. The Revolution for him is Fidel Castro and his happy band of bearded heroes taking potshots out in the Sierra Maestra" (39). The character of Mayta could not have made that statement after the Cuban Revolution officially embraced communism in 1961. Nevertheless, the real-life event that inspired Vargas Llosa actually took place in 1962 after the island's government had defined itself as socialist, and despite its Trotskyist filiation, it must be seen as one of the many offshoots of the Cuban Revolution in Latin America.

Vargas Llosa's liberties with the actual Jauja uprising go beyond chronology. Probably due to the many years that had passed since he first read about the guerrilla uprising, Vargas Llosa's account of the real Jauja uprising in "Transforming a Lie into Truth" is full of mistakes:

> The revolutionaries consisted of only two adults and some high school students. . . . One of the adult leaders was a 23 year old lieutenant of the Guardia Republicana; the other, a man in his early forties named Mayta, was the only one with a background of political militancy. First he had been in the Soviet faction of the Peruvian Communist Party; then he became a Maoist. When the Maoist expelled him he became a Trotskyist. . . . The lieutenant was a spontaneous revolutionary—with no ideological education. (68)

The apparently factual statements in the article are thus very close to the descriptions of Alejandro Mayta and Vallejos in the novel. However, Vargas Llosa gets the names and the number of leaders wrong. The uprising had actually been led by Jacinto Rentería, who, like the novel's protagonist, was a veteran radical Trotskyite operator; the peasant leader

Vicente Mayta Mercado, whose last name Vargas Llosa gave to the main character; and the (sub)lieutenant Francisco Vallejos Vidal.[15] In real life, by the end of the uprising Vallejos and Mayta were dead and Rentería was imprisoned.

This would-be rebellion had nearly been forgotten by the time Vargas Llosa published his novel. Because of the rebellion's small size, perhaps because of Rentería's affiliation with Trotskyites (always a minority movement within the Left), and because it was almost immediately repressed, few readers would have been able to make the connection between the actual rebellion and the events described in Vargas Llosa's novel. As we have seen, Vargas Llosa himself seems to have misremembered the events that he once read with amazement in *Le Monde*, if one is to believe "Transforming a Lie into Truth" or the plot of the novel itself.

As one progressively discovers during the act of reading, the apparently seamless identification between what Cohn calls the "fake objective level" and the Peruvian reality of the time of publication rapidly breaks down. It is true that the novelist—who, despite the assertion made in "Transforming a Lie into Truth," is never named—appears to resemble Vargas Llosa to a T: he lives in the upper-class Lima neighborhood of Barranco, jogs every morning, seems to have a very successful literary career (the prisoners in the Lurigancho jail name their ramshackle library after him), and so forth.

However, the novel also claims that the fictional Mayta is a classmate of the author. Thus, as Rybalka notes, when comparing Vargas Llosa with the fictional author, "there is a striking difference: their age" (126). In *The Real Life of Alejandro Mayta*, the protagonist is described as being "over forty" in 1958 (22). The real-life Vargas Llosa, born in 1936, would have been at least nineteen years younger.

But an even more devious deviation from the actual Peru of 1984 is the novel's depiction of the country's descent into violence. Peru in the 1980s experienced, at the hands of the Shining Path, the beginning of the bloodiest and most violent guerrilla uprising in the continent's history. The Shining Path started its operations as the country returned to democracy in 1980 after twelve years of military rule. (Peru had been governed by a military regime for a dozen years comprised of a leftist period from 1968 to 1975 under General Juan Velasco Alvarado that nationalized resources and implemented a thoroughgoing land reform, followed by a moderate period under General Francisco Morales Bermúdez from 1975 to 1980 that paved the way for a return to democracy in 1980.) Ironically, the civilian president elected in 1980 was no other than Fernando Belaúnde Terry, who had been deposed by the military in 1968. In a further irony, the Shining Path began their military actions by burning ballots during the first elections after the coup. However, these relatively mild acts of protest would soon be followed by ever-greater acts of violence. By the time Abimael Guzmán, the leader of the Shining Path, was captured and the insurgency defeated in 1992, more than seventy thousand people were dead, more than half at the hands of the supposedly Maoist insurgency.[16]

Therefore, passages such as the following are written with the expectation that the reader will find in them a thin fictionalization of the impact of the Shining Path and their violent actions: "Until a few months ago, political violence did not affect the slums on the outskirts of Lima as much as it affected the residential neighborhoods and the downtown area. But now most of the people assassinated or kidnapped by revolutionary commandos, the armed forces or the counterrevolutionary death squads come from these zones" (53). Although blackouts caused by blowing out transmission towers in the Andes had become a regular occurrence by the time the novel was published, the actual violence of the Shining Path in the early 1980s was not primarily concentrated in the urban areas, but rather in the countryside, as dictated by Maoist tactics.[17] Nevertheless, one can safely assume that despite the differences between the novelistic accounts and actual Shining Path practices, the contemporary reader would associate the violence portrayed at the start of the novel with the real-life violence exerted by the nominally Maoist group. This play with the identification of real-life Peru in the early 1980s and the fictional setting of the novel is further enhanced by the exactitude of the references to historical events and figures, both recent and distant.

Perhaps the best example of how Vargas Llosa creates a reality effect is the reference to Ernesto Cardenal, the poet and minister of culture at the time for the left-wing Sandinista government in Nicaragua, visiting Peru. Though critics have noted the animosity of Vargas Llosa's description—"He came on stage dressed like Che Guevara. . . . [H]e responded to the demagoguery of some agitators in the audience with more demagoguery" (79)—the reader is led to associate real and novelistic presences through the detailed and careful account of Cardenal's demeanor and discourse.[18] Even the novelist's intemperate descriptions of Cardenal help create this linkage between fiction and reality. After all, everyone knows that the Vargas Llosa of 1984 dislikes the Left. Moreover, this description of Cardenal implicitly tars the Sandinista minister, and the revolution he represented, with Cuban communist feathers, which, as we know, were in the process of losing their luster.

The sense of reality is so strong in the early chapters of the novel that it is easy to forget that the novelist and narrator is at least nineteen years older than the real-life Vargas Llosa and that the Shining Path was not particularly active in Lima.[19] Of course, in a few years Abimael Guzmán and his followers would take the war to the country's urban areas, including the capital, making this "reality effect" even stronger.

As one continues reading, one discovers that the cause of the violence in the diegesis, which progressively reaches doomsday level, has its origin in the unification of all parties of the Left, not in the violence of the Shining Path: "All the leftwing parties, Stalinists, Maoists, Trotskyists, accepted years later the idea of an alliance, joint operations, even combining in a single party" (99). While in the real world the Peruvian Left had united in 1980, they had not committed acts of violence, instead opting for participation in the elections of 1980 and, not without contradiction, accepting democratic processes and institutions. In fact, Alfonso Barrantes, the leader of the United Left (Izquierda Unida), had been elected mayor of Lima in 1980. The United Left, which had rejected revolutionary violence and was in the process of fully and absolutely embracing democratic processes, was presented in the alternate world of the novel as key to the process that led to a violent and dystopian Peru.

Yet Vargas Llosa's imagining of a violent United Left is not the main divergence between the country depicted in *The Real Life of Alejandro Mayta* and Peru during the early 1980s. Halfway through the novel any similarity with the reality of Peru, of any Peru, is completely gone as, in what resembles a right-wing catastrophic fantasy, the pseudo–Vargas Llosa wonders: "Could it be true that Cuban troops had crossed the Bolivian border? That for the last three days the rebels, along with the Cuban and Bolivian 'volunteers' who support them, have pushed the army back? That the Junta has warned the United States that if it doesn't intervene, the insurgents will take Arequipa in the order of days and from there will be able to proclaim the Socialist Republic of Peru?" (147). Needless to say, there has fortunately not been any direct military foreign intervention in Peru from Cuba, Bolivia, or the United States. Despite depicting an alternate reality, the novel links it with the actual historical events and characters presented in the novel—that is, the Cuban Revolution and Sandinista Nicaragua. Thus, real and slightly fictionalized events, such as Alejandro Mayta and Vallejos's attempt to start a guerrilla movement—are presented as leading to the apocalyptic Peru of the novel. As the novelist within the novel says to Vallejos's sister after describing the violence they are experiencing in the present of the narrative: "Let's go back to what brought me here. . . . The revolution that began to take shape during those years. The one Mayta and your brother were involved in. It was the first of many. It charted the process that has ended in what we are all living through now" (59).

*The Real Life of Alejandro Mayta* implies a fictional history of what could be called the Peruvian Revolution from its unheralded genesis in 1958 Jauja to its doomsday conclusion in a parallel Peru in 1984. According to the novel, any attempt at revolution, even one that is rapidly put out, is a step toward political apocalypse.

Perhaps the most important criticism leveled against *The Real Life of Alejandro Mayta* at the time of its publication came not surprisingly from the pen of the major Latin American critic of the time: Antonio Cornejo Polar. Cornejo Polar is best-known as the theorist of heterogeneity—that is, the rejection of a unified culture or identity as the basis for Peruvian nationhood, instead acknowledging "the vast differences that separate and sharply contrast their various social-cultural worlds, and which, in their many historical rhythms, coexist and overlap even within national boundaries" (*Writing in the Air* 2). Despite his stress on cultural heterogeneity, he maintained a personal identification with the Peruvian Marxist Left. Cornejo Polar's criticism of *The Real Life of Alejandro Mayta* orbits around the problems raised by the view of history implicit in the novel. Noting that the novel can be characterized as following "the code of melodrama"—perhaps evidenced, for instance, by the relationship between Mayta and his wife, who resents that he would marry her as a cover for his homosexuality, and by the hatred felt by the now-homophobic Senator Campos for Mayta, having been his lover twenty years earlier—Cornejo Polar adds: "It is clear that from this perspective one can narrate the adventure of a few more or less eccentric characters, but it is extremely doubtful that it [the code of melodrama] is useful to tell that *other* history, that of the violence in Peru, and even less, to reflect, even if indirectly, on its meaning" ("La historia como apocalipsis" 367). Cornejo Polar later adds: "The 'historia de Mayta' ['Mayta's history,' referring to the original title of the novel] marks the other history, that of the many and diverse manners that the Peruvian people have developed in order to subvert the established order, with the trait the novel assigns to the first: that of adventurism" (371). Vargas Llosa's literary mistake—reading history as melodrama and as adventure—ultimately implies the intellectual error of eliding the actual history of resistance and rebellion of oppressed Andean peoples. Collective struggle is thus transformed into individual action, social goals into personal fantasy, and history into story. One can add to Cornejo Polar's comments that narrating history within the code of melodrama would contradict the basic tenets of the "total novel," which, among other things, attempted to present a coherent social background for the story narrated.

However, what ultimately irks Cornejo Polar is what he sees as the ideology underlying the catastrophic vision of the novel, as well as its immediate predecessor in Vargas Llosa's oeuvre, *The War of the End of the World* (1981): a disenchanted, exhausted liberalism. According to Cornejo Polar, "All doors have been closed to liberal thought. . . . In consequence all options still open are all negative: it either renounces its principles, and falls into one of the many forms that, in Latin America, 'enlightened absolutism' has taken, or it gives up trying to understand history and determines that social process is irrational and, as such, incomprehensible" ("La historia como apocalipsis" 380). Thus, *The Real Life of Alejandro Mayta* represents Vargas Llosa's and liberalism's ultimate embrace of nihilism as the real-life world turns its back on the values and politics of all liberalisms. But Cornejo Polar's criticism is rooted in an alternative belief that history is rational and understandable, and that it is moving in a progressive direction—in fact, toward socialism.[20]

However, seen from our twenty-first-century perspective, when neoliberalism and, to a much lesser degree, other versions of liberalism are dominant, it is difficult to share Cornejo's belief in a progressive flow of history, even if he raises important questions about *The Real Life of Alejandro Mayta*. As we have seen, already in 1984 socialism was rapidly becoming residual. It became fully so in 1989, with the collapse of the Soviet bloc. Nowadays we are no longer sure that history has an arc, and even less so that it bends toward justice; but for most, socialism seems outside any possible political future.

In addition to chastising Vargas Llosa for his (relatively) new liberal beliefs, or simply acknowledging the novelist's embrace of postmodern indeterminacy, other critics expressed surprise in the novel's positive portrayal of Mayta. Unexpectedly, it is only a slight exaggeration to claim that for each negative criticism of *The Real Life of Alejandro Mayta* as an expression of Vargas Llosa's putatively conservative view of the world, one can find a critic that sees the novel as sympathizing with, if not actually endorsing, its revolutionary protagonist.

Robert Boyers, for example, concludes his essay on *The Real Life of Alejandro Mayta* as a political novel by noting, "For all of the novelist's oft-repeated insistence that 'all fictions are lies' and that we can never know anything with certainty, he cannot but affirm that there is something in Mayta which continues to compel and attract. The impulse to honor—with whatever misgivings—whatever is authentic in Mayta's passion for social justice is the center of Vargas Llosa's novel and the substance of the meaning that abides" (78). In other words, for Boyers, despite the author's actual politics and beyond his apparent embrace of postmodern ideas, the novel would ultimately celebrate the emotions that underpin the character's actions, no matter how counterproductive they may ultimately be socially. Boyers would thus agree with no less a figure than Roberto Bolaño, who argued that "Vargas Llosa's sense of humor, which leaps, in Balzacian fashion, even over his own political convictions; political convictions that give way in the face of literary convictions, which is something that only happens to real writers. And finally the kindness and compassion—which others might call objectivity—that Vargas Llosa shows his characters" ("Two Novels by Vargas Llosa" 324). For both the New York journalist and the Chilean novelist, Vargas Llosa's artistic integrity leads him to create a novel capable of leapfrogging his own political beliefs and prejudices.

Not only liberals find *The Real Life of Alejandro Mayta* to contradict Vargas Llosa's well-known political beliefs. Neil Larsen, perhaps the major US Latin Americanist Marxist, has proposed the strongest version of such a reading:

Even the anti-communist, quasi-*roman-à-clef The Real Life of Alejandro Mayta* cannot manage to forswear the metaleptic realism that, in the end, politely falsifies Vargas Llosa's doctrinal intent. . . . None of the elaborately contrived, meta-fictional devices that Vargas Llosa employs . . . to, it seems, put the brakes on this ideologically out-of-control narrative are sufficient to hide the fact that Mayta speaks the truth and should have succeeded. He is not the precursor to Abimael Guzmán, but what might have once been his rational, humane, essence. (166)

According to Larsen, Mayta would not only have been portrayed truthfully, as Boyers and Bolaño argue, but the character's ideas would have ultimately won over those of the author.

Perhaps the most surprising version of this kind of reading is provided by Roberto Massari, the Italian sociologist and founder of the Fondazione Internazionale Ernesto "Che" Guevara, when he states: "I hope I will be allowed to think in a purely hypothetical direction, but based on everything written and done by Guevara, among all contemporary novels of the new Latin American narrative, he would have welcomed with the greatest enthusiasm, the poetic fusion of existential pulsion and political rationalism represented in the splendid *The Real Life of Alejandro Mayta*" (30).[21] According to Massari, *The Real Life of Alejandro Mayta* joins in a loving textual embrace the region's iconic revolutionary and its best-known neoliberal. While all texts are polysemous, few are to this degree.[22]

Time has been kind to Vargas Llosa and to the *Real Life of Alejandro Mayta*. Not only because his repudiation of armed revolution is now shared by most Latin Americans or because belief in the free market and liberalism has become dominant throughout the region and in no place more so than in his native Peru, but also because many of the gestures that were surely meant as provocations to the Left have lost their intended frisson.[23]

The prime example of how what once could have seemed like attacks have now become part of our time's common sense is the novel's identification of Mayta as a gay man. Nowadays only residual *machista* leftists could be shocked by Mayta's gay identity. However, at the time of publication, Mayta's sexual orientation could be seen not only as offending left-wing heteronormativity, but also, even for the many unburdened by prejudices, as a reminder of the systematic persecution of gay people practiced by the Cuban Revolution, as well as in other Soviet and Communist countries. As Francisco Soto notes, "The doctrinaire rigidity of the Cuban Revolution made it adopt Stalinist ideological tenets, which regarded homosexuality as a decadent bourgeois ideological phenomenon that had to be eradicated" (286). This perspective is consistent with that expressed in the novel by Comrade Joaquín, the one working-class member of the minuscule Trotskyite group to which Mayta belongs. During the party meeting in which Mayta is expelled from the POWR-W, Comrade Joaquín states: "You can't do anything straight, because you aren't straight, you're just not a man, Mayta" (160). In the novel, even those presenting themselves as the alternative to mainstream communism share the prejudices that unfortunately also characterized those societies that claimed to be overcoming exploitation and discrimination.

As the quotation by Soto notes, there was a continuum between Cuba's homophobia and other aspects of its growing ideological hardening before and during the "grey five-year period." In fact, discrimination against gay men and lesbians and the ideological closing of the revolution that led to the Padilla affair and contributed to Vargas Llosa's break with the Cuban government went hand in hand.[24] A certain kind of leftist reader can come to the conclusion that, in Larsen's words, "Mayta speaks the truth and should have succeeded," precisely because, unlike many radicals in the 1950s or 1960s, she is able to see overcoming discrimination—based on gender, sexual preference or identity, race— as imbricated with achieving economic and social equality. This belief in the necessary connections between overcoming discrimination and eliminating exploitation is made explicit in one of the most utopian— in the best sense of the word—moments of the novel. As he is about to begin the uprising, Mayta, inspired by the enthusiasm of the young schoolboys who constitute the bulk of the would-be rebels, imagines a future utopia: "The peasant owners of their own lands by then, the workers owners of their own factories by then. . . . With discrimination and exploitation abolished, the foundations of equality established . . . millions of Peruvians would feel that now indeed they were progressing, the poorest first" (243). But also: "Social, moral, and sexual prejudices would give way little by little . . . in that crucible of work and faith that Peru would be in the future" (244). In *The Real Life of Alejandro Mayta*, Vargas Llosa is able to imagine what his protagonist describes earlier in the novel as "the true, the integral revolution. A revolution that will wipe out all injustice, a revolution that will guarantee that no one will have any reason to be afraid of being what he is" (196). Mayta's white-hot desire for justice surely appeals to any reader aware of how far we are from anything resembling a just world.

As was the case in Vargas Llosa's essays, in *The Real Life of Alejandro Mayta* armed struggle is connected to the figure of Che Guevara. One finds in the novel implicit references to Guevara and his theories and practices. And, pace Massari, these are not necessarily positive.

Duncan Green and Sue Branford, in their Latin American studies textbook *Faces of Latin America*, have seen a caricature of Che in the following imagined description of what Mayta would have been like had the uprising been successful: "His beard had grown, he was thin, in his eyes there was unconquerable resolve, and his fingers had grown calloused from squeezing the trigger" (*The Real Life of Alejandro Mayta* 132; Green and Branford 88). Enrique Krauze also explicitly compares Guevara with Mayta in his reading of the novel: "Similarly, in the 1960s, 'daring to fight' in Bolivia, Che Guevara chose poorly, in terms both of human and physical geography" (*Redeemers* 393). Daniel Bensaid notes that "*The Real Life of Alejandro Mayta* is . . . full of allusions to Latin America's contemporary history from the death of Che to the birth of the Shining Path." The traces of Guevara's life and figure in the text are not accidental. As Vargas Llosa acknowledges in his "Transforming a Lie into Truth" that the Cuban Revolution served as a backdrop to his early imagining of the novel, and he admits Che Guevara's belief that "the objective conditions for a revolution could be created by revolutionaries themselves" (68) is what ultimately animates *The Real Life of Alejandro Mayta*. According to Vargas Llosa, the real-life Mayta, Rentería, and Vallejos aimed to "establish a revolutionary focal point in the mountains, just as the Cubans had" (68).

Guevara's *foco*, the "focal point" in Vargas Llosa's quotation, is defined in *The Real Life of Alejandro Mayta*: "a small, well-armed, well-equipped vanguard, with urban support and clear ideas about their strategic goals, could become the focal point [*foco*] from which the revolution would radiate outward toward the rest of the nation—the tinder and flint that would spark the revolutionary blaze" (83–84, with modifications).[25] Later, Blacquer, a Peruvian Communist Party leader with whom the Trotskyite Mayta communicated, comments: "If the focal point had lasted longer, things might have turned out the way Mayta planned" (169, with modifications).[26] The failure of Mayta's rebellion becomes a stand-in for the failure not only of Che Guevara's Bolivian adventure but also of all Latin American guerrillas. As the novel argues, even when the *foco* succeeds and revolution breaks out, it only leads to greater violence and misery.

So, is it correct to conclude that his novelistic craft has, as Larsen argued, "politely falsified Vargas Llosa's ideological intent"? That, as Bolaño argued, the Peruvian novelist's literary "kindness and compassion" has led to such a sympathetic character that it undermines any attempt at creating a negative portrayal of the Left? Or that history has bent in the direction of Vargas Llosa's ideas to the point that his criticism of the Left has lost all its bite? Answering these questions affirmatively would not necessarily raise an objection from Vargas Llosa. After all, he has often acknowledged that in fiction "planning and conscious work were less important than the intervention of my unconscious" and that "the writer does not have the last word" ("Transforming a Lie into Truth" 68, 70).

Of course, despite this generosity toward the reader—a naive version of reader-response theory—in his essay for the *National Review*, the 2010 Nobel Prize winner assigns to his novel a polemical intention with a political edge: "How interesting that fiction can be both beneficial and damaging. In one way, the civilization's great literary achievements have enriched mankind . . . and have encouraged progress. . . . But at the same time fiction has been a major instrument of suffering, because it is behind all the dogmatic doctrines that have justified repression, censorship, massacres and genocide" ("Transforming a Lie" 69). And: "Why not, therefore, write a novel about the two faces of fiction, obverse and reverse?" (69). Even if Vargas Llosa claims not to be writing a political text, he contradicts himself by declaring his intent to present—and actually presenting, despite his "compassion" toward Mayta—radical politics as necessarily dogmatic, repressive, and even genocidal.

In his 2004 Irving Kristol Award reception speech—"Confessions of a Liberal"—Vargas Llosa expounds on what *liberalism* means to him:[27]

Thus, the liberal I aspire to be considers freedom a core value.
Thanks to this freedom, humanity has been able to journey from the
primitive cave to the stars and the information revolution, to progress

from forms of collectivist and despotic association to representative democracy. The foundations of liberty are private property and the rule of law; this system guarantees the fewest possible forms of injustice, produces the greatest material and cultural progress, most effectively stems violence and provides the greatest respect for human rights. According to this concept of liberalism, freedom is a single, unified concept. Political and economic liberties are as inseparable as the two sides of a medal.

While the novelist made this statement twenty years after the publication of *The Real Life of Alejandro Mayta*, it is, at least to my mind, a relatively accurate description of the political beliefs that, at least consciously, informed his life and writing in 1984. As we have seen, he was in the process of becoming, if he had not already become, the region's best-known liberal (in its Latin American sense of defender of the free market). From Vargas Llosa's perspective, the apparent minimalism of liberalism—free market and rule of law—would make it impossible to describe these political beliefs as a fiction, that is as "the dogmatic doctrines that have justified repression, censorship, massacres and genocide" ("Transforming a Lie" 69). However, the novel does not represent liberal politics as even as a default possibility.

In a passage that perhaps attempts to rephrase and ultimately answer the question first posed in Vargas Llosa's monumental *Conversation in the Cathedral* (1969)—"At what moment had Peru fucked itself up?" (3)—the narrator enters the Museum of the Inquisition. There he asks himself: "What secret thread links this all powerful institution, which for three centuries kept guard over Catholic orthodoxy in Peru . . . and the obscure revolutionary militant" (*The Real Life of Alejandro Mayta* 106). In this passage, the narrator lucidly describes the history of the institution and the political and ideological methods the Inquisition used to maintain "the spiritual purity" of Spanish South America (106). In particular, the novel notes the homeopathic doses of violence that characterized its activities: "they didn't in fact burn very many: thirty-five in three centuries" (107). However, "even though the Holy Tribunal didn't burn many people, it did torture an enormous number" (108). Through the threat of violence, the Inquisition created a system of informers and of intimidation that permeated colonial society. One could very well see in the reference to the Inquisition—an institution that represents the coming together of religion and politics, and that there-fore attempted to control what it meant to be a Spaniard and a Span-ish American during the colonial period—a postcolonial answer to the question posed in *Conversation in the Cathedral*. The colony, predicated on the imbrication of political violence and religiosity that enforced religious uniformity, would be the moment when Peru fucked itself (to continue with that novel's terminology). This enforcement of ideologi-cal uniformity would inform Peru's history of violence against any and all deviance and difference.

For the reader familiar with Peruvian culture and history, it is easy to hear in this the echo of José Carlos Mariátegui's identification and criti-cism of the survival of colonial ideology after independence.[28] However, Mariátegui also stressed the negative impact of the persistence of colo-nial institutions, such as the large haciendas and indigenous servitude, issues that are basically elided in Vargas Llosa's novel.

The mention of the Inquisition can also imply criticism of commu-nism as a later incarnation of precisely this conjunction of ideology and politics. In a perplexing twist, the passage presents a "mind meld" between narrator and protagonist, as Mayta also responds to the sights of the Museum of the Inquisition. A few paragraphs after his sexual identity has been discovered, he asks himself: "How many homosexuals could they have burned?" (106). The reader had just been presented with Senator Campos's pseudo-intellectual justifications for his ho-mophobia and, outside the text, knows about the repression against gay and lesbian people in Cuba and elsewhere. (The novel actually notes that in China, Mayta, as a gay man, "would have been shot" [195].)

Octavio Paz articulates the analogy between colonial Latin America and communism with great force in *Sor Juana, or, The Traps of Faith* (1982): "The total fusion of the idea [Catholicism] and power was at the root of the 'historical mission' of the Spanish empire, as today it is at that of the communist state" (30). The nobility of Mayta's ideas and the purity of his goals do not prevent him from becoming a victim of com-munism's fusion of ideas and power, even if represented by the minus-cule Trotskyist group to which he belongs. However, his experience is ultimately a synecdoche of what one could expect from communism in power. The points of contact between Paz in *Sor Juana* and Vargas Llosa in *The Real Life of Alejandro Mayta* may be more than coincidence. Var-gas Llosa declared, albeit only in 2007, that Paz's *Sor Juana* is "probably the best book of literary criticism that originated in Latin America" ("Una mujer contra el mundo").

The narrator's final comments on the visit to the museum do more than present a version of the postcolonial criticism of Peruvian society. For that matter, they do more than offer an analogy between colonial society and religion, on the one hand, and the narrative's (and potentially Peru's) communist present and future, on the other. After leaving the museum, the narrator notes: "Condensed in a few striking images and objects, there is an essential ingredient always present in the history of this country, from the most remote times: violence. Violence of all kinds . . . which have gone hand in hand with power here. It's good to come here . . . to see how we have come to be what we are, why we are in the condition we find ourselves" (109).[29] Now the connection between power and violence, between the state and violence, is clear. Mayta, regardless of how appealing his ideas, ultimately makes the mistake of using violence. Unwittingly, revolutionary politics becomes the intensification of Peru's failed politics—whether conservative or nominally liberal. Peruvian history, as Michel Foucault notes about humanity, "does not gradually progress from combat to combat until it *arrives at universal reciprocity, where the rule of law finally replaces warfare; humanity installs* each of its violences in a system of rules and thus proceeds from domination to domination" (emphasis added; 85).[30]

Throughout his career Vargas Llosa will defend the importance of political participation, of which his candidacy for the presidency in 1990 serves as example. Moreover, in his "Confession of a Liberal," representative democracy, and therefore politics itself, is a necessary condition of liberalism. But *The Real Life of Alejandro Mayta* presents a dire vision of the history of Peru—as a state and a society—as intrinsically linked to violence and ultimately to oppression. Regardless of the personal virtues of the revolutionary—and despite his obvious tactical mistakes, Mayta is sympathetic and humane—he is shown to be participating, even strengthening, the tradition of violence that in the novel characterizes Peruvian history and institutions.

In an unexpected turn of the screw, in the last chapter, the narrative is shown to be "fiction." The novelist/narrator admits to have never known Mayta nor, obviously, to have been his classmate or childhood friend. He only gets the opportunity to meet and talk with the novel's protagonist after the latter's last stint in prison. However, in a characteristic blurring of real-life fact and written fiction, this last chapter was motivated by the real-life author meeting the "living model of Mayta" (10)—one assumes he is now referring to Rentería—as Vargas Llosa acknowledged in the prologue to the 2008 edition of the novel. At least in the novel, the narrator is surprised by the "real" Mayta's lack of interest in talking about the Jauja uprising. However, "His voice and expression sweeten when he talks about the food kiosk he ran . . . in building 4 [in prison]. 'We created a genuine revolution,' he assures me with pride. 'We won the respect of the whole place. We boiled the water for making fruit juice, for coffee, for everything. We washed the knives, forks and spoons, the glasses, and the plates, before and after they were used. A revolution, you bet'" (294). In a novel that stresses the overwhelming presence of trash and filth, as many critics have noted, Mayta's emphasis on hygiene is significant. Garbage and violence are imbricated in the text; after all, both violence and garbage are presented as growing exponentially from the novel's chronological beginning to its fictive Armageddon. Moreover, in the last chapter, while the reality portrayed seems free from the kind of generalized violence described in the "fictional" section of the novel, the "real" world is still characterized by "garbage that is invading every neighborhood in the capital of Peru" (310).

Mayta's kiosk represents the "genuine revolution" that the novel ultimately celebrates. The other revolution—violent and Marxist—is shown in the novel to conclude in catastrophe and to expand the violence that has characterized Peruvian society since its colonial beginnings. Jean O'Bryan-Knight notes: "Mayta's choice of words here is significant. When the former leftist militant calls to mind a 'genuine revolution,' he thinks not of the leftist rebellion he organized in the highlands but of the successful small business he ran while locked up. In the immeasurable filth and depravity of the prison, he managed to build an oasis of honesty and safety that benefited both clients and proprietor" ("Let's Make Owners and Entrepreneurs" 53). Ultimately, the only revolution that breaks free from the thread of violence that characterizes Peruvian history—and all other histories—is the product of entrepreneurship. O'Bryan-Knight is again correct when she notes that "the characterization of Mayta in the final chapter also appears to owe much to the representation of the informal sector of Peruvian society that appears in Peruvian economist Hernando de Soto's widely read and highly influential book *The Other Path* (1987)".[31] The subtitle of de Soto's book is, after all, *The Invisible Revolution in the Third World.*[32]

In "Transforming a Lie into Truth," Vargas Llosa criticizes Marxism, because "in the novel the reader can perceive that this ideology is, in fact, a fiction—constantly rejected and falsified by objective reality" (70). In his foreword to de Soto and the Instituto Libertad y Democracia's *The Other Path,*[33] a book that has been called "the most important work of Latin American neoliberalism" (Devés 117), Vargas Llosa argues that de Soto's study proves that "the path taken by the black-marketeers—the poor—is not the reinforcement and magnification of the state but a radical pruning and reduction of it" (xvii). Moreover, "if we listen to what these poor slum dwellers are telling us with their deeds, we hear nothing about what so many Third World Revolutionaries are advocating in their name—violent revolution, state control of the economy. All we hear is a desire for genuine democracy and authentic liberty" (xvii). Neoliberalism, or, as Vargas Llosa prefers to call it, *liberalismo,* would be based on objective reality rather than on melodramatic codes. It would be listening to deeds not words. In this manner, *liberalismo* would not be a fiction imposed on reality that, according to Vargas Llosa, necessarily implies its falsification. Instead, it would be the perfect documentary translation of reality. Despite the brevity of the reference to Mayta's informal business, it represents the only baby steps out of the violent morass of Peruvian history to be found in *The Real Life of Alejandro Mayta.* This free-market "informal revolution" permits Vargas Llosa to insinuate a new liberal democracy capable of breaking free from the repeating cycle of violence that has characterized Peruvian society since colonial times. Moreover, it is consistent with the liberal/neoliberal advocacy that already characterized the Instituto Libertad y Democracia and Vargas Llosa's growing political participation. According to the Peruvian novelist, the promotion of the free market can help Peru and Latin America break free from ideology and from the tradition of violence—in other words, from political fiction.

## Manuel Puig *and* Kiss of the Spider Woman

Unlike *The Real Life of Alejandro Mayta,* which was written more than twenty years after the events it depicted, Manuel Puig's *Kiss of the Spi-*

*der Woman* responded to the totalitarian shifts in Latin American and Argentine politics as they were happening. Although it was published in 1976, just after the Argentine coup, it was mostly written before the Peronist administration had been deposed.[34] With perspicacity, Santiago Colás notes: "Puig's novel seems to prophetically confront this reality, though its publication coincided only with the beginning of the *Proceso* [the Argentine military government's plans to eradicate subversion]. This almost-prophetic character perhaps owes to the fact that the narrative was composed during the no-less-fearsome period of semi-official state-sanctioned terrorism that caused Puig's own self-exile" (76). One of the aspects of the book most surprising for readers is that the repressive Argentina depicted in the book is not that of the murderous military regime that took control of the country in 1976, but rather that of Isabel Perón's putative democratic government, which was in power in 1975 when the novel takes place. Despite its democratic provenance, Isabel Perón's government supported the most right-wing elements in the Peronist movement, including death squads.

In 1975, however, the coups in Chile and Uruguay had already taken place. One can, therefore, safely say that Puig is responding to the political turn of the early 1970s when the naive utopian hopes of many were dashed by the most brutal of military regimes. Even more darkly, *Kiss of the Spider Woman* implies that these military regimes participate in a repressive and corrupt political continuum with its putative democratic predecessors, which, in the Argentine case, had already begun the illegal extermination of young radicals, a process that would be continued and intensified after the military coup.[35]

From the perspective of this study, *Kiss of the Spider Woman* is relevant because it tackles the ethical and political need for, as well as the impossibility of, radical action. Written while some still held on, against wind and tide, to the possibility of making a revolution following in the footsteps of Cuba, Puig's novel imagines a postrevolutionary activism based the struggle for gender equality and full respect for all sexual identities.

In many ways, Puig was the last author one would have imagined dealing explicitly with the central political issues of the time. His narrative studiously avoided the kind of grand political topics that so stimulated Carlos Fuentes (the Mexican Revolution) and Alejo Carpentier (the Haitian Revolution, the French Revolution). Instead, Puig's breakthrough novel, *Betrayed by Rita Hayworth*, details the experiences of a sensitive and artistically oriented young gay kid growing up in the closed-minded hinterlands of the Argentine Pampas. Moreover, unlike Mario Vargas Llosa, who, regardless of what one might think of his neoliberal ideas, is undoubtedly the Boom writer who most clearly took up the mantle of the public intellectual, Puig, like García Márquez and Adolfo Bioy Casares, was "reticent to transform into an intellectual" (Gilman 58).[36]

However, *Kiss of the Spider Woman* participates in the political and ideological debates waged in the mid-1970s regarding the relevance of revolutionary politics. As José Miguel Oviedo notes: "*Kiss of the Spider Woman* represents a qualitative leap over the author's previous novels: while these were defined by a retrospective character completely foreign to actuality or historical reality, in his fourth novel, just as the Argentine dictatorship begins, he manages to insert political topics into the forms and concerns he had previously examined" (351). Thus, in addition to his well-established ability in delineating plots and fleshing out characters, the intertextual role he assigns to film as a specific set of real and imaginary works, and to the film script as an art form, the novel refers to the political reality of mid-1970s Argentina. It depicts the jailing of left-wing activists and would-be guerrilla fighters, as well as the use of physical and psychological torture against them; at the same, it clearly represents the ideas and beliefs of these radical youth.

The basic plot of *Kiss of the Spider Woman* is based, as Oviedo notes, "on a functional design of notable simplicity . . . : the concentration in a physical space of two completely foreign and different men" (351). Luis Alberto Molina, a gay window dresser, imprisoned for "corruption of minors," is placed in a cell with Valentín Arregui, "involved in promoting disturbances with strikers at two automotive assembly plants" (*Kiss of the Spider Woman* 149). (There is the clear implication in the text that Valentín belonged to an urban guerrilla group, though we are not provided any information that actually links him to acts of violence). At the end of the novel, Valentín is tortured, perhaps to death, while the political group to which Valentín belongs shoots and kills Molina (274). (Throughout the novel, Molina is called by his last name, while Valentín is called by his first.) Despite their differences—one of the main plot twists in the novel is that Molina has been placed with Valentín in order to spy on him for the government—their daily interaction in the cell, which, among other things, involves Molina's retelling of the plots of real and made-up films, leads both men to discover their common humanity and the possibility of expressing sexually their growing solidarity and affection.

The simplicity of the plot may help explain the ease with which the novel has been adapted into different media. It was rewritten by Puig into a play (1985); it was adapted into the Oscar-nominated movie *Kiss of the Spider Woman* (1985), directed by Argentine-Brazilian Héctor Babenco, with William Hurt as Molina, a role for which he won the Oscar, and Raul Julia as Valentín; and in what is a first for a Latin American novel, it was transformed into a Broadway musical created by playwright Terrence McNally and the songwriting team of John Kander and Fred Ebb, of *Cabaret* and *Chicago* fame.[37] (The musical, Kander, Ebb, and McNally all won Tony Awards in 1993.) Given the popularity of its adaptations and the role Puig played in the development of these versions of his original text—he wrote the play, participated in the development of the film, and collaborated in the very early stages of the development of the musical—it is tempting to see *Kiss of the Spider Woman* not only as a major Argentine or Latin American novel, but even more as what André Bazin called a "single work reflected through," in this case, four "art forms" (26).[38]

In addition to crossing artistic media, *Kiss of the Spider Woman*, in its different versions, has been embraced by readers and audiences from across the world. This widespread popularity has to do with the synchronicity of the novel's translation in 1979 into English with the development of new social movements. In particular, the growth and social repercussions of the gay and queer movements in the United States and Europe after the Stonewall Riots in 1969, when members of the LGBT community in New York City reacted to harassment by the local police, created a favorable social context for the reception of Puig's work, especially *Kiss of the Spider Woman* in its many adaptations.

Puig had himself been touched by the upsurge in queer activism inspired by the Stonewall Riots. In 1971, together with poet Néstor Perlongher and essayist Juan José Sebreli, he helped found the Frente de Liberación Homosexual (Homosexual Liberation Front).[39] One can, therefore, see his participation in public political debates as directly related to his evolving sense of what it meant to be a gay man in a sexually repressive and patriarchal society such as Argentina.[40] That said, *Kiss of the Spider Woman* reflects this growing awareness of the political valence of gay identity. In fact, Daniel Balderston and José Maristany declare it "the founding text of a post-Stonewall gay literature in Latin America" (208).[41]

Moreover, the novel's exploration of the intersections and tensions between politics and individual identity, its criticisms of patriarchy and of the role played by the internalization of patriarchal values in the reproduction and maintenance of an unjust society, led Colás to argue:

> We might, on account of Puig's attention to the interior spaces of repression, wish to situate him as a precursor to some postmodern women's writing in the Southern Cone: Diamela Eltit's *Lumpérica*, Marta Traba's *Conversación al Sur* and *En cualquier lugar*, Cristina Peri Rossi's *La tarde del dinosaurio* and *La rebelión de los niños*. For that matter, it may be worth noting that Puig himself conceived *Beso* as an attempt to understand Latin American, and particularly Argentine, patriarchy from the angle of women's internalization of oppressive structures. (78)

In addition to Puig's affinity with the burgeoning gay rights and queer liberation movements, the congruence of his writing, especially *Kiss of the Spider Woman*, with the values that guided the struggle for women's liberation helps explain the novel's international popularity. With the obvious exception of Isabel Allende's novels, generally seen by Latin American critics as best-sellers rather than as "serious" literature, *Kiss of the Spider Woman* is among the most successful Latin American novels published after the 1960s.[42] As a result, while all of Puig's works have been translated into English, only *Kiss of the Spider Woman* and its play version are currently in print. Moreover, the prestigious MLA Teaching Series includes two Latin American novels, *One Hundred Years of Solitude* and *Kiss of the Spider Woman*, out of a total of only three Spanish-language novels; the third being none other than *Don Quixote*.[43]

For obvious reasons, none of the other versions of *Kiss of the Spider Woman* incorporate a central aspect of the novel: the use of footnotes. With the exception of the notes included during Molina's telling of the fictional Nazi film (which serve to buttress the reality of the movie by providing what purport to be passages from a Tobis-Berlin press release), the footnotes appear to present in a direct manner the psychoanalytical and political underpinnings of the fiction presented in the diegesis. Additionally, they serve as a theoretical counterpoint to the actual narrative, often complementing the dialogue and actions of Molina and Valentín, but also, on occasion, presenting a psycho-political discussion that is contradicted by the fiction.

Despite the fact that the use of footnotes as a storytelling technique has a distinguished history in Latin American literature—for instance, they are occasionally used by Jorge Luis Borges—Oviedo argues that their use in the novel "interferes with the fluidity of the narration" (352). Leaving aside the footnotes that accompany the "Nazi film," which, as mentioned, add information regarding its production, Oviedo is correct in noting that the footnotes force the reader to keep in mind what could be described as two parallel discursive tracks: on one hand, the diegesis, on the other, the discussion regarding psychoanalytic attempts at understanding same sex desire. But these footnotes also defend gay sexuality as natural and do so by appealing to one of the privileged intellectual discourses in Argentina.

It is difficult to exaggerate the importance of psychoanalysis in Argentine culture. As Mariano Ben Plotkin reminds us, "Argentina today has one of the highest incidences of Freudian analysts in the world. Argentina also vies with France for first place in the number of Lacanian analysts" (1). More relevant than the number of psychoanalytic professionals is the dissemination of Freudian ideas throughout society: "From politicians to bank clerks, from soap opera stars to cab drivers, and even a few generals—everybody seems to use psychoanalytic concepts to express the concerns of everyday life. . . . For broad sectors of Argentine society, psychoanalysis has become an interpretative system . . . used to understand various aspects of reality" (Plotkin 1). By appealing to psychoanalysis in his attempt at understanding and presenting homosexuality, Puig reflects this intellectual consensus as he uses it to undermine the prejudices of the implied reader. The use of any other scientific discourse—biological, for instance, if there were evidence of a "gay gene"—would have been less effective in making Puig's case for an Argentinean reader. In the footnotes, Puig is attempting to change the reader's mind regarding same-sex desire, as well as providing the "scientific" underpinnings for the behavior of the two protagonists.

Furthermore, there is an additional political dimension to Puig's resort to psychoanalytic theories that dovetails perfectly with the actual plot of the novel. As Federico Finchelstein notes:

> Psychoanalysis became an identity of the liberal Argentina defeated by the military and Peronism. In a totalitarian context, psychoanalysis showed its emancipatory potential and became a counterpoint to reactionary conceptions of the sacred, competing with the right for spaces previously occupied by the state and competing also with the church for spaces traditionally occupied by religion. . . . Argentine psychoanalysis may have retreated to culture from politics, but this "retreat" posed a long-lasting resistance against the forces of authoritarianism. Standing against the return of the repressed, Argentine psychoanalysis was itself ultimately repressed. Its persecution by the military dictatorship shows that this idea of Freud as a target in an Argentine civil war was created to last. (*Transatlantic Fascism* 176)

Thus the novel takes up the discourse that buttressed opposition to totalitarianism, including Peronism—one must remember that Isabel Perón's regime is presented as the one that has jailed Valentín and Molina—as well as past and future military regimes.[44]

In the novel Molina proves his equal worth as a human being to Valentín by means of his actions, as well as by the stories he tells, and the footnotes attempt to do the same with the reader by appealing to psychoanalysis. While homophobia, together with anti-Semitism and misogyny, were, Finchelstein notes, central to the Argentine fascist imaginary, one can assume that many liberal and socialist readers also saw same-sex desire as abnormal.[45] After all, Argentina, like other Hispanic countries, has a deep patriarchal tradition that, as we saw in the previous section on *The Real Life of Alejandro Mayta*, plagued even those who sought to create a new and more egalitarian society. Nevertheless, secular liberals and non-Stalinist leftists still constituted a readership relatively open to changing their opinion regarding issues of sexual identity. The footnotes were written with them in mind.

The use of footnotes is not the only unusual aspect of the novel's text. Although *Kiss of the Spider Woman* also includes "police reports," the description of Valentin's hallucinations under the influence of morphine, interior monologues, and so on, most of the novel resembles a screenplay in structure, as was the case with the earlier *Betrayed by Rita Hayworth*.[46] (There are, however, major differences from the screenplay form in that there are neither indications of setting nor, more importantly, information regarding who is speaking.) Thus, in addition to the explicit references to popular cultural products, the novel reflects the formal influence of popular culture or, better said, of a specifically technical aspect of a popular art form. While this structural presence of the screenplay form in the novel reflects Puig's own training in film—like García Márquez, he studied at the Centro Sperimentale di Cinematografia in Rome, and, in fact, *Betrayed by Rita Hayworth* began as an attempt at writing a screenplay—it also shows the depth of Puig's involvement with this popular art form.

The novel begins with someone speaking: "Something a little strange, that's what you notice, that she's not a woman like all the others" (3). Again, the reader does not know yet that it is Molina who is speaking or, for that matter, that this begins his retelling of *Cat People* (1942), the first of the fabled collaborations between director Jacques Tourneur and producer Val Lewton. In this manner, the novel establishes an intertextual relationship with the kind of films that someone with intellectual pretensions like Valentín would have probably found of little interest, though he does not refer to the cinema in his discussions. It is not the films of Ingmar Bergman or Jean Luc Godard, directors that at the time occupied the center of the artistic film canon, nor those of the Hollywood auteurs, such as Alfred Hitchcock or Nicholas Ray, vindicated by such influential nouvelle vague figures as the same Godard or Francois Truffaut, that are cited in the novel. Instead, the "real" films retold in the novel—the Tourneur-Lewton horror movies *Cat People* and *I Walked with a Zombie*, but also John Cromwell's weepy *The Enchanted Cottage* (1945)—are not only Hollywood films, but also the kind of studio films that were only just beginning to be recuperated by critics at the time Puig began to write the novel in 1973.[47] However, Molina finds enormous experiential and perhaps allegorical value in the movies he retells.

One assumes that Puig actually believed *Cat People*, *I Walked with a Zombie*, and *The Enchanted Cottage* were works of artistic worth. According to Levine, he "enjoyed the campy excess" of horror films (41), an opinion that would seem to imply that he saw these B films as enjoyable but of limited artistic merit. However, as we will see, his writings prove that he valued at least some Hollywood B films, including those that escaped the auteurist critical revaluation of the 1960s. Thus, in "Cinema and the Novel," an essay that originally accompanied his published screenplays, Puig compares Tay Garnett's *Seven Sinners* (1936), "an unpretentious B-movie," favorably to William Wyler's *The Best Years of Our Lives* (1946), "a 'serious' spectacular which won a clutch of Oscars and was seen as an honour for the cinema" (399).[48]

While most critics today would make a much stronger case for the artistry of the Lewton-Tourneur collaborations and the Cromwell melodrama than the one Puig makes for Garnett's movie, the fact is that, regardless of Puig's actual opinion about these films, Molina's anti-intellectual discourse precludes such argumentation being made in the novel. In fact, the made-up movies belong to genres that are infinitely less prestigious. Not only do they include one belonging to a group of films generally seen as lacking any redeeming value—the Nazi propaganda movie titled *Her Real Glory*, but the other two—an improbable French car-racing movie that turns into a story about Latin American guerrillas and another belonging to the Mexican *cabaretera* genre— would, if real, belong to only marginally more esteemed genres. However, for Molina, the value of these movies—real and made-up—resides in the emotional and experiential uses he finds for them.

For Puig, the main difference between novel and film is that novels "always aim for the direct reconstruction of reality" and are characterized by their "analytical nature." Regarding film, he writes: "Synthesis is best expressed in allegory or dreams. . . . Cinema needs this spirit of synthesis so it is ideally suited to allegories and dreams. Which leads me to another hypothesis: can this be why the cinema of the 1930s and 1940s has lasted so well? They really were dreams displayed in images" ("Cinema and the Novel" 399). Puig's vindication of allegory is contemporary to that made by postmodern critics, such as Paul De Man, but is significantly different. Unlike deconstructive critics who saw in allegory an acknowledgment of the artificiality of literature, of its inability to establish a univocal and direct relationship between signifier and signified, Puig believed in the possibility of a fully realistic depiction: he claims that his novels aim at the direct reconstruction of reality.[49]

Unlike *Seven Sinners* and other Hollywood B films that supposedly embraced their roles as allegories, Wyler's *The Best Years of Our Lives* makes the categorical mistake of intending "a realistic portrait of US soldiers returning from the Second World War" ("Cinema and the Novel" 399). In other words, Wyler should have either adopted the cinematic allegorical style that, for Puig, permits "an unbiased look" at specific issues, or, if he needed to cling to realism, made a documentary or, perhaps more appropriately, written a novel on the topic.[50] By making a realistic film, Wyler cannot avoid *The Best Years of Our Lives* ending up becoming "a valid period piece" (399). (One assumes that the novel, because of the medium used for representation, would be in less danger of becoming obsolete.) Puig concludes his brief discussion of allegory versus realism in film by noting: "When I look at what survives of the history of cinema, I find increasing evidence of what little can be salvaged from all attempts at realism, where the camera appears to slide across the surface, unable to discover the missing third dimension beyond two-dimensional photographic realism. This superficiality seems, strangely enough, to coincide with the absence of an *auteur*" (399). Ironically, Wyler, one of the most awarded filmmakers in Hollywood history, is presented as a hack, while the studio "factory" director Garnett is praised for having made "a work of art" (399).

One could very well see *Kiss of the Spider Woman* as Puig's attempt at creating a text that, while presenting a realistic portrayal of two men trapped in a prison cell, as befits a novel, is at the same time also able to appropriate the allegorical dimension of film by making movies part of the daily reality the novel describes and analyzes. Without discounting myriad other possible interpretations, one assumes Puig would have wanted the films—both real and invented—to be read as allegories.

But if *Seven Sinners* "was an unbiased look at power and established values, a very light-weight allegory on this theme" ("Cinema and the Novel" 399), how should one interpret the films interpolated in the novel? As mentioned above, the novel begins with Molina recounting the plot of *Cat People*. This movie tells the story of Irena, a Serbian émigré—though Puig makes her Transylvanian in the novel—in New York. She marries Oliver Reed, an architect, despite her fear of being part of a lineage of cat women who transform into panthers when sexually aroused. She gets help from Dr. Judd but transforms into a panther when the psychoanalyst attempts to seduce her. Driven jealous by Oliver's friendship with Alice, another architect at the firm, Irena transforms into a panther and follows her, but does not manage to attack her. She is finally killed by a panther when she enters its cage in the Central

Park Zoo. Perhaps significantly, Molina identifies the male characters by their profession, while Irena is called by her name and Alice by the name of the actress who plays her: Jane Randolph. Moreover, reflecting Molina's subscription to traditional gender roles, Alice/Jane Randolph is misidentified by Molina as the architect's assistant rather than as a colleague.[51]

The possibility of seeing *Cat People* as an allegory is explicitly presented in the novel by Valentín rather than Molina: "But you know what I like about it? That it's just like an allegory, and really clear too, of the woman's fear of giving in to a man, because by completely giving in to sex she reverts a little to an animal, you know?" (31).[52] Valentín thus sees the plot of *Cat People*, as retold by Molina, as an allegory of female desire. Valentín—and, through him, Puig—agrees with Judith Butler, for whom allegory is the privileged mode for speaking about desire.[53] But given that modern allegories, unlike medieval ones, do not have a fixed dogmatic interpretation, the possibility of other readings is fully open.

The novel astutely illustrates the manner in which viewers—in this case, listeners—of movies ultimately identify with specific characters based on their own personal traits, needs, and desires. As a result, they are able to actualize the filmic allegory, adapting it to their specific context. Thus, in a key moment, Valentín and Molina discuss the characters who they feel represent them:

> —Who do you identify with? Irena or the other one?
> —With Irena, what do you think? She's the heroine, dummy. Always with the heroine.
> —Okay, go on.
> —And you, Valentin, with who? You're in trouble because the architect seems like a moron to you.
> —Go ahead and laugh. With the psychiatrist. But no making jokes now, I respected your choice, with no remarks. Go on. (25)

Molina's sense of being a woman is reflected in his identification with Irena.

That *Cat People* can also be seen as an allegory of Molina's desire is implied by the very first sentence of the novel: "Something a little strange, that's what you notice, that she's not a woman like all the others" (3). As we read on, we discover that Molina identifies not as a gay man but as a woman, and a traditional one to boot: "And since a woman's the best there is . . . I want to be one. That way I save listening to all kinds of advice, because I know what the score is myself and I've got it all clear in my head" (19). He, like Irena, the protagonist of *Cat People*, is a woman with a difference.

While today many would probably see Molina as transgender, the novel depicts male homosexuality, even in the case of someone who identifies with female gender roles, as another way of being a man. The novel agrees with Valentín's response to Molina: "Look, you're a man just as much as I am, so cut it out. . . . Don't go setting us apart" (58). However, as we will see, Puig, following the ideas of the radical psychoanalysis of the time, proposes what could be called pansexuality rather than fixed sexual identities.

As can be inferred from the description above, Valentín sees himself as an intellectual. One could even argue that he represents the fusion of intellectuality and action that, for many, found its greatest avatar in Ernesto "Che" Guevara. Furthermore, the fact that the cat woman kills the psychoanalyst can be seen as foreshadowing the destruction of Valentín's sense of identity that will take place as a result of his encounter with Molina. Of course, this leads to the construction of a new sense of self on the part of Valentín, but that lies outside the possible allegorical reading suggested by Molina's version of *Cat People*.

Puig's (and in the novel, Molina's) genius resides in choosing (and inventing) film plots that refer directly to the evolution of the characters' situation and relationship. The Nazi film, for instance, introduces the topic of spying on someone you (potentially) love. The auto racing film highlights the tensions between romantic desire and political necessity, which Valentín, as a revolutionary, believes must subordinate it. *I Walked with a Zombie* illuminates the romantic triangle between Valentín, his distanced lover, and Molina. And the Mexican *cabaretera* movie portrays romantic self-sacrifice and permanent separation on the part of the female protagonist and, through her, Molina.

That said, the importance of the films and, to a lesser degree, the song lyrics is that, as Molina says about the latter, "boleros contain tremendous truths, which is why I like them" (139). The truths they contain are the truths of desire, which, as Butler noticed and as the novel illustrates, cannot be stated directly, at least in everyday conversation. It is through films and songs that Molina and especially Valentín, whose revolutionary persona had been based on rejecting anything redolent of personal pleasure, are ultimately able to come to grips with the nature of their desires.[54]

The presence of a psychoanalyst in *Cat People* and the discussions between Molina and Valentín regarding sexual desire establish a connection between their conversations in the "main" text of the novel and the footnotes dealing with psychological and psychoanalytical theories regarding the origin of homosexuality.[55]

In "A Last Interview with Manuel Puig," the Argentine novelist spoke about the role of the footnotes in the novel. After being asked by US critic Ronald Christ whether the footnotes should be taken seriously, Manuel Puig responded: "Of course, of course. This information has been denied *violently* to people. . . . And you must remember that novel was destined, first of all, to a Spanish-speaking reader. So I said to myself: well the information's been violently denied, so I'll violently incorporate it into the narration" (573). The quotation points out how passionately Puig felt about the need to provide the reader with information about gays and lesbians beyond widely shared prejudices and stereotypes. Puig argues in the same interview that in the footnotes, "It's my voice, but not my judgment. I simply repeat, in a condensed form, the judgments of specialists" (573). However, all the "specialists" can be loosely classified as working within the intellectual boundaries of psychoanalysis: not only Sigmund Freud and first-generation psychoanalyst Otto Rank, but also figures of the second generation such as Anna Freud and Otto Fenichel, and even thinkers who, without being professionals in the medical field, embraced psychoanalysis as a tool with which to understand culture and society, such as Norman O. Brown and Herbert Marcuse. For Puig, when it comes to human behavior, scientific discourse is synonymous with psychoanalysis.

Rather than dismissing psychoanalysis or, as Puig himself claims, merely providing information for readers who have been denied access to scientific discussions on homosexuality or, worse, bombarded by homophobic discourses, the footnotes attempt to present and correct psychoanalytic discussions on the topic. Despite Puig's claim that the footnotes do not represent his "judgment," they show Puig as working within the Freudian tradition. This participation in psychoanalytic ideas is evidenced by his full acceptance of the central concept of psychoanalysis—the Oedipus complex—as the keystone to an understanding of same-sex desire.

In a characteristic Freudian move, Puig begins his review of academic views on homosexuality by rejecting biological explanations for its origin (*Kiss of the Spider Woman* 59–65nn).[56] He favors those interpretations that develop Freud's ideas in directions that contradict heteronormativity and patriarchy. Thus, he affirms the work of Brown and Marcuse:

> The qualification "polymorphous perverse" which Freud applies to the infantile libido—referring to the indiscriminate pleasure derived by the child from his own body or the body of others—has also been accepted by more recent scholars, like Norman O. Brown and Herbert Marcuse. The difference between them and Freud, as already indicated, lies in the fact that Freud considered it proper that the libido is sublimated and channeled into an exclusively heterosexual direction, definitely a genital one, while more recent thinkers approve and even favor a return to polymorphous perversity and to an eroticization that goes beyond the merely genital. (*Kiss of the Spider Woman* 205–6n)

According to the footnotes, psychoanalytic theory can be used to ground a defense of pleasure and sexuality in all its myriad forms. Following Marcuse, Puig contends that the key is not to restrict this polymorphous perversity but to imagine ways it could be made compatible with living within a social community.

Puig rejects the argument that heteronormativity is necessary because "a humanity without bounds of restraint . . . could never organize itself" (164n) by referring favorably to Marcuse's then-popular fusion of Marxism and psychoanalysis:

> It is here that Marcuse interjects his concept of "surplus repression," designating by such a term that part of sexual repression created to maintain the power of the dominant class, in spite of not proving to be indispensable to the maintenance of an organized society attending to the human necessities of all its constituents. Therefore, the principal advance that Marcuse presupposes in opposition to Freud would consist of the latter's toleration for a certain type

of repression in order to preserve contemporary society, whereas Marcuse deems it fundamental to change society, on the basis of an evolution that takes into account our original sexual impulses. (164–65n).

Behind the apparently neutral recounting of psychoanalytic explanations for same sex desire, the footnotes show Puig's support for radical change in sexual mores and social structures.

In particular, Puig approves of the ideas proposed in "a recent work of the Danish doctor Anneli Taube, *Sexuality and Revolution*" (207n) that conclude his survey of psychoanalytic ideas regarding homosexuality. According to Taube:

The rejection which a highly sensitive boy experiences toward an oppressive father as symbol of the violently authoritarian, masculine attitude is a conscious one. The boy, at the moment when he decides not to adhere to the world proposed by such a father—use of weapons, violently competitive sports, disdain for sensitivity as a feminine attribute, etc.—is actually exercising a free and even revolutionary choice inasmuch as he is rejecting the role of the stronger, the exploitative one. Of course, such a boy could not suspect, on the other hand, that Western civilization, apart from the world of the father, will not present him with any alternative model for conduct, in those first dangerously decisive years—above all from three to five—other than his mother. . . . In the case of the girl, on the other hand, who decides not to adhere to the world of the mother, her attitude is due to the fact that she rejects the role of being submissive, because she intuits it as humiliating and unnatural, without realizing that once that role has been excluded, Western civilization presents her with no other role than that of oppressor. But the act of rebellion by such a girl or boy would be a sign of undeniable strength and dignity. (Puig, *Kiss of the Spider Woman* 207–8n)

While Taube continues mainstream Freudian thought by placing the Oedipus complex at the core of the development of sexuality and identity, her belief that children can consciously reject following the gender-corresponding parent as a model contradicts Freud's central discovery: that of the unconscious. However, her political reading of psychoanalysis continues and complements that provided by Marcuse.

Taube's importance does not reside only in her being the last theoretical voice included in the footnotes, but also by a fact not disclosed
to the reader in the text: Taube is a fictional theorist, and her opinions
can be read as representing Puig's. As the novelist states in "A Last Interview": "I advanced an idea of my own; but I wanted to present it under
a very respected name, not a fiction's writer's name, and well . . . it's
there" (574).

However, even if an act of rebellion, the identification of the child
with the non-gender-corresponding parent is not necessarily politically
progressive, if one wants to use such terminology regarding gender
identity. After all, according to Puig as Taube, this "act of rebellion"
does not ultimately destroy the dyad of submission and oppression;
it just changes the gender of one of its participants. This decision, as
the footnotes argue, "causes the future male homosexual, for example,
after rejecting the defects of the repressive father, to feel anguished
about the necessity for identification with some form of conduct and
to 'learn' to be submissive like his mother. The process is identical for
the girl: she repudiates exploitation, and because of that she hates to be
like her submissive mother, but social pressures make her slowly 'learn'
another role, that of the repressive father" (210n). This leads "male
homosexuals" to exhibit a "submissive spirit, a conservative attitude, a
love of peace at any cost, even the cost of perpetuating their own mar-
ginality . . . whereas what has been characteristic of female homosexuals
is their anarchical spirit, violently argumentative, while at the same time
basically disorganized" (213n). Underlying Puig's discussion of the gender dyad is a belief in the need to break free from it, especially because
these models of conduct are ultimately linked to specific social and class
formations. Thus Puig as Taube notes: "Yet both attitudes have proven
not to be deliberate, but compulsive, imposed by a slow brainwashing in
which heterosexual bourgeois models for conduct participate—during
infancy and adolescence—and later on, at the point of adopting homosexuality itself, 'bourgeois' models for homo-sexual conduct" (213n).
Needless to say, here Taube is perfectly describing Molina's behavior.

In a gesture that connects gay liberation with the liberation of
women, Puig concludes the footnotes with the following comment:
"Much of the [*sic*]—fortunately, suggests Doctor Taube—began to
change throughout the decade of the sixties, with the emergence of the
woman's liberation movement, when the resulting judgments tended to

discredit—in the eyes of such sexual marginals—those unattainable but tenaciously imitated roles of 'strong male' and 'weak female.' The subsequent formation of homosexual liberation fronts is one proof of that" (213–14n). Thus, from the footnotes one can gather a psychosocial view of sexual identity that sees gender roles as connected to specific social and economic systems. In other words, while there is no explicit reference to the author of *Capital*, Puig in the footnotes continues to weave together Marx and Freud in ways that characterize the views of some of his references, such as Marcuse.

Even if there's no mention of Marx or any exclusively Marxist writer, the footnotes show a surprising tolerance toward then-existing socialism's distrust of gays and lesbians by noting that it originates in the prevalence of bourgeois models: "This prejudice, or perhaps truthful observation, concerning homosexuals placed them on the periphery of movements for class liberation and political action in general. The socialist countries' mistrust of homosexuals is notorious" (213n). However, while Puig seems to understand, without necessarily justifying, the reasons underlying this discrimination against gay people, he notes the contrast between Lenin's and Stalin's attitudes toward sexuality by citing Dennis Altman: "Altman emphasizes that in spite of Lenin's concern for sexual liberty in the USSR, his rejection of anti-homosexual legislation for example, such legislation was reintroduced in 1934 by Stalin, and as a result, the prejudice against homosexuality—as a type of 'bourgeois degeneration'—held fast in a number of Communist parties of the world" (196n). Anyone with any knowledge of the 1960s new Left in Latin America and beyond knows that ideas associated with Lenin were seen in a positive light, but those associated with Stalin were marked by the kiss of death.[57]

Though Puig attempts to reconcile sexual and political revolution in the footnotes, the political contours of this radical and egalitarian utopia are never fully described. On the other hand, Puig makes clear the radical nature of the sexual utopia he envisions. We have already seen his stress on the positive possibilities found in the polymorphous perversity of human sexuality. In fact, in the footnotes, it is this polymorphosity, not an exclusively gay identity, that is seen as the true key to sexual liberation. He again cites Altman approvingly: "Finally, Altman underscores the lack of any form of identity for the bisexual in contemporary society, and the pressures that he suffers from both sides, given that bisexuality threatens equally the exclusively homosexual forms of bourgeois life as well as heterosexual forms, and this characteristic would explain the reason why avowed bisexuality is so uncommon" (196n). It is not surprising, then, that when Ronald Christ described the relationship between Molina and Valentín as "a homosexual affair in an Argentine prison," Puig objected by noting "I wouldn't call it a 'homosexual affair.' In that cell there are only two men, but that's just on the surface. There are really two men, and two women. I agree with Theodore Roszack when he says that the woman most desperately in need of liberation is the woman every man has locked up in the dungeons of his own psyche" ("Last Interview" 571). In the interview, he is repeating a reference he had earlier made in the footnotes.[58]

Polymorphous perversity, which has bisexuality as its main but not exclusive expression, represents the sexual aspect of the utopia that informs the footnotes, as well as other of Puig's public statements. In "A Last Interview," Puig goes as far as arguing:

> For me, the only natural sexuality is bisexuality; that is, total sexuality. It's all a matter of sexuality, not homosexuality, not heterosexuality. With a person of your own gender, with a person of the opposite gender, with an animal, with a plant, with anything. Just as long as it's not offensive to the other party. I see both homosexuality and heterosexuality as specializations, as limiting matters. I see exclusive homosexuality and exclusive heterosexuality as cultural results, not as a natural outcome. If people were really free, I think they wouldn't choose within the limits of one sex. At the same time, I believe in the couple, whether heterosexual or homosexual. I think that with one person you develop things in time, sex also becomes much, much richer, more refined. I don't mean monogamy necessarily, but . . . (574)

Again referring to Roszack, Puig describes the breakdown of limitations in sexuality: "All of the above would represent the most cataclysmic reinterpretation of sexual life in the history of humanity, inasmuch as it would involve a restructuring of all that concerns sexual roles and concepts of sexual normality that are currently in force" (*Kiss of the Spider Woman* 196n). In the footnotes, these changes in sexual mores promise to actualize "the convenient but—until a few years ago—

merely potential parallelism between the struggle for class liberation and the one for sexual liberation" (196n).

Thus, according to Kimberly Chabot Davis, "Puig might be called proto-queer in his desire to move beyond the limits of either/or identity choices to embrace a 'natural' bisexuality" (5). One can also see in his embrace of polymorphosity proof of his participation in the sexual utopian thinking that arose in the late 1960s and flourished during the early 1970s.[59] But, despite Puig's insinuation that it is possible to link class revolution and sexual revolution, the footnotes concentrate almost exclusively on sexual liberation and, in particular, male same sex desire as one possible expression of human sexuality as valid as all others.

While the footnotes are where Puig deals theoretically with the issue of sexual orientation and, at least in principle, with its relationship with radical politics, one could see in the diegesis of the novel a narrative development of these theoretically based ideas and hopes. After all, one could find in the encounter between the queer Molina and the revolutionary Valentín an acting out of the struggles for sexual liberation and political liberation theorized in the footnotes. The novel would thus show revolutionary politics as represented by Valentín to be flawed by not taking into account an individual's subjective and sexual needs, while Molina, despite his psychological and emotional intuitiveness and basic human decency, seems completely unaware of the need for social and political change.

One is tempted to see in the evolution of both characters a coming together of sexual and political utopias. After all, by the end, Valentín and Molina have become lovers, and Molina has attempted to help Valentín's revolutionary group. As Balderston and Maristany argue: "Explicitly focused on the political maturing of a gay man, Molina, and of the changing perspective of an imprisoned revolutionary, Valentín Arregui, who comes to see the place of sexual oppression in the society he is struggling to change, Puig's novel depends for its force on identity categories that it ultimately questions" (208). *Kiss of the Spider Woman* could thus be seen as solving in its diegesis the problems that have in real life haunted the Left: how to reconcile political revolution and individual liberation. Again, Balderston and Maristany make this point: "The novel exemplifies the connections made among struggles for liberation in the New Left and uniquely dramatizes those struggles in the prison house dialogue. Puig's novel is arguably the first in which a gay character is given the status of a political subject, and in which the struggle for a new society explicitly includes a vision of the place of gay people in that society" (209). I would, however, argue that the representation of sexual and political liberation in the novel's text proper is much more complicated than Balderston and Maristany acknowledge.

One could see in Valentín's development from puzzlement at same-sex desire to an embrace of the polymorphosity celebrated by Puig precisely as representing this changed perspective. Valentín and Molina's sexual affair is not presented as leading to the political prisoner's discovery of his unacknowledged gay identity. Instead, after having sexual intercourse with Molina, Valentín says, "The more I think of it, the more I am convinced that sex is innocence itself" (221). But if Valentín evolves from what the novel portrays as a restrictive heterosexuality into a full embrace of the life-affirming potential found in a "total sexuality," Molina is still bound by a feminine version of gay identity.

More importantly, against Balderston and Maristany, Molina does not show a "political maturing" similar to Valentín's "sexual maturing."[60] Thus his decision to provide the urban guerrilla group the information that Valentín inexplicably possesses is in no moment presented as the consequence of an awareness of the need for social change. Instead, as Puig notes, "Molina's just the last of the romantics, the last of the romantic women" ("Last Interview" 574), and sacrificing one's life for the captive lover's cause is the ultimate romantic act.

The novel insinuates a similar interpretation. In the midst of the morphine-fueled hallucination that concludes *Kiss of the Spider Woman*, Valentín has an imaginary conversation with his true love Marta to whom he recounts an equally imaginary exchange with his mother:

"Yes," well . . . she's asking me if it's true all that stuff in the papers, that my cellmate died, in a shootout, and she's asking if it was my fault, and if I'm not ashamed of having brought him such awful luck, "What did you answer her?" that yes, it was my fault, and that yes, I am very sad, but that there's no point in being so sad because the only one who knows for sure is him, if he was sad or happy to die that way, sacrificing himself for a just cause, because he's the only one who will ever have known, and let's hope, Marta, how much I wish it with all my heart, let's hope that he may have died happily,

"For a just cause? hmmm . . . I think he let himself be killed because that way he could die like some heroine in a movie, and none of that business about a just cause," that's something only he can know, and it's possible that even he never knew, but in my cell I can't sleep anymore because he got me used to listening to him tell films every night, like lullabies, and if I ever get out of here sometime I'm not going to be able to call him and invite him over to dinner, he who had invited me so many times. (279)

Marta and, through her, Valentín and perhaps the novel as a whole present Molina as acting out of romantic attachment rather than as the result of a growing awareness of political injustice or a belief in the goals of the urban guerrilla movement. Without denying Molina's nobility, his helping the urban guerrilla group is shown as a futile and arguably mistaken act. It is true that Valentín's actions before being imprisoned—union organizing—and afterward—going on a hunger strike over the killing of a fellow prisoner—seem to be those of an exemplary social activist.[61] However, despite the footnotes' hope for class liberation that would also imply sexual liberation (and vice versa), the novel presents Valentín's political group in the worst possible terms. In the novel, Valentín convinces Molina to provide information to his revolutionary group. (Though one cannot help but wonder how someone who has been in jail for two and a half years could be in possession of any new and important information.[62]) The novel's "police report" explains what happens as agents stop to arrest Molina: "Subject demanded to see credentials. At that moment, however, several shots were fired from a passing automobile, wounding CISL agent Joaquin Perrone, along with subject, both of whom immediately fell to the ground. . . . Of the wounded, Molina expired before arriving patrol unit could administer first aid. . . . The impression of other members of the patrol unit is that the extremists preferred to eliminate Molina to avoid the possibility of a confession" (274). If Valentín is shown to suffer from the self-repression that, according to the novel, is promoted, if not required, by the Marxist ideology espoused by his urban guerrilla group, Molina is presented as the ultimate victim of revolutionary ideology.

If any of the characters develop politically, Valentín is the most likely to have done so. At the start of the novel he appears to be a dogmatic

Marxist, but by the end of the novel he no longer seems to see in the class struggle an exclusive political option. Thus, when he is informed that Molina will be leaving prison, Valentín suggests that he join a political group regardless of its actual ideology:

> —When you're out of here, you'll be free, you'll be with people. If you want you can even join up with some kind of political group.
> —That's ridiculous and you know it; they'd never trust some faggot . . .
> —Anyway, there's a lot of different types of groups for political action. And if you find one that appeals to you, join it, even if it's a group that just does a lot of talking. (215)

Not only is the rigid heterosexual gone by the end of the novel, but the doctrinaire Marxist seems to have been replaced by someone who, rather being committed to achieving maximalist revolutionary change, now sees politics as a form of self-expression and identity building, and sees changing social mores regarding sexuality independent of the class struggle as a valid option.

Against the explicit desire expressed in the footnotes for a class liberation imbricated with a sexual liberation, a desire that Puig shared with numerous radicals in the late 1960s and throughout the 1970s, the novel's story debunks existing revolutionary politics. Despite Valentín's personal values, based on not exploiting or abusing anyone, his revolutionary group has no scruples in killing Molina.[63] And there is no other radical political option considered throughout the narrative.

Santiago Colás notes the importance of this discussion about the possibility of revolution in Puig's *Kiss of the Spider Woman*:

> *Beso* clings to this utopia [of radical political change] on one level, but on another level, it tells the tale of this utopia's impossibility and of the tragedy of believing in its inviolable realization. In this sense, *El beso de la mujer araña* represents . . . a turning point in recent Latin American narrative from a Latin American modernity, critical but still within the logic of European modernity, to a Latin American postmodernity that operates from beyond the exhaustion of those paradigms, when hope lay not in a totalized utopia of a dramatic leap, but in the laborious critical procedure of "de-" and "re-" constructing history. (75)

While Colás is correct in noting the manner in which Puig prob-
lematizes 1960s revolutionary beliefs, which had by 1976 been shown
to be grossly flawed, he exhibits a similar optimism regarding postmodernity in the 1990s. (His book, published in 1994, is, after all, titled
*Postmodernity in Latin America: The Argentine Paradigm.*) If the 1960s
radicals believed in armed insurrection as the shortcut to utopia, those
of the 1990s often believed that the world could be changed by cultural
means, deconstructing gender and other hierarchies. As Colás states,
"The 'hybrid cultures' of postmodernity in Latin America redefine the
meaning of popular culture—rejecting ahistorical essentialisms and
myths of authenticity—in terms of 'sociocultural representativity.' This
means accepting a new inclusiveness. It means not prescribing or cir-
cumscribing but 'permitting' genuinely popular culture to draw on even
the most 'tainted' of mediums in its attempts to combat political and
economic marginalization" (17). For many, Madonna—or, to be more
accurate, Shakira and the mass popular culture she represents—had replaced Che Guevara as a symbol in the struggle against the inequalities
that have marred the region's societies.

Perhaps reflecting a sensibility shaped in the 1950s and 1960s, *Kiss
of the Spider Woman* privileges film and boleros as the central popular
art forms with which to attempt to understand desire. We have already
seen how a movie such as *Cat People* becomes the mediator by means of
which the frustrated conscious and unconscious desires of both Valentín
and Molina become explicit. While Valentín identifies with the psychia-
trist, it is Molina, who by telling the films, catalyzes the intellectual and
emotional changes that lead the activist from Marxist logic to humanist
sexual solidarity. By portraying desire through allegory, movies become
a kind of collective dream. And, as we know, dreams are the royal road
to the unconscious.

The power of the retelling of *Cat People* or of the use of Mario
Clavel's bolero "La carta" (My letter) resides in their dovetailing with
the desires and needs of the novel's characters and, through them, of the
reader. Puig's point that these existing works of popular art represent
the unconscious of each individual is thus presented in the strongest
possible way.

After realizing how the lyrics of "My Letter" resemble the hidden
meaning of a letter sent in code to him, Valentín notes: "Know something? There I was laughing at your bolero, but the letter I got today

says just what the bolero says" (137).[64] And as we saw, Molina sees boleros as telling "tremendous truths." These truths are precisely those of desire. Thus, popular culture and politics are ultimately valued for their ability to help people discover what they truly mean and who they truly are.

Not without contradiction, the counterpoint between the footnotes and main text, between psychology and politics, between mass culture and revolution, ends up resolved in a politics of identity and of self-discovery implicitly presented as compatible with an ever-more-enlightened liberal politics, where even groups that only "do a lot of talking" are able to incorporate queer views and needs into the social conversation. The class struggle is no longer the exclusive or perhaps even the primary motor for social change.

———

*Kiss of the Spider Woman* and *The Real Life of Alejandro Mayta* question the figure of the revolutionary. Instead of describing a larger-than-life figure helping lead Latin America to a new age of justice and equality— a Mozart capable of putting "this recklessness to order," as Cortázar puts it ("Meeting" 429)—Vargas Llosa and Puig bring the revolutionary down to earth. Mayta and Valentín, though sympathetic, are flawed figures who do not have all or even most of the answers to politics, even less so to life or art. Even though Mayta is able to imagine an "integral revolution" that would eliminate gender and other biases and democratize productive resources, this vision is presented as a noble dream, completely delinked from any possible political or insurrectional activity. In fact, Vargas Llosa portrays all radical activity as leading to social destruction. Puig's novel depicts politics similarly. Thus Valentín, rather than possessing political truth, is shown as a flawed individual who is able to learn about life and even politics, as evidenced by his finding value in political groups that just do "a lot of talking." Moreover, his revolutionary group is revealed to be callous and cruel. By questioning the figure of the revolutionary, both novels reject the belief in maximalist revolution that characterized the ethos of the 1960s. But if destroying capitalism and replacing it with new modes of production is no longer considered the privileged road to a full and equal modernity, what is to be done?

While, fortunately, neither work can be classified as political propaganda, there are political implications that, while not identical, are at least comparable and perhaps compatible. On the one hand, *Kiss of the Spider Woman* ultimately embraces the centrality of personal and sexual discovery for individual development, the potential of popular culture for this purpose, and the role of political activity, but not activity described in radical or subversive terms, in contributing to this process. On the other hand, the only moment of optimism in *The Real Life of Alejandro Mayta* is in its description of the "real" Mayta as an informal entrepreneur running a food kiosk in prison. The novel even describes it as a "genuine revolution" (294). Given this, could not a political activity rooted in the promotion of the free market be seen as a way out of the violence and intolerance of Peruvian history? In both cases, the underlying political horizon seems to be a liberal democracy capable of incorporating individual voices, including queer ones, and open to the promotion of new laws and policies within the existing economic system.

What is clear is that maximalist revolution is no longer a possibility.[65]

# 4

# Revolution after the Demise of Revolution

*Roberto Bolaño and Carla Guelfenbein on Social Change*

The concluding section of this study looks at the works of two Chilean authors: Roberto Bolaño (1953–2003) and Carla Guelfenbein (1958– ), whose novels reflect the structure of feeling that characterizes the region after the absolute demise of any and all revolutionary hope. Both Bolaño and Guelfenbein were personally marked by Salvador Allende's attempt at pouring revolutionary wine into Chile's old democratic institutional bottles, by Augusto Pinochet's murderous military coup that overthrew the socialist government, and by the new regime's implementation of the radical free-market policies developed at the University of Chicago.[1] Both experienced exile, even if Bolaño's was, at least at first, for economic rather than political reasons. However, if Bolaño is the most admired Latin American writer of the last decades, not only in the region but throughout the world, Guelfenbein, despite winning the prestigious Alfaguara Award in 2015 for her *In the Distance with You* (2015), is often seen as a commercial writer.[2]

In spite of their common backgrounds, Bolaño and Guelfenbein can be seen as representing two diverging attitudes to literature and revolution. And while gender is central to their differences—indeed, Guelfenbein has claimed to practice "women's writing"—there are other equally significant distinctions between the writers.[3] Nevertheless, Bolaño and Guelfenbein have written novels and other texts that can be read as reflections on Allende's socialist government, perhaps the last moment during which truly revolutionary change seemed clearly possible for the region.

### Roberto Bolaño

In 1996, Roberto Bolaño, a then-unknown Chilean writer, published two books with major Spanish publishing houses: *Nazi Literature in the Americas*, an encyclopedia of fictional fascist writers, was issued by Seix Barral, the editorial house that had played a central role in the development of the Boom of the Latin American novel in the 1960s, while Anagrama put out *Distant Star*, which developed one of the entries in *Nazi Literature in the Americas* into a novel exploring the imbrication of art and fascism in Pinochet's Chile. Although these books did not make the best-seller lists, they were very positively reviewed in the major newspapers of the Hispanic world, such as the Spanish *El País* and the Argentine *Clarín*.

Bolaño's early succès d'estime became full-blown canonization two years later when *The Savage Detectives* took Hispanic literary circles by storm. Not only did this novel win the prestigious Herralde Award for 1998, but the following year it received the Rómulo Gallegos Prize as the best novel published during the previous two years. As had been the case with the first two Rómulo Gallegos awards, given to Mario Vargas Llosa and Gabriel García Márquez in 1967 and 1972, respectively, the prize consecrated Bolaño as a living master.[4] Bolaño, who was twenty-six years younger than García Márquez and seventeen years younger than Vargas Llosa, was now acknowledged by writers and critics alike as the one truly major Spanish-language writer to have appeared on the scene since the heyday of the Boom in the 1960s and 1970s. His influence shows no sign of waning. As Wilfrido H. Corral argued in 2013: "He is the master of the new generations" ("General Introduction" 12).

This central position is evidenced by no less a figure than the celebrated Spanish novelist Enrique Vila-Matas, who, on the occasion of Bolaño's untimely death due to liver failure in 2003, wrote:

He lived life in a way that taught us how to write. . . . I remember that . . . many of the texts I was about to send for publication . . . went through a last minute revision, provoked by my sudden suspicion that perhaps Bolaño would read them. . . . [T]hanks to the feeling that Bolaño read everything, I began living in a state of constant literary exigency, because he had placed the ribbon very high and I didn't want to disappoint him. Because of this I witnessed how, for example, a text . . . I considered of secondary worth began to grow in different directions and was transformed into the best of my novels. And all because of the heights at which Bolaño placed the ribbon. (48–49)

While one cannot discount the element of postmortem exaggeration in Vila-Matas's words, the fact that the Spanish author had been born in 1948, five years before Bolaño, and had published his first novel in 1973, twenty-three years before *Distant Star*, brings home the impact that the Chilean author had on Spanish-language literature.

Bolaño's importance within the field of Spanish-American and Spanish literature can be explained by the manner in which his novels achieve the literary goals implicit in the writings of many of the best novelists of the region during the 1980s and 1990s. As Ignacio López-Calvo notes: "Bolaño is also well known for having rejected magical realism and especially the writing of post-Boom authors who imitated García Márquez's techniques" (8). Moreover, Bolaño shares this rejection of magical realism with "the McOndo group (Alberto Fuguet, Sergio Gómez, Edmundo Paz Soldán, and Jaime Bayly) as well as the Crack group (Jorge Volpi, Pedro Ángel Palou, Ricardo Chávez Castañeda, Eloy Urroz, and Ignacio Padilla)" (8). In fact, Bolaño can be seen as evincing in a convincing manner the most important traits of these two groups of writers. His work thus seamlessly achieves a fusion of the McOndo group's embrace of international pop culture and the Crack writers' tony European ambitions.

But Bolaño's success was not limited to the Spanish-speaking world. Like the writing of his Boom predecessors, especially García Márquez, Bolaño's works have been hailed internationally. While Bolaño's novels began to be translated into major European languages before his death in 2003—*Nazi Literature in the Americas* was translated into German in 1999; *By Night in Chile* was translated into French and English in 2002—and received excellent reviews, the Chilean author's canonization as a major figure in world literature began in earnest later with the translation of his longer novels: *The Savage Detectives* and the posthumous, one-thousand-page opus, *2666*, published in 2004.[5] In fact, the English translation of *The Savage Detectives* was named one of the ten best books of the year by the *New York Times* in 2007. Bolaño's *2666*, originally published in Spanish in 2004, received the same award in 2008. As the hip Brooklyn-based journal *N+1* commented in 2008: "Bolaño's canonization has taken place so rapidly and completely, and with so little demurral, that one can only reluctantly pile aboard the bandwagon. But Bolaño is the real thing, as urgent, various, imaginative, and new as any writer active in the last decade. The question is: why not canonize anyone else?" ("On Bolaño" 10).

Although the review answers its own question—"real thing," "urgent," "imaginative," and the like—the international acceptance of Bolaño's work, the issue that puzzled the *N+1* coterie, merits further discussion beyond this acknowledgment of its undeniable quality.[6] After all, other Spanish-language writers with comparable novelistic achievements, such as the Argentine Ricardo Piglia and the previously mentioned Vila-Matas, have not had a similar impact in the United States.

Sarah Pollack, among others, notes that Bolaño has been read in a manner that continues and renews the exoticization of Latin America that many, including the Chilean novelist, criticized:

> The yellow butterflies and floating beauties of García Márquez's fiction form no part of the scenery in Bolaño's novel. . . . I would argue, however, that from them a new and equally reductive image of Latin America is emerging in the U.S. collective imagination, one that *The Savage Detectives* unintentionally feeds. An extravagant cast of characters populates its pages: a bisexual poet named Luscious Skin, a Uruguayan exile who hides for a week in a bathroom stall during the 1968 police occupation of Mexico City's national university, an institutionalized architect who communes with a dead poet, a pimp who regularly measures his phallus with his knife. These personages may not be born with pigs' tails, but for many U.S. readers they certainly feel exotic and belong to a reality far removed from their own. (360)[7]

While Pollack attempts to clear Bolaño of any responsibility for fueling this exoticist view of Latin America, the fact is that he concentrates on the excessive aspects of the region's reality, such as the violence fueled by the drug trade and the right-wing repression of the 1970s, rather than on its preponderant mundanity.

However, in addition to the appeal of the exoticism found in his novels, the way he singles out spectacular and tragic moments in the region's history such as the Chilean dictatorship and the rise of the femicides in Northern Mexico and his success in synthetizing the literary evolution of Latin America during the last two decades, Bolaño's success can also be attributed to his synchronicity with the current political mores and emotions of Western culture.

In an essay as much critical as descriptive, Jacques Rancière complains about the "ethical turn," celebrated by so many as the aesthetic privileging of human beings over abstract politics, and of means over ends, as rejecting the possibility of politics itself.[8] For earlier artists, revolution, whether understood as violent or democratic, was a future "cut in time" ("Ethical Turn" 201) that implied the possibility of political progress. However, as Rancière notes:

> With the ethical turn, this orientation is strictly inverted: history becomes ordered according to a cut in time made by a radical event that is no longer in front of us but already behind us. If the Nazi genocide lodged itself at the core of philosophical, aesthetic and political thinking some four or five decades after the discovery of the camps, the reason is not only that the first generation of survivors remained silent. Around 1989, when the last remaining vestiges of this revolution were collapsing, the events until then had linked political and aesthetic radicality to a cut in historical time. This cut, however, required that the radicality, could be replaced only by genocide at the cost of inverting its meaning, of transforming it into the already endured catastrophe from which only a god could save us. ("Ethical Turn" 201)

For Rancière, the fall of socialism led to the end of the belief in the possibility of social change.

As the principal European historical example of politics as genocide, the Holocaust—"the already endured catastrophe," as Rancière puts it—has become the limit against which all reflection must cede and to which it must endlessly return. Literature has thus become "an unprecedented dramaturgy of infinite evil, justice and reparation" (Rancière, "Ethical Turn" 185). "Evil" is presented here as existing in potentia in any attempt at significant political or social transformation. The Holocaust—better said, another holocaust—is always implicit in any move toward substantive political change.[9] Bruno Bosteels, who analyzes this "ethical turn" in Latin America, ably summarizes its logical consequence: "Ethics, then, no longer founds the internal consistency of a political process within a specific situation but instead becomes a new external point of authority from which all militant processes can be found guilty of dogmatism, authoritarianism, or blind utopianism" (309). The artistic examples given by Rancière are unsurprisingly all from Europe and North America—a sign of the times: two films, Lars von Trier's *Dogville* and Clint Eastwood's *Mystic River*, are given pride of place. While Bosteels examines several Latin American narrative and critical works by such figures as the Mexican writers Sabina Berman and Paco Ignacio Taibo II, he omits any mention of our author. However, Roberto Bolaño is one of the main examples of this replacement of politics with ethics, not only in Latin America or Spain, but in world literature.

It is true that Bolaño did not shy from dealing with the most traumatic political moments and issues of the last decades in Latin America. The topics he depicted, on occasion with unflinching accuracy, include the Pinochet dictatorship in both *Distant Star* (1996) and *By Night in Chile* (2000); the youth upheaval and its repression in Mexico in 1968 in *Amulet* (1999); and the serial killings of women at Ciudad Juárez in his posthumous *2666* (2004). Frequently, the topics of his novels are precisely those which for other writers—such as Taibo II in *1968* (1991), Elena Poniatowska in *Massacre in Mexico* (1975) (Mexico in 1968), or Antonio Skármeta in *The Postman* (1985) (Pinochet coup)— have been occasion for political denunciation or reflection. However, unlike Taibo or Skármeta during the 1970s and early 1980s, Bolaño is far from being a traditional committed writer. Instead, he is the prime Latin American example of how to write about politics in a postpolitical manner. In a manner analogous, though not identical, to the films and texts examined by Rancière, Bolaño throughout his novels replaces political commitment with ethical evaluation, and the appeal for change with the call for mourning. This is, to my mind, one of the reasons Bolaño's novels have been embraced throughout the world.

The paradigmatic example of this rejection of politics in Bolaño's work is his 1999 novel *Amulet*, which presents a sui-generis look at Mexico City in 1968. Often overshadowed by other more famous events of 1968—the Prague Spring, which raised and buried the hope of a "socialism with a human face," and May 1968 in Paris, the last European radical uprising, which gave birth to the postpolitical ideas and world in which we live—Mexico also saw the rise of a radical movement during that fateful year.[10] The organization of the 1968 Olympic Games, the first located in what was then called the Third World, generated resistance among the more politically aware members of the population, especially the radicalized students of the Mexican capital. One must remember that the hopes raised by the Cuban Revolution, by the Vietnamese struggle for independence, and by the social and sexual liberation characteristic of the international youth movement of the 1960s had led many young people to dream of utopia as around the corner, or at most only a couple of revolutionary blocks away. While the cry of "no queremos olimpiadas, queremos revolución" (we don't want Olympics, we want revolution) was often chanted during the summer and fall of 1968 (Poniatowska 21), the Mexican student movement also illustrates how notions of revolution and utopia made politics possible, including politics proposing progressive changes that were not directly revolutionary. As Taibo notes:

> The student program was very brief, consisting famously of six points that resounded throughout the country . . . : freedom for political prisoners; repeal the law against "social dissipation," which was used to justify the jailing of political dissidents; dismissal of police leadership; apportionment of blame for repressive measures; compensation for the wounded and for the families of those killed; and abolition of the riot police. This set of demands had a second meaning . . . the call for democracy. The right of citizens to live in society was being won in the streets and imposed upon a repressive power structure. (48–49)

But, as we will see, this political, democratic, and reformist dimension of Mexico's 1968 is completely absent from Bolaño's novel.

Narrated as a visionary monologue told by Auxilio Lacouture, the self-designated Uruguayan mother of Mexican poetry, *Amulet* is presented as "a story of murder, detection and horror" (1).[11] She adds, "Told by me, it won't seem like that. Although, in fact, it's the story of a terrible crime" (1). However, in the Spanish original, instead of "murder, detection, and horror," Bolaño had written "una historia policiáca, un relato de serie negra y de terror" (*Amuleto* 11); a literal translation would have been "a detective story, a noir and horror fiction." Given the year the novel is set, one might assume that the crime that sets in motion the novel's detective story is the massacre at Tlatelolco. There, on October 2, 1968, between three hundred and four hundred demonstrators of all ages and from all classes were killed by the police and military acting under the orders of then-president Gustavo Díaz Ordaz.[12]

Of course, Tlatelolco is mentioned in the novel. In the monologue, the reference to the massacre is made by Auxilio while trapped in a public bathroom as the military occupy the leading Mexican university—UNAM—precisely in 1968: "Now the tears are running down my ravaged cheeks. I was at the university on the eighteenth of September when the army occupied the campus and went around arresting and killing indiscriminately. No not many people were killed at the university. That was in Tlatelolco. May that name live forever in our memory!" (22).[13] However, Tlatelolco is not the crime that concerns Bolaño.

The real crime is mentioned at the very end of the novel, when Auxilio has an allegorical vision that encapsulates Bolaño's view not only of the student movement of 1968 but of the radical Latin America of the 1960s: "Then I heard a murmur that rose through the cold air of evening in the valley toward the mountainsides and crags, and I was astonished. They were singing. The children, the young people, were singing and heading for the abyss" (182). Later, after describing the fall of the children into the chasm, the novel clarifies the passage's meaning: "And although the song that I heard was about war, about the heroic deeds of a whole generation of young Latin Americans led to sacrifice, I knew that above and beyond all, it was about courage and mirrors, desire and pleasure. And that song is our amulet" (184).

As in a good detective novel, Bolaño presents a corpse—in this case a generation worth of corpses—and a culprit, whose identity is a surprise. The criminal is not the Díaz Ordaz government, which actually ordered the killing of the students and other demonstrators, or the Southern

Cone dictators—Pinochet, Videla, and so on—who murdered tens of thousands. Instead, as the passage illustrates, the implicit villains of the allegory are the unnamed Pied Piper–like leaders that led the students into the abyss.[14]

In his reception speech for the 1999 Rómulo Gallegos Award granted to *The Savage Detectives*, Bolaño explains the allegory later found in *Amulet*. After providing a description of his own writing as an act of mourning, he is much more explicit regarding the criminals in his generation's detective saga:

> To a great extent everything that I have ever written is a love letter or a farewell letter to my own generation, those of us who were born in the 1950s and who at a certain moment chose . . . militancy, and we gave the little that we had—the great deal that we had, which was our youth—to a cause that we thought was the most generous cause in the world and in a certain way it was, but in reality it wasn't. . . . [W]e had corrupt leaders, cowardly leaders. . . . [W]e fought for parties that if they had won would have sent us straight to labor camps, we fought for and put all our generosity into an ideal that had been dead for more than fifty years, and some of us knew it, and how could we not when we'd read Trotsky or were Trotskyites, but we did it anyway because we were stupid and generous . . . and now those young people are gone. . . . All of Latin America is sown with the bones of these forgotten youths. ("Caracas Address" 35)

Despite Bolaño's disdain for the Pinochet regime, expressed in *Distant Star* and *By Night in Chile*, in his "Caracas Address" these unidentified leftist leaders are the real criminals in the whodunit of the Latin American 1960s and 1970s.

Bolaño's speech is to a great degree an expression of the disillusionment with the Left that characterized Western thought after the fall of the Soviet bloc. In fact, even long-standing leftist critics of real existing socialism had been quick to embrace the free market after 1989.[15] That said, there is much in Bolaño's address with which it is difficult to disagree. For instance, the revolutionary guerrilla tactics of the 1960s were often characterized by the irrational embrace of strategic violence as necessarily leading to popular revolutionary uprisings, as seen in Ernesto "Che" Guevara's *foco*. This unfounded belief in the possibility of willing revolt into being was, of course, based on the flawed argument that in Latin America the objective social conditions were so unjust and unequal that it took only a spark to start a revolution. These absurd tactics (mis)led many young Latin American radicals to their death. However, even if one were to identify isolated or even frequent instrumental uses of violence by leftist leaders and movements, one must remember that Guevara's ideas were actually based on his own experience as a revolutionary and as a guerrilla leader, as well as in his disillusionment with democratic processes as he saw the reformist president Jacobo Arbenz toppled from power in Guatemala and the improbable success of the Cuban Revolution.[16]

In *Amulet* and the "Caracas Address," Bolaño presents the Latin American youth of the 1960s and 1970s as passive followers of leaders who criminally misled them. In both texts, students lack agency and are depicted as being incapable of making up their own minds. In fact, their pusillanimity is such that, at least in the "Caracas Address," they are capable of following these unworthy leaders even though they know the ideas proposed have been disproven by history and are ethically wrong. These unnamed leftist leaders are thus presented as responsible for the murder—implicitly in *Amulet*, much more clearly in the "Caracas Address"—of Bolaño's generation.

Moreover, the novelist makes clear in his Rómulo Gallegos speech that, regardless of how tragic the defeat of the region's radical movements may have been, the consequences of their triumph would have been at least as disastrous. Again, one can point to the example of Cuba as giving credence to Bolaño's statements, even if he makes no reference to the island in his address. As we have seen, censorship and so-called reeducation camps for homosexuals and dissidents had become part of Cuba's political reality. Moreover, by 1998 the utopian hopes that had been placed in the island's revolution had long faded.

Bolaño presents labor camps, corruption, and abuse as necessary consequences of the success of all and any Latin American leftist movements.[17] However, as the example of the Mexican student movement indicates, he is presenting a gross simplification of the politics of the 1960s and 1970s. Continuing with Bolaño's metaphor in *Amulet*, one could argue that together with the violent and repressive notes that would reach their tragic crescendo in the Shining Path's bloodbath in Peru during the 1980s and early 1990s, the region's youth also sang a different melody that could have been orchestrated into something positive and new.

For instance, the Mexican students did not call for a Soviet Mexican republic, but for the democratization of the country. Mutatis mutandis, this was the case for many of the region's radical movements. Allende's attempt at reconciling revolutionary politics and democratic processes and values in Chile is a clear case in point. Thus, what was destroyed was not necessarily the creation of a Warsaw Pact in Latin America, which would perhaps have justified Bolaño's rueful allegory and his comments in the "Caracas Address." What died in the 1960s and 1970s was the potential construction of something different, as exemplified in the embrace of a potentially radical and egalitarian democracy by the students and their sympathizers in the Mexico of 1968.[18]

In what I believe constitutes the best interpretation of the political and ideological ground from which Bolaño developed his narrative, Jean Franco notes: "These novels [*The Savage Detectives* and *2666*], not to mention the brief novels that preceded them, represent a remarkable though possibly quixotic effort to redirect the whole literary enterprise and not only that, but do so in a moonscape of political and social disaster that encompasses post-coup Chile, the German retreat from Russia during the Second World War, Tlatelolco, Pinochet's Chile, the death cult in Ciudad Juárez and even the First Liberian War" ("Questions for Roberto Bolaño" 207). But these disasters are not presented in Bolaño's novels as discrete and unrelated events. Instead, the Nazi regime is presented as the origin for many of the later events mentioned by Franco.

This connection between Nazism and later injustices, in this case the Pinochet regime, is most explicitly made in *Distant Star*. Thus Bibiano, a character in the novel, notes that the last name of Carlos Wieder, the right-wing, mass-murdering air force captain and poet in *Distant Star*, "meant 'once more,' 'again,' 'a second time,' and in some contexts 'over and over'" (40). It is obviously not accidental that Bolaño gave this character a German last name. Earlier in the novel, when Wieder begins his aerial exploits—in addition to murder, he *skywrites* poetry—he flies a Messerschmitt over one of Pinochet's concentration camps, leading one of the inmates to cry: "The Second World War is returning to the Earth . . . it's the second returning, returning, returning" (26–27). Bolaño also presents Nazism as the ultimate origin of present horrors in many other works, including the femicides in Ciudad Juárez (renamed

Santa Teresa) in *2666* and, again, the Pinochet dictatorship in *By Night in Chile*.[19]

Federico Finchelstein argues the following about the role played by Nazism in our author's works: "As Bolaño understands it this history goes from Hitler to Pinochet and from the Spanish Civil War to extreme violence against women in Mexico and many other places. This idea of fascism as a foundational trauma for Latin American history is remarkably present in his work *Nazi Literature in the Americas* and eventually, and especially so, in *2666* where fascism is the source of all present violence and suffering" ("On Fascism, History, and Evil in Roberto Bolaño" 24). It may be worthwhile to compare Finchelstein's comments on Bolaño with one of Theodor Adorno's best-known dictums. For Adorno, Auschwitz undermines the possibility of poetry because it "represents the final stage of the dialectic of culture and barbarism" (34). In other words, the Holocaust is the end result that evidences the horror implicit in Western culture even at its most enlightened. But, as Finchelstein points out, for Bolaño, the Holocaust, more than being the culmination of history, is a traumatic event that is tragically and cyclically reenacted in Latin America and elsewhere.

As Franco notes in her "Questions for Roberto Bolaño," these returns of the Holocaust—Tlatelolco, Chile, Ciudad Juárez—are figuratively and literally the grounds on which Bolaño builds his narratives. One could see his literary obsession with Nazism as an accurate reflection of real-life social tendencies. Not only did the Chilean and the Argentine dictatorships tap fascist ideas and practices, but today we are experiencing the return of fascism throughout the Western world. However, the great Chilean writer does not attempt to historicize Nazism or fascism. Instead, these returns represent traumatic horrors that exemplify Rancière's "dramaturgy of infinite evil, justice, and reparation." One must, however, add the caveat that while the evil is always infinite, justice is rarely if ever achieved, and reparation is unthinkable.

Bolaño's dismissal of politics is allegorized in a strange episode in *Amulet* involving Arturo Belano, Ernesto San Epifanio, and the King of the Rent Boys.[20] Belano is the author's literary alter ego and, in what amounts to a flash-forward in Auxilio's narrative, has returned from Pinochet's Chile; San Epifanio is a gay poet; and the King is nothing but the glorified pimp of male prostitutes in the neighborhood of Guerrero. According to the novel, "The King had bought Ernesto's body, which meant . . . that he now belonged to that monarch body and soul . . . and if he did not accede to his new owner's demands, the judgment and the wrath of the King would fall upon him and his family" (83). Ernesto explains the reason for the King's hold on him: "He said there comes a time in the life of every gay man in Mexico when he goes and makes an irredeemably dumb-ass mistake, and then he said that he had no one to help him, and that if things went on the way they were going he'd end up a slave to the king of the King of the Rent Boys in Colonia Guerrero" (83).

The anachronistic language—with its references to kings and slaves—grants the episode the patina of parable or allegory, even if here it is presented as part of the plot. Moreover, it is a parable that deals with politics and the law. This is clearer in the Spanish original than in the English version. "Demands" is originally "requisitoria" (*Amuleto* 74), that is, "requisitory." This word, according to *Merriam-Webster*, is "a demand, usually in writing, made by a prosecutor that a sentence be passed against an accused party, and stating reasons for the demand." Even more relevant, "judgment" is actually "justicia" (*Amuleto* 74), that is, "justice," the only time in the novel when this word is used.

The absence of the word "justice" in *Amulet*, except in this passage, is surprising since the real-life Mexican students were looking for justice. As we have seen, among the demands of the students was the bringing to justice of the police and military responsible for violent acts against students and their sympathizers, and the granting of monetary compensation to the relatives of the victims. Moreover, after the massacre at Tlatelolco and other massacres and abuses on the part of the government, the search for justice for the students has been an ongoing cause of the Mexican Left. But all of these explicitly political concerns are of no interest to Bolaño.

Bolaño's stress on the fear of physical harm as constitutive of the authority of the King of the Rent Boys evokes philosophical discussions on sovereignty that go back to Hobbes, if not earlier. Jacques Derrida comments on and develops Hobbes's reflection on the role played by fear in the constitution of sovereignty:

> Fear always exceeds corporeal presence. . . . And if you take fear to the limit of the threat either exerted or felt, i.e. terror, then you have to conclude that terror is equally opposed to the state as a challenge as it is

exerted by the state as the essential manifestation of its sovereignty. . . . There is at bottom only fear, fear has no opposite. . . . The political subject is primarily subjected to fear. . . . And fear is primarily fear for the body, for the body proper, for one's own proper body. (71)

It is fear—the constitutive emotion of politics according to Hobbes and Derrida—of what the King of the Rent Boys could do to Ernesto and his family that constitutes the basis of his power. In the novel, the pimp is king and judge, an absolute sovereign. His decisions cannot be appealed because they are by definition just, simply because they originate from him. They are justice itself, as Bolaño notes. Justice, politics, and the law are presented as based on "fear for the body" and for the bodies of one's relatives.

However, despite the anachronistic language present in this passage, the actual politics of the 1970s still show up indirectly. Ernesto San Epifanio asks Belano for help because—like the real-life Bolaño—he had been imprisoned in Pinochet's Chile. As Ernesto says to Belano, "Whatever the King can do to me you've seen it multiplied a hundred times or a hundred thousand" (84). Ernesto assumes that Belano, having survived the violence of a worse authority, has no fear of the King of the Rent Boys. Ernesto believes that Belano is outside the economy of fear that girds the sovereignty of the King.

More importantly, the novel thus establishes a connection between the King of the Rent Boys and the Chilean dictator. The difference between them is presented as one of degree, not kind. The pimp and the general are both criminals and sovereigns. In fact, one can argue that they are sovereigns precisely because they are criminals. Of course, all should agree that Pinochet and the Argentine generals were morally nothing more than brutal gangsters, just like the King of the Rent Boys, even if they had greater means to exercise their wrath. However, one can argue that for Bolaño the King of the Rent Boys represents all sovereigns, even those elected democratically and committed to the most progressive ideas of the time. In what has been called his final interview Bolaño was asked what he would like to say to Salvador Allende. His answer: "Little or nothing. Those who have power—even for a short time—know nothing about literature; they are solely interested in power. I can be a clown to my readers, if I damn well please, but never to the powerful" (102).

Of course, anyone who has read *Distant Star* or *By Night in Chile* knows that for Bolaño there are differences between Allende and Pinochet. In other moments, he will express admiration for the socialist president. For instance, in an interview published posthumously in 2005, he presents a different portrayal of Allende:

> His figure, in what concerns me, has changed vastly over time. I remember September 11, 1973: in one moment, I'm waiting to receive weapons to go and fight and I hear Allende say . . . "Go forward knowing that, sooner rather than later, the great avenues will open again and free men will walk through them to construct a better society." In that moment, it seemed terrible to me, almost like a betrayal committed by Allende against those of us young people who were willing to fight for him. With time, that's one of the things that has ennobled Allende: saving us from death, accepting death for himself but saving us from it. I think that has made him huge in an immense way. ("Positions Are Positions" 77)

Allende, to his credit, did not lead the youth to the abyss. Instead, he was the one who jumped into it. In Bolaño's telling, it was not a political decision but an ethical one that determined Allende's greatness. However, when Bolaño considers Allende as a politician, he is, in principle, not that different from the King of the Rent Boys or Pinochet. The difference between them is quantitative, not qualitative. Politics is by definition the kingdom of crime.[21]

It is, therefore, not difficult to see Bolaño's work as a whole as implicitly rejecting the state—as represented by the King of the Rent Boys, Pinochet, and even Allende in his political role. Bolaño is part of an intellectual continuum that dismisses the state as a possible instrument for social and political change, a continuum that includes such otherwise heterogeneous bedfellows as libertarians, (some) neoliberals, anarchists, many postmodernists, and Michel Foucault.[22]

Rejecting politics together with espousing an ethical criticism of existing reality is what characterizes Bolaño's narrative: not only *Amulet*, but also *Distant Star, By Night in Chile*, even *2666*. In *By Night in Chile*, the troubled narrator, the literary critic Sebastián Urrutia Lacroix, makes a comment that, despite coming from a villainous character, expresses perfectly the view of real politics found in Bolaño's works:

"Sooner or later everyone would get their share of power again. The right, the centre, and the left, one big happy family. A couple of ethical problems, admittedly. But no aesthetic problems at all. Now we have a socialist president and life is exactly the same" (102). Despite the thousands dead, the tens of thousands tortured, the Pinochet dictatorship culminates in political collaboration. Trapped by his ethical rejection of politics, Bolaño is unable or perhaps unwilling to note the underlying economic reasons for this consensus. According to Andrés Solimano, writing in 2012:

> During the past twenty-five years, the strong policy consensus in Chile has been that economic growth is predicated on ensuring macroeconomic stability—low inflation, low fiscal deficits, and moderate current account deficits. The underlying view was that a sufficient condition for growth to proceed was to have a stable macroeconomics framework. . . . This principle was, of course, an underlying message of the Washington Consensus, a message that was highly influential in Chile. Although the Concertación governments adopted some variations of the orthodoxy of the Consensus, mainly in the 1990s (such as taxes on capital inflows, managed exchange rates, and gradual disinflation), the economic teams of the socialist presidents of the 2000s embraced that same orthodoxy when they assumed leadership positions in the democratic governments. (61)

The cultural consensus described by Urrutia is predicated on the acceptance of existing social and economic structures. This common belief in the impossibility of revolution or, for that matter, even reform, has led to the disappearance of any deep political differences among left, right, and center.

Bolaño's description of pre-Pinochet Chile also stresses a similar hypocritical continuity despite superficial political differences. Leftists, like Neruda, and rightists, like Urrutia and his mentor the older literary critic Farewell, are all presented as belonging to the same clique, getting together for evenings of food, literature, and debauchery. Urrutia continues his description of Chilean culture:

> Now we have a socialist president and life is exactly the same. The Communists (who go on as if the Berlin Wall hadn't come down), the

Christian Democrats, the Socialists, the right and the military. Or the other way round. I could just as well say it the other way round! The order of the factors doesn't alter the product! No problems! Just a little bout of fever! Just three acts of madness! Just an unusually prolonged psychotic episode! (*By Night in Chile* 102)

Before and after the Pinochet regime (and the Allende socialist experiment) the country's cultural elites constituted "one big happy family."

Be that as it may, one cannot deny the criticism of what one could call the Chilean cultural consensus present in *By Night in Chile*. This implicitly critical view of a contemporary and neoliberal Chile differentiates Bolaño from, for instance, the Vargas Llosa of *The Discreet Hero* who explicitly celebrates the analogous embrace of the free market in Peru.[23]

According to Chilean critic Raúl Rodríguez Freire, the political purpose of *Amulet* and, more generally, of all Bolaño's narrative is "to remember, as all people affected by that violence that Michel Foucault called racist have done or should do, that violence that in name of the one has attacked the other, its other" (37). For Rodríguez, Bolaño's novels serve as acts of remembrance of the Left's history:

In all his novels, Bolaño talks about memory, inheritance, and generations; and he does this in order not only to look back, but even more so in order to look forward. He does so in order to look at those who are not with us, whether these be dead youths, or those who are to come, to be born. And this is the same as . . . talking about justice. It is finally the same as talking not only about the struggles of memory, but, even more fundamentally, about the memory of the struggles; of these in their complexities and achievements, of which there were not few, and also in its mistakes, its betrayals. With responsibility. (43)

Bolaño's works provide a history, perhaps even a genealogy, of the Left in all its warts and glory; it is a history that, according to Rodríguez, is in danger of being forgotten during a moment of confusion and waning influence and expectations among those on the left.

According to the Chilean critic, Bolaño's work reminds us of a history of insurrection and repression and, therefore, provides a call for justice that can serve as a foundation stone for reconstituting a new and better Left. In fact, Rodríguez offers a brief list of the events in this history that Bolaño's work memorializes: "The massacre at Tlatelolco happened; the concentration camps happened; Roque Dalton was murdered by his comrades—like so many others—and the left forgets or does not remember" (41–42). However, Rodríguez's list is problematic.

Is this a list of sins of the Left? The reference to Roque Dalton's unjustifiable murder at the hands of nominal comrades seems to insinuate this. If that is the case, is he blaming the Mexican Left for Tlatelolco? As we have seen, Bolaño blamed the "leaders" of the Left for the death of its militants. Regardless, the Mexican Left did not forget this massacre. Is Rodríguez's mention of "concentration camps" a reference to Cuba's Unidades Militares de Producción (Military Units of Production), which were used to "reeducate" those the government considered malcontents?[24] If so, these undoubtedly merit total condemnation and remembrance so that they may never be repeated. However, outside Cuba, and in particular in the case of Chile and the other Southern Cone countries, there were other, arguably more deadly camps that, as with the massacre at Tlatelolco, were part of a brutal process of attempting to destroy the Latin American Left.

Furthermore, while Rodríguez sees the recollection of these disparate events as necessary to the historical reconstitution of the Left, in Bolaño's "Caracas Address," the reference to labor camps and to the leaders responsible for them and for the death of the region's "youth" helps justify the Chilean novelist's rejection of radical politics as "an ideal that had been dead for more than fifty years" (35).

Bolaño's writings present these events as removed from any social context or evolution. What Franco writes about *The Savage Detectives* applies to his work as a whole:

> Because grand narratives no longer sustain the carefully engineered plot, the fabula is sustained through chains of petits récits, records of casual encounters thanks to which information that may be trivial or, occasionally, momentous is passed on as anecdote, shouldering out. History with a capital H. As Johns, one of Norton's lovers in *2666*, states "no se trata de creer o no creer en las casualidades. El mundo entero es una casualidad" (*2666* 122–23). But history is not thereby eliminated; rather it is broken down into episodes and reminiscences. ("Questions for Roberto Bolaño" 211)

Bolaño's novels are paradigmatic examples of this postmodern rejections of grand narratives. Moreover, these episodes can be seen as recurrences of an incurable, insuperable trauma. The episodes and reminiscences harken back to foundational moments of social violence—such as the Holocaust—that in being reenacted destroy the optimistic progressive dreams of humankind. Bolaño's elision of the radical and democratic aspects of Mexico's insurgency of 1968 reflects this view of history as the eternal return of an intrinsic horror.

As we have seen, Auxilio describes *Amulet* as the "story of a terrible crime," but, even more than the betrayal of the Left by its leaders or the killing of students at the university and Tlatelolco, at their deepest level all of Bolaño's novels attest to another even more terrible crime: the violence implicit in all and any human society. What Rancière writes about novels and films after the "ethical turn" fully applies to Bolaño's oeuvre: "The aim . . . is no longer to preserve the promise of emancipation. On the contrary, it is to attest endlessly to the immemorial alienation that transforms every promise of emancipation into a lie, which can only be realised in the form of the infinite crime, art's answer to which is to put up a 'resistance' that is nothing but the endless work of mourning" ("Ethical Turn" 200).[25] One finds in the "Caracas Address" an explicit acknowledgment of this aim: Bolaño describes his novels as a "love letter or a farewell letter." Love and farewell are intrinsic to any act of mourning.

Despite their supreme artistic achievement, Bolaño's novels exemplify in their work of mourning one of the main characteristics of contemporary Western literature and art. They represent the most successful examples of a Latin American artistic response to the infinite crime that always turns emancipation into lies. In their Latin American estrangement of topics and moods characteristic of much contemporary literature resides, to a great degree, their worldwide success.

As Corral perceptively notes, "In Bolaño there is no clear evidence that he desires the collapse of the prevailing order, or that he believes there would be great changes if it were overthrown" (*Bolaño traducido* 253). His novels imply that we have always been living in a postcatastrophic moonscape. The "cut in time" of historical trauma, while best exemplified in his work by the Nazis and the Holocaust, is also associated with Aztec human sacrifices, the Crusades, the Spanish conquest, and the killing of youthful leftists during the 1960s and 1970s, for which his work mourns.[26] His novels are the perfect expression of our time when we believe that we are always living after the catastrophe but cannot imagine a way out. For Bolaño, another world is not possible.

### Carla Guelfenbein

In his introduction to an interview with novelist Carla Guelfenbein, Ezekiel Trautenberg notes, "In her novels, Guelfenbein explores topics such as exile, memory, and personal and collective trauma; often referring aspects of her own life history" (131). However, "exile, memory, and personal and collective trauma" can also describe aspects of the lives of all those who experienced and escaped from the brutal Southern Cone dictatorships of the 1970s. These terms can also characterize the literature that attempts to deal with that "personal and collective trauma," such as the novels of Roberto Bolaño. Moreover, as Ángel Rama had already noted in 1981, "If we consider the deep roots of contemporary mass migrations, together with the modern realities of exile, we can see how the rigid boundaries between exile and migration disappear" ("Literature and Exile" 11). If the case of the Cuban diaspora, especially during the 1960s and 1970s, can be seen as in some ways parallel to those of the later Chilean, Argentinean, and Uruguayan exiles, the Central American migration to the United States during the 1980s and 1990s also showed how "the exile is . . . one who voluntarily abandons his land to avoid persecution, prison or death, or, more frequently, in order to continue his work in a country that provides more appropriate conditions. . . . Although among exiles, members of the intellectual sector . . . are more notorious, laborers, white collar workers, students, and even businessmen are much more numerous" (11). Today, as neoliberal democracy has, at least in appearance, made military dictatorship unfeasible in Latin America, exile is now primarily the result of economic and even security reasons, as widespread drug- and gang-related crime has become as prevalent as dictatorial repression once was.[27] Thus "exile, memory, and personal and collective trauma" are now thematically part and parcel of the literature produced by a Latin American diaspora that includes not only authors of Southern Cone or Cuban provenance, but also exiles, emigrants and their descendants from every single country in the region.

Like Bolaño, Guelfenbein left Chile when she was young, but in her case exile was in response to the repression of the Pinochet regime. Her father, an architect, had helped design low-income housing during the Allende government; her mother, a philosophy professor and socialist militant, was "disappeared"—kidnapped and tortured in the Tres Alamos detention center—for three weeks, immediately after having been diagnosed with cancer. The family escaped to London in 1977.[28] Guelfenbein's life was, therefore, that of the political rather than the economic exile. Despite its obvious hardships, she was able to thrive and take advantage of the educational—and other—opportunities available in her new home in England. Her international upbringing is clearly reflected in her novels, which, though primarily set in Chile, are characterized by cosmopolitan wanderings and multinational identities.[29] While the author of *Distant Star* also peoples his novels with wanderers, they, like the author himself, are often marginal intellectuals, regardless of their actual abilities, rather than the often-affluent, always worldly, intelligentsia of Guelfenbein's works.[30] Though one can always find exceptions in their works, both authors here reflect their own personal situations as migrants.

Not surprisingly, Guelfenbein's route to literary stardom was very different from Bolaño's. Instead of the voyage, unequalled in the annals of Latin American literary history, through marginal, even working-class, bohemia that was Bolaño's Mexican Infrarealist and early Spanish literary career, Guelfenbein's route to literary stardom follows a pattern that, despite certain idiosyncrasy, is clearly attuned to the neoliberal reorganization of cultural production in Chile and elsewhere. After her return to her native country, Guelfenbein, who had studied biology at the University of Essex and design at Saint Martin's School of Arts, worked first in advertising and then as the art and fashion director of Chile's *Elle* magazine. Before becoming a novelist and even afterward, she worked and published in the privileged creative venues of our contemporary world: advertising, a transnational magazine, the main Spanish-language book publisher (her novels are, from the beginning, published by Alfaguara). While she would only publish her first novel—*El revés de mi alma* (The other side of my soul)—in 2002, she rapidly became a best-selling author in Chile. Her pan-Hispanic consecration came in 2015 when her novel *In the Distance with You* won the Alfaguara Award.

All of her literature, including *In the Distance with You*, uses the formulas of the romance genre. Thus, if Bolaño created a literature that was ruthlessly indifferent to literary fashions—even if he still participated in the cultural Weltanschauung of our time—Guelfenbein's novels use the traits and tics of one of the least respected commercial genres. The question that divides critics is whether she continues or subverts the romance genre. But one can see her appropriation, if not necessarily subversion, of this best-selling genre as a response to the neoliberal demand that literature participate in book and culture markets.

That said, the palette of topics and emotions Guelfenbein explores is clearly set within the parameters of the romance novel, even if the characters and historical setting of her novels are obviously unusual for the genre. Despite her novels' awards and sales success, their loose use of romance tropes and plots has led many readers to question the value of her narrative.[31]

During an interview given as part of the publicity tour for her novel *Nadar desnudas* (To swim naked) (2013), Guelfenbein stated: "Allende did not want to put make-up on Chile. He wanted to change it from the roots up and eliminate its deep social differences" ("La dictadura chilena"). While the Chilean novelist does not use the word *revolution*, her description of Allende's goals illustrate the maximalist definition of the term as "bringing about a wholly new social order" (Williams, *Keywords* 273). From the perspective of "the ethical turn," Allende's government was, despite its noble goals, destined for failure and a violent conclusion, like all attempts at radical social change. Guelfenbein, in contrast, presents sympathetically the socialist government's goal of creating an equal and just society.

In the interview, in addition to acknowledging the positive utopian dimension of Allende's government and the Pinochet regime's role in closing this historical possibility, she stresses the brutality of the military dictatorship: "It was a dream that went to shit, that was taken apart very violently, with many dead, disappeared, tortured, and exiled. We intellectuals and artists have to always return to that historical movement so as not to view the possibility of it ever being repeated" ("La dictadura chilena"). Despite her sympathetic acknowledgment of Allende's true ambitions, she signals that the main concern of her writing is to remind readers of the violence of the Pinochet regime and thus forestall the return of similar brutality. What is important to her is denouncing the dictatorship's violence rather than examining Allende's frustrated attempt at revolution within democracy and evaluating what perhaps remains relevant. It is, after all, described as a dream rather than as a frustrated possibility. In *Nadar desnudas*, as well as in her other novels, Guelfenbein is ultimately more concerned with the effects of political and social violence on individual psyches than with the actual political and historical backgrounds of said violence.

Although *La mujer de mi vida* (2005) and *In the Distance with You* (2015) make reference to the brutality of the Pinochet dictatorship, only *Nadar desnudas* is (partially) set during the Allende presidency. The novel thus represents Guelfenbein's fullest engagement with the historical events that so deeply marked her own life. Equally important, it also attempts to connect the Chilean coup of 11 September 1973, an event that could seem ancient history set in a remote country, with one of the most dramatic events of the twenty-first century, the attack on the Twin Towers on 11 September 2001.[32]

In the interview with Trautenberg, Guelfenbein speaks of the relationship between narrative and history:

> Literature is made up of small histories. The other [option] is writing History, with a capital H.[33] When one wants to write history one writes about the great social movements, about the lives of those characters who are in the forefront of history, regarding whom their intimacy is unimportant, what matters are the broad strokes with which history moves. But literature has the possibility of choosing its movements, its characters, to enter the inside these characters. This is what defines literature. . . . And the intersection between small history and History with a capital H has always interested me. (134)

As we saw in the discussion of *The Real Life of Alejandro Mayta*, in Spanish, as in other Romance languages, the word *historia* means both history and story. Thus one could also read the quotation above as dealing precisely with the distinction between *historia* as story, that is as fiction, and as history, defined as a record of actual events of social significance. In other words, Guelfenbein is here stressing that what happens to her characters—their love affairs, joys, disappointments, psychological disjunctions, and so on—takes place within larger national and international contexts that give meaning to these personal and interpersonal experiences.

This definition of her narrative as based on "the intersection between small history and History with a capital H" almost seems to be referring to Jean Franco's analysis of Bolaño's novels quoted above. For Franco, Bolaño's writing ultimately dissolved history (with or without a capital H) into "information," into ultimately meaningless facts. On the other hand, Guelfenbein claims that her writing firmly sets individual stories within historical and social patterns and developments, in other words, within "History with a capital H."

Guelfenbein thus presents her writing in terms reminiscent of Vargas Llosa's early novels, which so brilliantly depicted the manner in which his characters' lives were imbricated with Peru's social reality. However, in *Nadar desnudas*, as well as in Guelfenbein's other novels, the stress is placed on individual stories, on psychology and interpersonal relations, even if "History with a capital H" helps determine the parameters within which these develop. "History with a capital H" is, however, never fully explored.

The title of the novel, *Nadar desnudas* (To swim naked), refers to a passage in the novel in which two young women break into the Stade Francais, Santiago de Chile's posh private sports club, and decide to have a swim in its pool. The nocturnal swim, described in lush prose that highlights the activity's potential sensuality, establishes the relationship between Sophie, the artistically oriented eighteen-year-old daughter of Diego, one of Salvador Allende's closest advisors, and Morgana, the twenty-two-year-old daughter of diplomats representing Francisco Franco's Spanish dictatorship. When Morgana becomes Diego's lover, the girls grow apart, perhaps because of Sophie's inchoate desire for Morgana, as well as the former's oedipal inability to tolerate her father having a long-term relationship with her friend. Later, unable to cope emotionally with Morgana's pregnancy, Sophie leaves for Paris, where she had grown up and where her mother still lived.

The background to this affair is the Allende regime and the resistance leveled against it. The novel thus presents the growing violence and activity of the anti-Allende forces—including the "marcha de las cacerolas vacías" (march of the empty pots) of 1 December 1971, the failed coup attempt of June 1973, and the military coup itself on 11 September 1973. In fact, Morgana gives birth to Antonia, her daughter with Diego, on September 13. Before attempting to escape from Chile, Morgana hands Antonia to her mother and diplomat father.

Subsequently, she and Diego are shot by the military before they are able to leave Chile.

The second part of the novel is framed by 11 September 2001. Because of the trauma caused by her relationship with Morgana and by Morgana and Diego's tragic end, Sophie, now an established artist in Paris, has led a life of emotional and physical isolation. Spurred by the destruction of the Twin Towers and the loss of life she witnesses on television, she contacts and meets her half-sister Antonia, who, unlike Sophie, is happily married with two children and lives in the Spanish resort island of Lanzarote. However, the politically conservative Spanish grandparents who raised Antonia had, from their perspective, sanitized the past by telling her that her parents had died in a car accident in Spain. In fact, Antonia did not know her father had advised Allende or even that she was born in Chile. Despite the awkwardness of Sophie's attempt at reaching out to Antonia, which almost flounders when Sophie decides to return to Paris, the novel ends on an optimistic note: Sophie, disregarding her flight's last boarding call, stays behind talking with her half-sister.

The longest reference to Allende is also the one that best presents the novel's positive portrayal of his socialist government. It is found toward the beginning of the novel:

> When Allende was elected president, Diego wrote him a letter expressing his ideas. Those days he lived between Madrid and Paris. He had met him years earlier, when Diego was still a young pup, and whenever they ran into each other, they expressed respect for each other's ideas. Diego had been close to Dubček during the Prague Spring, supporting his attempt at creating "socialism with a human face." He had also been present during the Soviet Invasion and had seen the tanks aiming their guns at unarmed students. Allende showed interest in Diego's critical positions, in his studies in political science at the Sorbonne, in his experience and enthusiasm, as well as in the fact that he combined these with good doses of skepticism. "Come," Allende answered him by mail. (37–38).

If, for Bolaño, the Latin American Left, including Allende's administration, one assumes, had been tainted by the original sin of Stalinism—"we fought for parties that if they had won would have sent us straight to labor camps"—Guelfenbein's Allende is at the antipodes. Instead of a repetition of the Russian Revolution (1917) or even the Cuban Revolution (1959), Allende's Chile is presented as aligned with the Czech revolution of 1968 that attempted to create "socialism with a human face."

Bolaño implicitly links Mexico's radical prodemocracy movement of 1968 with what could be called a Stalinist manipulation of the region's young and candid activists—as exemplified in *Amulet*'s image of them being led, as if by the Pied Piper, into the abyss. Guelfenbein, on the other hand, sees the Chilean road to socialism as an attempt to reconcile equality and liberty (and, of course, fraternity) that includes but is not limited to the Prague Spring. While this is a noble genealogy, it is also one of political failure.

The first public tensions between the four core Boom writers and the Cuban Revolution originated precisely in 1968 over the Soviet invasion of what was then Czechoslovakia—even if, unlike the later Padilla affair, the conflict did not lead to a parting of ways between the writers and the Cuban government. In August 1968, Vargas Llosa, always the most outspoken of the group, did not hesitate to publish "Socialism and the Tanks," an article castigating Fidel Castro's support for the Russian intervention.

In reality, Castro's support signaled the Cuban government's full alignment with the Soviet bloc and its abandonment of the political independence that it had exhibited until then.[34] But for Vargas Llosa, it additionally represented the rejection of the island's "Third-Worldist" anti-imperialist stance and its promise of a different kind of socialism: responsive to local reality and characterized by individual freedom. "Socialism and the Tanks," especially its conclusion, presents the seed of the future Nobel Prize winner's political disillusionment that would flower during the Padilla affair in 1971:

> It is distressing to see Fidel reacting in the same conditioned and reflex way as the mediocre leaders of the Latin American Communist parties who rushed to justify the Soviet intervention. Doesn't the Cuban supreme commander understand that if he allows the USSR the right to decide the type of socialism suitable for other countries and to import its choice by force, then what has happened in Prague could happen tomorrow in Havana?

To many sincere friends of the Cuban revolution, the words of Fidel have seemed to us as incomprehensible and as unjust as the noise of the tanks entering Prague. (82)

The notion of "Cuban exceptionalism" that had, for many, justified the passionate support granted to the revolution was put seriously in question by the government's approval of the Soviet invasion of Czechoslovakia and the destruction of the Prague Spring. In fact, earlier in the article Vargas Llosa claimed, "The violation of the sovereignty of the Czech people by the USSR has been less bloody but no less immoral than that committed against the people of Santo Domingo" (79). By comparing US support for the toppling of Juan Bosch's progressive government in the Dominican Republic with Soviet military action against Dubček, Vargas Llosa equates Soviet and US American "imperialism." For Vargas Llosa, the Cuban government was betraying its Martí-an—that is, anti-imperialist—reason for being.

But Vargas Llosa was not the lone Boom writer impacted by the Prague Spring and its destruction. His fellow literary musketeers—Carlos Fuentes, Gabriel García Márquez, and Julio Cortázar—had all gotten on a train to Prague on 8 December 1968 with the purpose, in Fuentes's words, "to support our friend Milan Kundera and the impossible battle for the Prague Spring" (*This I Believe* 259). In 2005, Fuentes, with a rosy historical view based on the diminution of his political expectations, wrote: "In Czechoslovakia, the Prague Spring won the battle, even beyond its own original desires, when the Soviet empire fell, and when Václav Havel, one of the leaders of the dissidence in '68, won the Presidency" ("68: modelo para armar"). Fuentes is, of course, writing as if neoliberal democracy and "socialism with a human face" had ultimately been shown to be identical.[35]

Perhaps surprisingly, given his later closeness to Fidel Castro, García Márquez was also shocked by the suppression of the Prague Spring. According to his biographer Gerald Martin: "Czechoslovakia was a far more serious matter for García Márquez than the events in Paris because it seemed to demonstrate that Soviet communism was incapable of evolution" (*Gabriel García Márquez* 337). During those days he wrote to his close friend Plinio Apuleyo Mendoza, the future coauthor of the neoliberal screed *Guide to the Perfect Latin American Idiot* (1996): "My world collapsed but now I think maybe it's better like this: to demonstrate, without nuances, that we stand between two imperialisms, equally cruel and voracious, is in a certain sense a liberation for one's conscience" (qtd. in Martin, *Gabriel García Márquez* 338). Perhaps reflecting their growing friendship, García Márquez is here agreeing with Vargas Llosa's belief (at the time) of the equivalence between US and Soviet imperialism.

The case of the third visitor to Prague, Cortázar, is more ambiguous. While he too was disappointed by Soviet invasion, he would progressively become an ever more dedicated activist for all revolutionary causes. Even though in a notorious interview with Rita Guibert of *Life*, he stressed that "every imperialist system was hateful to me" ("Julio Cortázar" 287), he was much more concerned with US imperialism than with Soviet intervention in Europe or elsewhere.[36] Cortázar notes: "Here in Paris I have had plenty of opportunity to see with what energy illusions about North American 'civilization' are being introduced; this has happened in Moscow also, and, too much perhaps, in Czechoslovakia" (287). For the Argentine novelist, US imperialism was particularly heinous: "When you ask me point blank what difference I see between the Soviet intervention in Czechoslovakia and that of the United States in the Dominican Republic and Vietnam, I reply by asking whether any of *Life*'s reporters had seen children burned with napalm in the streets of Prague" (287). While Cortázar saw the Soviet invasion as imperialist, he believed that the Soviet Union was a more benign imperial master than the United States. Be that as it may, the disappointment caused by the squelching of the Prague Spring did not stop García Márquez or Cortázar from continuing their vocal support of the Cuban government.

Conventional views, obviously on the right but also on the left, saw Allende's Chile as a follow-up to Castro's Cuba, and as the second red domino falling in the Americas.[37] Guelfenbein, in contrast, traces a different ideological and intellectual lineage, one directly opposed to that of the Soviet Union. Instead, she follows a leftism characterized by the embrace of human freedoms. While it would seem unlikely that in real life a Czech politician would have had a Chilean adviser, in *Nadar desnudas* the fact that Diego "had been close to Dubček" is precisely why Allende seeks his counsel. Rather than being a dogmatist, Allende is implicitly presented as sharing Diego's critical and skeptical positions. If not, why would he have asked him to be his advisor? The analogy is clear: both Allende and Dubček strove to create a "socialism with a human face" and both were defeated by what García Márquez called "two imperialisms, equally cruel and voracious." I am tempted to find in Guelfenbein's linking of Allende's Chile with the Prague Spring an indirect connection with other movements of 1968, particularly those in France and Mexico, that attempted to marry freedom and socialism.

However, the novel also represents a hard, intransigent Chilean Left, ironically composed of university students. When Morgana, Diego, and Sophie are escaping from the "marcha de las cacerolas," the right-wing demonstration led by women, they hear students aggressively chanting "las momias al colchón, los momios al paredón" (right-wing women to bed, right-wing men to the firing squad, 74). As a way of marking the protagonists' distance from this violent and sexist view of socialist politics, the three protagonists are shocked by the chant and run away from the counterdemonstrators.

Guelfenbein's view of Allende has a basis in historical fact. As Joan Garcés notes, "The government of the Unidad Popular between 1970 and 1973 was one of the most developed instances of economic and social democracy till then practiced within a pluralist and representative political system, of a socialist orientation" (9). Peter Winn adds, "Equally revolutionary was the increase in popular power that characterized Allende's Chile. Workers and peasants administered their work places, dwellers led their shantytowns, indigenous people challenged decades of discrimination and oppression" (19). Moreover, this popular empowerment did not mean a lack of concern with economic equality. As Winn again notes, "By 1972, Chile had become one of the most egalitarian societies in Latin America" (18).

However, and perhaps contradicting Guelfenbein's attempt to separate Allende from Soviet-style communism, Castro, by then the main Latin American representative of this socialist brand, was a friend of the Chilean socialist and visited the country in 1971. According to Winn, Castro "delighted in his role as the senior revolutionary in the region, expressing freely his analyses and advice" (133). As Bolaño has the right-wing priest Urrutia declare in *By Night in Chile*, in 1971 "Fidel Castro came on a visit and many people thought he would stay and live in Chile forever" (81). Winn adds, "Castro's presence pleased the left, but it was a two-sided sword. While it could be used to galvanize the left in support of Allende's Chilean revolution, it also could serve to mobilize its opponents" (133). And it did.

Regardless of the actual effects of Castro's visit on Chilean politics, the relationship between Allende and Castro was characterized, as Garcés notes, by "respect and friendship," despite their "differentiated tactical structures" (172). However, there were significant political and institutional divergences between the socialist governments: "The Cuban and Chilean revolutionary processes were opposed regarding the question of the armed apparatus of the State. The basis of this discrepancy was the interrelationship among the popular movements in their revolutionary phase, the professional armed forces, and the counterrevolution" (Garcés 172). In addition to Allende's principled embrace of his country's democratic institutions and processes, the main difference between Castro's Cuba and socialist Chile resided in the relationship between the armed forces and the revolutionary processes in each country. In Cuba, Batista's armed forces had been destroyed and then substituted by a new army fully subordinated to the revolutionary government, but in Chile, the professional armed forces, while nominally subordinated to the president as head of state, did not suffer any structural transformation after Allende's inauguration. Castro's concerns about Chilean "fascism" (Garcés 172) would become reality on 11 September 1973 when Pinochet, who had ironically been among those who had met the Cuban leader during his visit, deposed Allende.

While Guelfenbein is correct in stressing the uniqueness of the Chilean socialist experiment—it was, after all, the one historical example of an elected leader committed to a thoroughgoing socialist revolutionary transformation of society—Allende himself seems to have seen his government as participating in a radical continuum that included the Cuban Revolution. This does not, however, mean that the Chilean socialist experiment, had it managed to continue, was bound to share in the intellectual closing that unfortunately characterized Cuba.

As we saw earlier, *Nadar desnudas* presents several important moments in the breakdown of the social fabric of Chile caused and promoted primarily by the Right. Perhaps the most relevant one is the notorious "marcha de las cacerolas vacías" (march of the empty pots) in 1971. According to Garcés, the march was organized by "the semi-clandestine organization 'Poder Femenino' [Feminine Power]. . . . Thousands of women from residential neighborhoods went into the streets with empty pots on which they banged as they marched. . . . The opposition political parties, including both the Christian Democracy and the Partido Nacional, refused to take responsibility for a demonstration they knew had as its goal to create widespread disorder in the streets of Santiago" (64). Winn adds that the demonstration was "protected by the neofascist paramilitary group Patria y Libertad [Country and Freedom]" (135), while Garcés describes Poder Femenino as "an organization financed and manipulated by the intelligence services of the United States" (164n9).[38] As Winn notes, the marcha de las cacerolas signaled that "the period of easy revolutionary advance had ended and the battle for Chile had begun" (132). The disruptive tactics first essayed in the marcha de las cacerolas have become part of the repertoire of political demonstrations across the political spectrum.[39]

Guelfenbein describes the march in great detail, presenting the women demonstrators as violent and irrational. Morgana and Diego "run into a march of screaming women." "Morgana notices a halo of ferocity on their faces. Their eyes are bloodshot, they open their mouths and scream, and their tense throats vibrate as they state their slogans. They carry pots, pans, rolling pins hang from ropes tied around their necks. They wear pots, baskets and net bags, as helmets. Their chants, progressively harsher and more strident, surround them. 'There is no meat, asshole; no milk, asshole; what the fuck's happening, asshole'" (71). The novel never describes the actual political connections underlying the march—that is, there is no mention of the neofascist Patria y Libertad or even of Poder Femenino. This passage does, however, depict the march as a group descent into barbarism. Faces have become expressions of violence—bloodshot eyes and screaming mouths. Dress—and one must remember that these are upper-class women for whom fashion and elegance are traditionally of great importance—has become a parody of military uniform and tribal garb. Even language has diminished into screams, slogans, and profanity. Given the potential for violence they see in the demonstrators, Morgana, Sophie, and Diego hurriedly escape the demonstration.

Guelfenbein, however, also presents what paradoxically could be called the utopian dimension of the right-wing protests: "A troop of older women sing the national anthem as they laboriously make their way. If one had not heard their violent screams, one would think that their souls were charged with the desire for kindness and beatitude"

(72). In fact, one could argue that it is precisely because of their screams and their hatred for Allende and for his supporters that they are able to feel beatitude. Theirs is a utopia based on hatred and exclusion; or, perhaps, better put, it is a utopia for them and a dystopia for their class and political enemies.

This passage parallels one found in *The Real Life of Alejandro Mayta*. Although Vargas Llosa's novel can be read as much as a parody as a description of a guerrilla fighter's personal and political life, the passage in question also presents the utopian core that underlies Mayta's actions: "Lulled by the happiness of the adolescents"—the students of the Colegio San José who joined Mayta and Vallejos in their attempt to start a revolution—"he let his imagination run wild" (242). Mayta goes on to imagine what the new socialist Peru he is struggling to create would be like: "Every day the chasms that separated the proletariat from the bourgeoisie, the whites from the Indians, blacks and Asiatics, the coastal people from the mountain and jungle people, the Spanish speakers from the Quechua speakers would be bridged just a bit more" (243). And: "Social, moral, and sexual prejudices would give way little by little and it wouldn't matter to anyone, in the crucible of work and faith that he would be living with Anatolio" (243–44). As we saw in an earlier chapter, we are here dealing with, as Žižek writes, "Revolution . . . not experienced as a present hardship . . . but as the present hardship over which this future happiness and freedom already cast their shadow" (247). Of course, in the case of *The Real Life of Alejandro Mayta* this short circuit between reality and utopia is ultimately undermined by the fact that the revolutionaries consist of a small group of teenagers, two unenthusiastic peasants, an out-of-shape man with altitude sickness (Mayta), and only one individual who knows how to fight and lead (Vallejos). Moreover, the reader is by this moment in the novel aware that the well-meaning actions of Mayta will lead to unforeseen apocalyptic consequences years later.

But what calls my attention is the nature of the utopia. If for Mayta it is based not only on economic equality but also on the inclusion of all Peruvians by eliminating all types of discrimination and, as a consequence, constructing a true community, for the Chilean demonstrators it is based on eliminating difference, maintaining inequality, and rejecting Allende and his sympathizers. However, given the generic requirements of the romance novel, Guelfenbein does not explore these topics, despite the fact that Morgana sees "one of the Chilean friends of her mother" among the right-wing women (73).

As mentioned above, the novel's two sections are framed by 9/11/1973 and 9/11/2001. Despite their obvious differences, both events could be seen as connected. After all, the first inaugurated our neoliberal world by means of a brutal military coup sponsored by the United States, while the second was a massive and deadly terrorist attack against the World Trade Center, a symbol for our economic system. However, rather than signaling a weakening of neoliberalism, the attack on the World Trade Center has led to a renewed imbrication of the military and the state with corporations in the United States, to the destabilization of the Near East, to the concomitant increase in migration and Islamophobia, and, ultimately, to the rise in the West of neofascist movements and leaders.

However, the novel finds in these two events a different connection. Thus, in the first part of the novel, Sophie answers Morgana's questions about what, if anything, Diego feared by stating: "of disappearing. . . . Of not leaving tracks, that all forget him, that someday the extraterrestrials will come for him" (35). Of course, it would be the Chilean military and their secret police, not ET, that would come for Diego and Morgana. Later in the novel, a day after the massive terrorist attack on the Twin Towers, Sophie, now a world-famous artist, has a conversation with her assistant Gerard: "They say there are hundreds of disappeared. The word *disappeared* burrowed into her, leaving behind a trail of emotions that twists her face into a grimace" (198). In Sophie's mind and in the structure and plot of the novel as a whole, both 9/11s are identified with the idea of disappearance—that is, of individuals whose death is ultimately unaccounted and therefore impossible to grieve.

In fact, Sophie had managed to weave a new life for herself by forgetting Chile and her friendship with Morgana and even her relationship with her father. The events of 9/11 and in particular the "disappearances" caused by this catastrophic act of terrorism force Sophie to remember her father and her best friend, in other words, to "reappear" them: "They again: Diego and Morgana's greatest fear was to disappear. A fear neither could ever explain. Its intensity could be seen in each one of their gestures and their acts. It was fear that joined them and which gave urgency to their lives. In their desire to live fully they seemed not

to care that they infected every instance with the possibility of its ending" (201). The 9/11/2001 attack helped Diego and Morgana return to
Sophie's mind and emotions.

In seeing a connection between the disappeared of 9/11/1973 and
9/11/2001, Guelfenbein was probably influenced by Chilean American
writer Ariel Dorfman. The coauthor of *How to Read Donald Duck* has
stressed in numerous essays this resemblance between the Chilean coup
and the attack on the Twin Towers. In an essay anthologized in a collection significantly titled *Chile: The Other September 11* (for chronological
reasons *United States: The Other September 11* would have been more
accurate) Dorfman writes about the two tragic events:

> I recognise . . . something deeper, a parallel suffering, a similar pain,
> a commensurate disorientation, echoing what we lived through in
> Chile as of that September 11. It's most extraordinary incarnation—I
> still cannot believe what I am witnessing—is that on the screen I see
> hundreds of relatives wandering the streets of New York, clutching
> the photos of their sons, fathers, wives, lovers, daughters, begging
> for information, asking if they are alive or dead. The whole United
> States has been forced to look into the abyss of what it means to be
> *desaparecido*, with no certainty or funeral possible for those beloved
> men and women who are missing. ("The Last September 11" 2).

For Dorfman, the horror of this second September 11, in addition
to being "the explosive conclusion" to "the United States' famous exceptionalism," also opens the possibility "for Americans to overcome
their trauma and . . . to admit that their suffering is neither unique nor
exclusive, that they are connected, as long as they are willing to look at
themselves in the vast mirror of our common humanity, with so many
other human beings who . . . have suffered similar situations of unan-
ticipated and often protracted injury and fury" (3–4). In other words,
the terrorist attacks should have led the United States to realize that it
was not isolated from the experiences and suffering of the rest of the
world and, therefore, to embrace policies and actions that would help
humanity as a whole, not only limited national and, in truth, class and
group interests.[40]

Both Dorfman's and Guelfenbein's association of 9/11/1973 with
9/11/2001 falters when considering the underlying reasons for the *dis-*

*appeared* associated with each date and the event it represents. Unlike New York's *disappeared*, who were victims of a terrorist attack that, at least from their perspective, was not only unexpected and unforeseeable but also unrelated to their own actions, the Chilean *disappeared* are the victims of state repression and disappeared precisely as the result of their real or, in many cases, purported political activity.[41] While in the case of New York's 9/11, the terrorist act is an intentionally macabre and horrifying public spectacle, in the case of Chile, the state's desire to hide its responsibility for the fate of those it kills underlies this macabre innovation in repression. Moreover, in the case of the brutality of 9/11/1973, and in its representation in *Nadar desnudas*, the violence of the coup is far from unexpected. The novel presents the "prehistory" to Pinochet's coup, and its description of the march of the pots evidences the passion of the opposition to Allende. In addition to the march of the pots, the novel mentions the "failed" coup of 29 June 1973, which included among its victims Argentine journalist Leonardo Henrichsen.[42] Furthermore, the novel details how Diego, who is close to the president of the Republic, is followed by what can only be military or secret police. In fact, the level of intimidation and fear is such that when Diego decides to face the agents in a car tailing him, Sophie screams at him "'You cannot do that daddy!' . . . It was the first time Morgana had heard her call him that. 'They are going to kill you'" (51). The reader is thus not surprised when Diego is actually beaten in the novel or, for that matter, when the coup actually succeeds.[43] From the plot of the novel, Diego and Morgana should have feared the military rather than extraterrestrials for their possible disappearance.[44]

However, despite the stress in *Nadar desnudas* on the continuity between precoup right-wing military and police actions and the repression of the Pinochet regime, the novel does not help us understand the reasons behind the coup. While the reader is probably aware that the economic interests of many in the Chilean upper classes are threatened by the measures proposed and executed by Allende's government, the concrete policies of the Socialist administration are never mentioned, nor the manner in which these policies would affect these upper classes. In fact, Diego's actual work for Allende remains unspecified.

In the novel, as Sophie fills in Antonia about her parents' past, she thinks to herself:

She wanted to tell her that her grandparents committed an injustice, that Diego was noble and upright, a man who wanted to change the world. However, she would also have to tell her that if he had lived, he would have renounced his ideals—as did so many of his generation; and, perhaps would have also abandoned her [Antonia] and her mother. She would have to tell her that each of these betrayals would have left its mark: a more clearly marked rictus, the wrinkles on his brow deeper, a more severe grin, and in his eyes, instead of their golden shine, one would find cynicism, disappointment, or complacency. (240–41)

There is an element of historical truth in Guelfenbein's imagining of what Diego's life could have been. After all, the converts from the Left to neoliberalism were legion during the 1980s and 1990s. However, for many converts—Vargas Llosa can serve as an example—underlying their turn toward neoliberalism was not only disillusionment with real existing socialism, or even the fall of the Soviet bloc, but also the belief that the free market actually was the most just and efficient way of organizing society.

As we have seen, Guelfenbein expressed a negative view of the neoliberal world created by the Chilean military regime. In fact, Sophie's description of the negative effects of this change on Diego, perhaps reflects Guelfenbein's estimation of our current world. However, Sophie ultimately presents Diego's imaginary evolution as necessarily leading to the abandonment of his nondogmatic and humane version of socialism. Neoliberalism may be deplorable, but it is the only option. However, it is Sophie, presented as a damaged character toward the end of novel, rather than the narrator or any other "authorial" voice, that presents this version of the inevitability of neoliberalism. The question then remains: Given that we live in a neoliberal world, what is to be done?

The novel's conclusion leaves little doubt that the only solution Guelfenbein can imagine is ultimately individual, rooted in the realms of the personal and emotional. As mentioned above, *Nadar desnudas* ends with Sophie disregarding her flight's last boarding call:

Suddenly she feels incapable of getting up, picking up her bag and walking toward her boarding gate. And it is not until she hears her name called on the loudspeakers that she realizes that she does not want to leave Antonia. It is a realization that surprises her but, at the

same time, produces a feeling of infinite tranquility. . . . She looks
at Antonia: her missing half. What unites them in a manner that
transcends formalities is not a story, it is the glow of someone who
looks for her origin, the same origin. If she is able to communicate to
her what she feels, perhaps, Antonia may be able to forgive her. (276)

The novel finds in interpersonal relations an answer to 9/11/1973 and
to the world it had created. Sophie had become emotionally stunted by
the disappearances of Diego and Morgana, but by the end of the novel
she is able to remember and celebrate their lives and establish a potentially deep personal connection with her sister. To put it somewhat
crassly, the solution to the coup is family. It is in the family, perhaps in
the reconstitution of the family, that the disappearances executed by the
Chilean dictatorship can be undone by acts of remembrance. Despite
her admiration for Allende and her opposition to the coup and the
world it created, Guelfenbein's novel is ultimately incapable of imagining any possible political alternative. Paradoxically, the only alternative
to a privatized public sphere is the private sphere.

Dorfman, too, in a later iteration of his essays on the two 9/11s,
provides an answer to the coup and, one would imagine, to the neoliberal world it inaugurated. Presenting Chile's response to 9/11/1973
as a rebuke to the wars with which the United States responded to the
destruction of the Twin Towers, he writes:

> Chile also could have responded to violence with more violence. If
> ever there was a justification for taking up arms against a tyrannical
> overlord, our struggle met every criteria. And yet the Chilean people
> and the leaders of the resistance—with a few sad exceptions—decided
> to oust General Pinochet through active nonviolence, taking over
> the country that had been stolen from us, inch by inch, organization
> by organization, until we ultimately bested him in a plebiscite that
> he should have won but could not. The result has not been perfect.
> The dictatorship continues to contaminate Chilean society several
> decades after it lost power. But all in all, as an example of how to
> create a lasting peace out of loss and untold suffering, Chile has
> shown a determination to make sure that there will never again be
> another September 11 of death and destruction. ("Epitaph for Another
> September 11" 17)

In this passage, Dorfman is implicitly accepting neoliberalism. He does reject the violence of the dictatorship and, perhaps surprisingly, the possibility of a violent response against oppression, and he acknowledges that unspecified aspects of the Pinochet regime have somehow survived to the present. However, there is no mention of the economic system that the military government set in place and that continues to our day. What Idelber Avelar states about the Brazilian dictatorship and the return to democracy in that country is even more apropos to the case of Chile: "The definition of the dictatorship as 'authoritarian state' made room for the next step, an oppositional class alliance hegemonized by neoliberal-conservative forces, leading to a redemocratization that never interrogated the economic model imposed by the military" (57–58). While one cannot deny the importance of the return to democratic processes and institutions, the exclusive focus on their implementation and their effect on the respect for "human rights" ultimately obfuscates the important economic and cultural continuities between the Southern Cone dictatorships and the democracies that replaced them in the 1980s and 1990s.

Despite their differences, Bolaño and Guelfenbein ultimately share in the rejection of politics, particularly radical politics. This is far from unusual in contemporary Latin American culture. In fact, it is difficult to think of any of the major contemporary writers as personally supporting any radical political movement. Although it is difficult to ascribe any utopian possibilities to the Latin American populist governments of the last twenty years, it is not an accident that it was writers like Elena Poniatowska or Eduardo Galeano—that is, younger contemporaries of the Boom masters—rather than Guelfenbein or Bolaño, who were found in Hugo Chávez's populist demonstrations. The well-known phrase by Alberto Fuguet and Sergio Gómez, also contemporary Chilean novelists, from their notorious "Presentación del país McOndo," is in principle still relevant: "If some years ago the options of the young writer were picking up either the pencil or the carbine, today the most distressing choice is that between Windows 95 and Macintosh" (13). Revolutionary politics, even if attempting to work within democratic frameworks as Allende did, is no longer even a theoretical possibility.[45]

However, as we saw in earlier chapters, Fuguet and Gómez's description of earlier Latin American writers as potential guerrilla fighters is misleading. It is true that there were numerous revolutionaries who were writers, and not only in potentia, as in the case of Ernesto "Che" Guevara, who was the author of such widely read narratives as *Episodes of the Cuban Revolutionary War* (1963) and the posthumous *The Motorcycle Diaries* (1993). The case of Javier Heraud (1942–1963), a gifted twenty-one-year-old poet who joined the guerrilla Ejército de Liberación Nacional and was killed by the police in the Peruvian jungle, can also serve as an example.

Nevertheless, Latin American intellectuals and writers have in their literary and scholarly work expressed caution regarding the uncritical embrace of maximalist revolution as often as they denounced injustice and misery. This caution began with Martí, whose idealistic belief in the possibility of humane social improvement within capitalism led him to reject revolution—though he would die in the struggle for Cuban independence—and Mariátegui, whose embrace of revolutionary violence was countervailed by his insistence on the need for radical cultural activism and education, and it continued with the Boom novelists, who, despite their personal commitment to the Cuban Revolution, expressed in their novels darker views on social activity.

The question that remains is whether Fuguet and Gómez's enthusiastic embrace of neoliberalism, Guelfenbein's resigned acceptance, or even Bolaño's pessimistic tolerance are appropriate to a period such as ours. After all, we are living in a moment in which the inequality produced by free-market policies threatens the existence of democracy itself, be it neoliberal or otherwise. Moreover, the ecological limits of our economic system are becoming every day more evident as fires rage and hurricanes blow with strengths never previously seen.

# Notes

## Introduction

1. An example of this belief that the socialist revolution was around the corner is given by no less a figure than Ángel Rama, surely the major Spanish-language literary critic of the period, who, in an essay from 1964 originally published in the Cuban *Revista Casa de las Américas*, wrote: "Our period is obviously one of imminent or already-in-process revolution." ("Diez problemas"). (In this case, as in that of all the works not listed in Spanish or Portuguese in the Works Cited, the translation is mine).

2. According to Carlos Rangel, "To understand how the noble savage was transmuted into the good revolutionary, we have to understand the supposed relation between man before the Fall and after redemption. These two states are not merely related: they are identical. The stage in between is a parenthesis, an interruption in man's natural beatitude. The first days will be like the last; the end of history will return to the golden age" (15).

3. Rafael Rojas has also made this point. "The greatest Latin American writers identified with Chilean democratic socialism. . . . So evident was their hope in the so-called 'Chilean path' as was their rejection toward Augusto Pinochet's military coup against the legitimate government of Allende, September 1973" (*La polis literaria* ch. 3). It is also worth emphasizing that the dictatorship's economic model was developed by US-trained professionals. As David Harvey reminds us, after General Pinochet's 1973 coup "a new approach was called for. A group of economists known as 'the Chicago boys' because of their attachment to the neoliberal theories of Milton Friedman, then teaching at the University of Chicago, was summoned to help reconstruct the Chilean economy. The story of how they were chosen is an interesting one. The US had funded training of Chilean economists at the University of Chicago since the 1950s as part of a Cold War programme to counteract left-wing tendencies" (8). They would transform Chile into a neoliberal workshop where policies were developed and tested. Harvey, after noting

that Chile's "neoliberalism" became more "pragmatic" after the debt crises of 1982, argues: "All of this, including the pragmatism, provided helpful evidence to support the subsequent turn to neoliberalism in both Britain (under Thatcher) and the US (under Reagan) in the 1980s. Not for the first time, a brutal experiment carried out in the periphery became a model for the formulation of policies in the centre" (9).

4. One example among many of his use of "revolution" for the struggle for independence from Spain is found in the "Programmatic Principles of the Socialist Party": "The independence revolution more than a century ago was a movement in solidarity with all peoples subjugated by Spain. The socialist revolution is a movement of all the peoples oppressed by capitalism. If the liberal revolution, nationalist in nature, could not be achieved without a close union between South American countries, it is easy to understand that the historical law in an era of stronger linkages and interdependence of nations, requires that the social revolution, internationalist in its nature, operates with a much more disciplined and intense coordination of proletarian parties" (237–38).

5. Unbeknownst to Williams, Mexican Nobel laureate Octavio Paz has made complementary points regarding the meaning of revolution. According to Paz: "The word revolution calls up many names and many meanings: Kant, the Encyclopedia, the Jacobin Terror, and most vividly of all the destruction of the order of privileges and exceptions and the founding of an order based not on authority but on the free exercise of reason. The old virtues went by the names of faith, fealty, honor. . . . Revolution is a word for a new virtue: justice. All the other new virtues—liberty, fraternity, equality—are based on it" ("Revolt, Revolution, Rebellion" 142). While Paz, curiously, omits any reference to socialism, he stresses that notions of revolution necessarily have a philosophical and rational component that underpins the claims of the newly established society as striving toward justice.

6. For instance, the Indian scholar Aijaz Ahmad argues: "For the historic 'New Left' as it arose in Britain, the reference points had been Hungary and Suez . . . ; in the United States, those sorts of energies had been associated first with Cuba and then with Vietnam, with the ambiguous liberalism of the Democratic Party itself becoming a very considerable issue. In France, terminologies were slightly different, but the wars in Indochina and Algeria had played the same constitutive role in the imaginations of the Left before the ascendancy of structuralism—in the perspective of High Gaullism, of course. Literary debates in these three cultures presumed those realities up to, and somewhat beyond, 1968" (2). One can note, however, that there is a chronological evolution in

play here. By the late 1960s, Cuba and Vietnam (or Indochina) had replaced Hungary, Suez, and Algeria as "reference points" in Europe and North America.

7. While there has been considerable debate about the composition of the Boom and its possible definition, for heuristic reasons this book is mainly interested in the group of writers—García Márquez, Fuentes, Vargas Llosa, and Cortázar—who, in addition to being what could be loosely called modernist novelists and being seen by readers and critics as constituting an identifiable group, were also united by bonds of friendship and collaboration.

8. One must remember that the eighty guerrilla fighters who arrived in Cuba with Fidel Castro and Ernesto "Che" Guevara were rapidly decimated by Batista's forces, although perhaps not down to the apostolic twelve, as has been claimed. According to Richard Gott, "The *Granma's* landing had not gone unnoticed by the authorities. Within hours of its arrival, the embryonic guerrilla group was under attack from the air and on land. Several were killed, while 22 were captured and later put on trial. The sorry remnant struggled through the swamp in disarray. According to legend, just 12 of them had survived, though this was an underestimate" (155).

9. Fidel Castro called Cuba "free territory of America" starting with the "The Second Declaration of Havana" in 1962. By 1966, Castro had begun calling Cuba the "first free territory of America," for instance, in an interview with Mario Menéndez Rodríguez (Castro, "Mexican Magazine Has Exclusive with Fidel").

10. According to David F. Schmitz, the Eisenhower administration debated in 1953 how to promote development and democracy in Latin America without creating situations that could favor the spread of Communism: "The solution to the dilemma of how to bring social change and an evolution toward democracy without setting off revolutions and aiding the spread of communism was to be found in supporting strong leaders who would heed American advice. The rule of various dictators, therefore, was viewed positively by the new administration" (184).

11. In Patrick Iber's words, "Even when U.S. policies were nominally committed to producing liberal outcomes and political democracy, their outcomes could still be illiberal. For that reason, the history of Latin America has often played an important role as a corrective to more triumphal accounts of U.S. victory in the Cold War, where it can serve either as a reminder of the mournfully high cost of a just victory or as evidence to support the argument that, as dreadful as the politics of the Soviet Union were, justice was not the point of the struggle at all. The

historian John Coatsworth has calculated that between 1960 and 1990 anti-Communist Latin America was more repressive than the Soviet bloc when measured by the numbers of political prisoners, victims of torture, and executions of political dissenters. Although U.S. policies were not always the proximate cause of this violence, and the Latin American Right had its own reasons for the actions it took to suppress political opponents, the United States both aided dictatorships and helped bring them about, and the climate of paranoid anti-Communism that the United States encouraged was a significant factor in the darkness of Latin America's Cold War years" (12).

12. As any reader of Williams knows, he seems to reserve the term "structure of feeling" for that agglutination of ideas and emotions that, while informing discourse, are still not fully explicit, that remain under the surface, and that apparently are developed individually in response to specific social evolution. The Cuban Revolution, on the other hand, was a rapidly institutionalized and institutionalizing event. It obviously originated as a response to the dissatisfaction with Latin American reality—perhaps the true structure of feeling of the time—and was successful in transforming it into concrete revolutionary actions and, later, institutions, including government itself. (One could perhaps even claim that there was a similar dissatisfaction with the real existing society throughout the Western world.) Moreover, it consciously tried to mobilize this dissatisfaction into support for the Cuban Revolution and for revolutionary activity throughout the region, and it was successful in doing so for several years. The following quotation makes clear Williams's original conception of "structure of feeling": "It is a structured formation which, because it is at the very edge of semantic availability, has many of the characteristics of a pre-formation, until specific articulations—new semantic figures—are discovered in material practice: often, as it happens, in relatively isolated ways, which are only later seen to compose a significant (often in fact minority) generation; this often, in turn, the generation that substantially connects to its successors. It is thus a specific structure of particular linkages, particular emphases and suppressions, and, in what are often its most recognizable forms, particular deep starting-points and conclusions" (*Marxism and Literature* 134).

13. Cortázar's *A Manual for Manuel* (1973), the other novel by one of the four major Boom writers that attempts to represent Latin American radical activity, is, however, set in Paris, in addition to being one of the least critically and commercially successful of the Argentine writer's novels.

14. Cuban novelist Leonardo Padura, a major contemporary novelist in his own right, comments: "The Chilean Roberto Bolaño, perhaps the greatest narrator in the Spanish language of recent generations . . . left an oeuvre composed of several novels and short story collections, but especially two works, that, in my opinion, compete with—and in many cases surpass—the mythic works of the Boom of the Latin American novel" (276). (The "two works" singled out by Padura are *The Savage Detectives* and *2666*.)

*Chapter 1*

1. One of the questions in Latin American history is why it took so long for the United States to be seen as at least as much a threat as an example. As early as 1829, Simón Bolívar had written about "the United States, which seems destined by Providence to plague America with miseries in the name of Freedom?" (173). The Mexican-American War (1846–1848) should have seemed enough proof to warrant skepticism regarding the intentions of the United States toward its southern neighbors. Nevertheless, for many in Latin America it was only the Spanish-American War in 1898 that made evident the United States' true aims toward the region. Ironically, only the defeat of Spain made the United States visible as the new empire. An example of this growing sense of the United States as an imperialist threat is Rubén Darío's foundational agitprop poem "A Roosevelt," published in 1904, which responded to that country's involvement in the separation of Panama from Colombia.

2. According to Vargas Llosa: "Mexico is the perfect dictatorship. The perfect dictatorship is not communism. It is not the USSR. It is not Fidel Castro. . . . [I]t is a hidden dictatorship. . . . It has the characteristics of a dictatorship: the permanence not of a man, but of a party. . . . And of a party that is unmovable" ("Vargas Llosa: México es la dictadura perfecta"). The Peruvian novelist made these statements during the "Encuentro La Experiencia de la Libertad" organized by Octavio Paz in Mexico in 1990 to celebrate the fall of Communism. Vargas Llosa's statements led to a sharp response from the Mexican poet.

3. Brazilian scholar José Luís Fiori notes, "After 1930, especially after the Communist Parties of Latin America adopted a democratic and reformist strategy for the conquest of power and the transformation of the capitalist system, the relationship of the left, and its core intellectual production, with developmentalism was transformed. This happened in almost all nations of the continent" (241). An extreme example of this permanent truce with "bourgeois" politics is provided by the relationship

of the Peruvian Communist Party with conservative candidate—and later president—Manuel Prado during the presidential elections of 1939 and the beginning of his government. According to Raúl Palacios Rodríguez, "The communist leadership that had supported him during the electoral campaign (due to a strange mixture of interests) was present when the main public positions were assigned. . . . Blinded by their support, one of them called Prado 'the Peruvian Stalin'" (31).

4. Elena de Costa notes: "Ernesto Cardenal, poet, liberation theologian and then Minister of Culture showed his organizational skills by promoting popular culture as a vehicle for a new national identity, a project that was a major part of Sandinista government policy. The government-sponsored poetry workshops invited participants, including the newly literate, to express their experience in poetry. . . . This discourse about the collective sphere averts what is called a 'culture of silence' in which there is an erasure of memory of such significant events by creating a culture of dissent and witness, of mutual affirmation through the voice of the community. The Nicaraguan poetry workshops were organized by the Ministry of Culture throughout the country as an experiment (not only in the rural sectors), but also among the army, the police force, the air force, the state secret police and Somocista prisoners" (634).

5. Some readers may feel tempted to add another date: 1999. This was the year when, having been elected on a platform rejecting neoliberal economic policies and promising to improve the lives of the poor, Colonel Hugo Chávez was inaugurated as president of Venezuela. Chávez's coming to power was seen by some as some as the start of a turn toward the political left on the part of the region, often known as "The Pink Tide." However, while Chávez had friendly relations with Luiz Inácio Lula da Silva (Lula) in Brazil (2003–2011) and Michelle Bachelet in Chile (2006–2010), both of their governments implemented policies consistent with free-market ideas. In South America, only Evo Morales's pro-indigenous government (2006– ), Rafael Correa's government in Ecuador (2007–2017), and perhaps the governments of Peronist presidents Néstor Kirchner (2003–2007) and Cristina Fernández de Kirchner (2007–2015) could be seen as close allies. Despite the renewal of leftist enthusiasm generated by the Pink Tide, it also created a significant backlash in Mexico and Peru, where putative links with Chávez led to the defeat of progressive candidates. However, as was the case with the Cuban Revolution and the Nicaraguan Revolution, the appeal of the Pink Tide has, at the time of writing, completely faded. In fact, despite Chávez's claims to represent a "socialism for the twenty-first century," Pink Tide politics could be seen as populist rather than strictly

socialist or even anticapitalist. The Pink Tide was by definition not revolutionary in the sense of this word as used in this study.

6. Be that as it may, Sandinista political influence outside Central America, where it temporarily became a model for guerrilla movements in El Salvador and Guatemala, was limited at best. As the different Southern Cone right-wing dictatorships folded back into democracy, liberal, if not neoliberal, parties came to power. Even in Peru, where that unicorn of political entities—a nominally progressive military government—had been in power, especially during the period led by General Juan Velasco Alvarado (1968–1975), the winner of the first democratic elections (1980) was Fernando Belaúnde, the liberal president who had been deposed in 1968. Rather than a turning point in the history of Latin American radicalism, the Sandinista revolution can be seen as a kind of St. Martin's summer for revolution.

7. I will deal briefly with the Central American revolutions of the 1980s and 1990s and the Peruvian Shining Path in Chapter 3, "The Fall of the Revolutionary and the Return of Liberal Democracy."

8. There were Latin American Marxists before Mariátegui. One can note, for instance, the group of Argentine intellectuals associated with the Argentine Socialist Party founded in 1896, such as Juan B. Justo, Alfredo Palacios, and José Ingenieros.

9. There is only one, rather perfunctory, mention of Martí in all of Mariátegui's writing. In an article titled "The Unity of Indo-Hispanic America," Mariátegui writes: "The identity of Hispanic-American people finds one expression in intellectual life. The same ideas, the same emotions circulate through all of Indo-Hispanic America. All powerful intellectual personalities have an influence on the continental culture. Sarmiento, Martí, and Montalvo do not belong exclusively to their respective countries; they belong to Hispanic America. The same that can be said of these thinkers can be said of Darío, Lugones, Silva, Nervo, Chocano, and other poets. Rubén Darío is present throughout Hispanic-American literature" (448). The lack of engagement with Martí is reflected in the list, which includes authors who will also not be mentioned by Mariátegui elsewhere, such as the Ecuadorian liberal Juan Montalvo, as well as cultural figures he actually disliked, such as the Peruvian poet José Santos Chocano.

10. It thus makes perfect sense that, as Maarten van Delden notes, "With the triumph of the Cuban Revolution in 1959, Martí acquired a new role in Cuban culture and politics. Fidel Castro quoted so extensively from the writings of the man now known as the *héroe nacional* that the poet Heberto Padilla called him the Pierre Menard of Cuban politics.

The organic intellectuals of the Revolution labored hard to prove that if Martí were alive today he would be supporting Fidel" ("José Martí: The End of a Myth" 32).

11. According to John Kirk, before the Cuban Revolution, Martí was seen as primarily a moral and ethical example of *Cubanía*, rather than read for his political or policy insights: "He was thus viewed as a great and selfless Cuban, determined to do all in his power to help his country, and if necessary, to give his life for the patria; a noble—but somehow alienated—patriot; in short, a Cuban version of Don Quixote" (131). The enthusiasm Martí felt for the United States—at least during part of the 1880s—has made it possible for pro–United States Cuban exiles to also claim him in their struggle against the Castro regime.

12. See Martí, "[Cartas de Martí] Nueva York, 29 de marzo de 1883," 237 note a. Obviously, the misspellings of Marx's last name are the responsibility of the Argentine newspaper *La Nación* and reflect the absence of the German thinker from Latin America's cultural radar.

13. An excellent example of a Marxist debunking of Martí is that by Afro-Cuban scholar and union leader Pinto Albiol. According to him, "Martí was a petit bourgeois. . . . [A]ll of his work is impregnated by an opportunistic ecleticism. . . . [H]e weeps with the poor, but he doesn't want to eliminate poverty; he loves deeply the black brothers and sisters, but he does not want to eliminate the material cause that keeps them as social inferiors; he wants a republic with all and for the benefit of all, but does not want to eliminate social classes" (27).

14. For a highly critical view of the intellectual juggling that the Cuban Revolution's need to yoke together Martí and Marx forced on Marinello, see Carlos Ripoll's "The Falsification of José Martí in Cuba," especially 5–6.

15. For instance, in José David Saldívar's *The Dialectics of Our America* (1991), Martí is brought into dialogue with Said, Bhabha, and Fernández Retamar himself.

16. The three best-known English translations are severely abridged. I am referring to those included in *Inside the Monster*, edited by Philip S. Foner; *The José Martí Reader*, edited by Deborah Shnookal and Mirta Muñiz; and *José Martí: Selected Writings*, edited by Esther Allen. Foner only presents the section dealing with Marx—one page out of ten; Shnookal and Muñiz present a slightly longer selection dealing with the whole memorial—three pages; and Allen, though presenting a more complete selection, eliminates the references to the funerals of Payne and George Elliot. A similar abridgement is practiced in Spanish. For instance, *José Martí: Sus mejores páginas*, edited by Raimundo Lazo, only

includes the section that deals with the memorial for Marx, as does *Marx en la Argentina: Sus primeros lectores obreros, intelectuales y científicos*, edited by Horacio Tarcus.

17. Throughout this essay I will refer to Esther Allen's translation, "Tributes to Karl Marx Who Has Died," ("Tributes"). However, when dealing with passages omitted by the English version I will quote from the Spanish "Carta" (cited as "Carta").

18. The best-known use of the epithet worm is explained by Beatriz Varela, "The third and last familiar name that we will cite for the Cuban-Americans is *gusano*, 'worm,' an appellation that makes them swell with pride and with which they all want to be identified. Castro had applied it in the sixties to the *contrarevolucionarios*, that is, the enemies of the Revolution, because *worms* crawl and they represent the most inferior animal in the zoological scale. In fact, he still uses *gusano* with other insulting terms like *anti-social, lumpen, scum*, etc. to refer to those who have abandoned their country to reside in the United States" (152).

19. Implicit in Martí's letter is the notion that European monarchical and repressive systems justified much more aggressive political action on the part of the workers of the old world. This may help explain the apparent contradiction of the pacifist Martí admiring the undeniably violent leaders of Spanish American independence, such as Simón Bolívar, or his leading the independence armies in Cuba up to his untimely death in 1895. In the case of Spanish America and Cuba, the Spanish colonial governments and their institutions did not permit the kind of melioristic politics Martí generally favored. Only violence was left as a method for the independence struggle.

20. Bosteels has noted that this distinction between American and European workers is a constant throughout the Cuban poet's writings: "Martí, in chronicles from the same period, will time and again reiterate this distinction in organizational style of the workers' movements in Europe and America" (33).

21. Given this emphasis on "soft remedies," it is surprising to read Martí's description of Bakunin, a celebrant of propaganda by the deed, as "tender and radiant" ("Tributes" 132).

22. Jrade quotes from a two-page version included in the anthology *Marxism in Latin America* rather than from the complete letter (27).

23. On Marx's presence in the US press, see Foner, "Introduction," *When Karl Marx Died: Comments in 1883* (New York: International Publishers, 1973), 61–66.

24. The optimistic vision of US modernity present in this "Carta" from 1883 contradicts Rafael Rojas's overall characterization of Martí's US

writings as making use of "the biblical metaphor of the sea monster and its entrails to signal that at the heart of North American life, profit, the passion for money, the market and its rhythms, urban sprawl, and dehumanization caused by technology, announce the cataclysm of spiritual institutions" (*José Martí* 16). At least in this text, Martí sees US politics as self-correcting.

25. For heuristic reasons, I have omitted any discussion of gender in Martí's "Carta." As discussed earlier, the Cuban poet mentions the decision by the board of trustees of Columbia University to establish a college for women. (This decision would be fulfilled in 1889 with the founding of Barnard College.) For Martí, this raises the question of women's full participation in public life, including politics and the workplace. Martí quotes approvingly a woman activist who replies to a preacher who argues for the subordination of women: "And what of my mind, which grasps all that yours grasps" ("Tributes" 134). He also seems to agree with an "ardent female reformer" who argues for the participation of women in politics because "the Board of Education, the police stations, and all the positions of state that are poorly managed by ambitious and unloving men would be better off in the hands of women, in whom the development of reason does not extinguish tenderness—which is indeed a great gift in governance" ("Tributes" 135; with corrections). Moreover, he is aware of the economic pressures that make women enter the workplace: "No one looks askance on the toughening of the feminine soul, for that is the outcome of the virile existence to which women are led by the need to take care of themselves and defend themselves from the men who are moved by appetite. Better that the soul be toughened than that it be debased" ("Tributes" 135). Despite the fact that Martí's arguments—unavoidable incorporation of women into society as workers and students, intellectual equality, and moral superiority of women—seem to point toward the full support of equality, including suffrage for women, Martí seems unable to take that step. Martí's hesitation regarding the education of women or their participation in politics originates in his adscription to Victorian moral values that see the public sphere as necessarily degrading. He is also emotionally invested in a conventional hierarchical view of gender relations threatened by women's participation in the public sphere. In what must be the silliest phrase in all of Martí's works, he concludes his reflections on the condition of women—in *La Nación*, the first published section of the "Carta"—by asking: "What will become of men on the day when they can no longer rest their heads on a warm, female bosom" ("Tributes" 136).

26. According to Christopher Conway, "There is a broad consensus among scholars that this event was key in radicalizing Martí's already critical attitudes toward the US, setting the stage for his later, more urgent missives against US imperialism in Latin America" (35). Among these scholars, one can mention Bosteels (34–35), Fountain (101, 120), and Lomas (254).

27. However, not all critics see Martí as fully changing his mind regarding the working-class struggle of the time. For instance, Alfred López writes about "an unmistakable ambivalence in Martí's writings regarding questions of class and class conflict, an undecidability that has allowed both sides in the Cuban culture wars to read Martí selectively to support their position and to claim him as their founding father. The truth is much more inconclusive and much less politically convenient: *Martí never made up his mind about these difficult issues* or at least never reconciled these conflicting impulses in his thought and works" (16). Francisco Morán, in his attempt at debunking the cult of Martí, argues regarding his description of the working class: "He not only *exported* this distortion [characteristic of US journalistic coverage of the US working class during the Haymarket affair], but even when his chronicles were not published or read in the United States, they form part of [the kind of journalism] published in the overwhelming majority of the North American press during the [Haymarket] affair, and were written in the midst of the same passion and in contact with it. Martí's chronicles— and not only those dealing with Chicago [Haymarket affair]—belong to that corpus, and, in that sense, belong to the work of an *American writer*. In other words, in particular Martí's chronicles on worker strikes and Haymarket supported the elite narrative that defended law and order and, in consequence are equally responsible [as US journalism] for the debilitating effect that the trial and execution of the anarchists of Chicago had for the worker movement" (518).

28. In "Our America" ("Nuestra América"), published in 1892, Martí expresses his fear of US imperialism: "The disdain of the formidable neighbor who does not know her is our America's greatest danger" (295). However, even in this essay, which has frequently been read as proposing a postcolonial political and cultural reorganization of Latin America, Martí's main solution to the danger of US imperialism is to make sure that the latter's population has more information about Latin America: "It is urgent—for the day of the visit is near—that her neighbor come to know her, and quickly, so that he will not disdain her. Out of ignorance, he may perhaps begin to covet her. But when he knows her he will remove his hands from her in respect. One must have faith in the best

in man and distrust the worst" (295). Here Martí clearly discounts the obvious possibility that greater knowledge about the region's resources could further whet imperial appetite, even if the reason given for optimism—"faith in the best in man"—is extremely weak. Martí's belief in the necessarily positive result of communication and dialogue, already present in the "Carta," is here repeated in his (extremely) optimistic evaluation of North-South (American) relations. And, as we saw above, Martí sees dialogue and "love" as the key to the supersession of Latin America's colonial heritage and ills.

29. This point has been made by many authors, including Harry Vanden and Marc Becker: "Mariátegui implemented a new theoretical framework that diverged from the doctrinaire ideology adopted by most of the Latin America Communist parties—an approach that attempted to apply a mechanical interpretation of Marxist strategy to a national reality. He broke from a rigid, orthodox interpretation of Marxism to develop a creative Marxist analysis that was oriented toward the specific historical reality of Peru and Latin America in the 1920s. Mariátegui did not believe that Marxism was a finished project" (13).

30. In his *La agonía de Mariátegui*, surely the most outstanding study of the Peruvian Marxist, Alberto Flores Galindo analyzes the response to Mariátegui's work by Vittorio Codovilla, the main apparatchik of the Soviet-led Third International in South America, as representative of the official Communist view on Mariátegui's ideas. When the Italian Communist received a copy of Mariátegui's masterwork *Seven Interpretative Essays on Peruvian Reality*, he claimed that "Mariátegui's works had very little value" (27). Flores Galindo adds: "Codovilla was uncomfortable with, couldn't tolerate, a book in whose title the words 'essay' and 'Peruvian reality' were joined. The word essay implied a style that recalled the writings of bourgeois and reactionary authors such as [José Enrique] Rodó or [Pedro] Henríquez Ureña. Moreover, it implied a certain tentativeness, the provisional character of the statements, and evidently a man such as Codovilla, who couldn't accept mistakes, could tolerate uncertainty even less. . . . Reality was neatly demarcated, so one knew one had to do one thing or the other. The correct [political] line did not admit discussion. 'Essays' were left for intellectuals" (28). For the Stalinists, Communism consisted of universally applicable measures.

31. While the APRA (as a political party) became later known as the Partido Aprista Peruano for the 1931 elections, held after the Augusto Leguía regime (1919–1930) had been overthrown, for the scheduled 1929 elections Haya's party was called Partido Nacionalista Libertador or Partido Nacionalista Peruano. Curiously, both names were used

in the documents issued by Haya and his collaborators. Thus, the candidacy's platform, "Esquema del plan de México," called the party "Partido Nacionalista Libertador," while a communiqué proclaiming the candidacy, issued in the small Andean city of Abancay, called it "Partido Nacionalista Peruano."

32. The basic principles of the APRA as published by Haya de la Torre in the British Communist magazine *Labour Monthly* in 1926 were as follows:

1. Action of the countries of Latin America against Yankee imperialism.
2. The Political unity of Latin America.
3. The nationalization of land and industry.
4. The internationalization of the Panama Canal.
5. The solidarity of all oppressed people and classes of the world. (756)

33. In his *Seven Interpretative Essays*, Mariátegui noted about Haya: "Writing this paper, I find in Víctor Raúl Haya de la Torre's book *Por la emancipación de la América Latina* (For the emancipation of Latin America) concepts that coincide absolutely with mine on the agrarian question in general and the Indigenous community in particular. We start with the same views, so it is imperative that our findings are also the same" (99). However, only a year later, in 1929, Mariátegui will write to fellow Marxist Moisés Arroyo Posadas: "Based on his claims to be a revolutionary Marxist, I gave Haya excessive credit and trust. I have learned afterward that when it comes to Marxism he has learned nothing" (*José Carlos Mariátegui. Correspondencia* 611). In fact, Haya and the APRA party would arguably become the first mass populist party of Latin America. That said, some apparently still see in Haya a Marxist. In a bizarre moment in his otherwise important *Marx and Freud in Latin America*, Bruno Bosteels includes "José Carlos Mariátegui and Víctor Raúl Haya de la Torre in Peru" among "the major recognized figures behind the various Communist (Marxist-Leninist, Trotskyist, Guevarist, Maoist) parties in Latin America" (23, 24).

34. Luis Alberto Sánchez, the influential literary critic and historian, is an exception to this rather simplified vision of the split between Mariátegui and those explicitly aligned with socialism and the APRA group after 1928. While he and Mariátegui had famously clashed regarding the importance of *indigenista* literature (that is, novels, poetry, and plays that represented and defended Andean indigenous populations), Sánchez remained a friend and confidant, even after Haya's first candidacy. After Mariátegui's death, however, he would become the main APRA intellectual. There have long been questions regarding Haya's 1928

"candidacy," given the fact that he could not actually become a candidate. According to APRA scholar Eugenio Chang Rodríguez: "In reality, Haya's candidacy was part of a program of distraction. . . . This trick hid the true purpose of a projected armed rebellion" (327). Thus, simultaneously with the electoral campaign, Felipe Iparraguirre, reputed to be a former captain in the Peruvian army living in El Salvador, arrived surreptitiously in Talara, a city in northern Peru, to organize a military insurrection under Haya's instructions. The uprising failed. Haya notes in a private letter dated 1929, "In his last letter he [Iparraguirre] advised me of the formation of an army based on 2,500 workers in Talara. I would have received an agreed telegram to travel to Peru immediately" (qtd. in Manrique 79). Although Haya assumed that Iparraguirre had been tortured and perhaps executed, in reality he had simply been deported after being captured (Manrique 81).

35. Mariátegui writes in *Seven Interpretive Essays*: "It is worthwhile repeating that this formula of breaking up large estates in favor of small properties is neither utopian, nor heretical, nor revolutionary, nor Bolshevik, nor vanguardist, but orthodox, constitutional, democratic, capitalist and bourgeois. It has its origins in the liberal ideals that inspired the constitutional laws of all democratic bourgeois states. And the countries of Central and Eastern Europe, where the crisis of the war led to the pulling down of the last ramparts of feudalism with the support of Western capitalism that since then used precisely this group of countries to oppose Russia in an anti-Bolshevik bloc of countries (Czechoslovakia, Romania, Poland, Bulgaria, etc.), have enacted agrarian laws that restrict, in principle, land ownership, to a maximum of 500 hectares" (71).

36. In his significantly titled "Mariátegui, marxista-leninista" (1943), Jorge del Prado, himself a leader in the Peruvian Communist Party, defended his former friend from the criticisms that had long been leveled by the Communist International and its representatives since his Mariátegui's death: "It is surprising how similar is the definition of Leninism proposed by Mariátegui—when formulating with principles of our [Communist] Party in 1928—to that provided by Stalin in his *Foundations of Leninism* from 1925, despite [*Foundations of Leninism*] having been published four years earlier. Mariátegui could not have known [*Foundations of Leninism*] since it was only in 1931 that translations into Spanish—or any of the other languages he spoke—became available" (75). One must add that Mariátegui had called the party Socialist, not Communist, thus violating the rules of the Third International.

37. Not only did Mariátegui refer on several occasions to Gobetti, but, according to the English translation, he even wrote about his "great spiritual affinity" with the Italian writer in *Seven Interpretive Essays on Peruvian Reality* (182). The translation, however, does little justice to Mariátegui's original phrase: "Gobetti, uno de los espíritus con quienes siento más amorosa asonancia" (191). A literal translation would be "Gobetti, one of the spirits with which I feel [a] more amorous connection."

38. Mariátegui continuously referred to Sorel as a central figure in the history of socialist thought. In "Henri de Man and the Crisis of Marxism," Mariátegui writes: "The true revision of Marxism, in the sense of the renovation and continuation of the work of Marx, has been done, in theory and practice, by another category of revolutionary intellectual—Georges Sorel, in studies that separate and distinguish what is essential and substantive in Marx from that which is formal and contingent" (189).

39. Despite Mariátegui's insistence on Sorel's socialist bona fides, his actual politics were much more ambiguous. Paradoxically, for Sorel, proletarian violence, fueled by the belief in the "general strike" (the specific "myth" he championed), leads to a heightening of the class struggle and therefore to the renewal of the bourgeoisie's beliefs in its own myths (private property, democracy, the market): "It is here that the role of violence in history appears to us as singularly great, for it can in an indirect manner, so operate on the middle class as to awaken them to a sense of their own class sentiment" (90). Heightened opposition— capitalists holding onto their own myths, workers embracing the violence of the "general" strike—is the only way to a well-functioning society: "If a united and revolutionary proletariat confronts a rich middle class, eager for conquest, capitalist society will have reached its historical perfection" (Sorel 92).

40. Throughout *Reflections on Violence* (1908), Georges Sorel's best-known work, the French writer stresses what he perceives as the necessary rejection of parliamentary democracy on the part of the working class, instead proposing class struggle and violence as its necessary politics. For instance, according to Sorel, "Electoral democracy greatly resembles the world of the Stock Exchange; in both cases, it is necessary to work upon the simplicity of the masses, to buy the cooperation of the most important papers, and *to assist chance* by an infinity of trickery" (221). Mariátegui, in fact, valued Sorel for, among other things, his attack on the social-democratic embrace of parliamentary democracy: "Sorelism, as a return to the original sentiment of class struggle, as a protest against

parliamentary pacification, bourgeoisfied socialism, is a type of heresy that is incorporated into dogma" ("The Process of Contemporary French Literature" 180).

41. Historian Peter Klarén, in his study of the origins of the APRA party, writes about the legendary and multitudinous 1931 meeting at the Acho Bullring, and notes the central role in the development and growth of the APRA movement played by Haya's rhetorical prowess and charismatic leadership: "As he [Haya] reached the end of his speech, he paused briefly and then, to the delight of the mass, closed with the words 'sólo el Aprismo podrá salvarnos' (only Aprismo can be our salvation)." And: "To thousands of Peruvians in 1931 that emotion packed-packed phrase touched a vital cord. Unsettled by the impact of the depression and moved by the constant revolutionary rhetoric of Víctor Raúl Haya de la Torre, the spell-binding orator that winter afternoon in Acho, they flocked in ever increasing numbers to the fledging Peruvian Aprista Party" (xi).

42. The preamble of the "Esquema del plan de México" notes that Peru is "subjugated today by the tyranny of the national landowners and foreign imperialism represented by the regime of Don Augusto B. Leguía" (290). The sixth point stresses "the return of the land to the Peruvian people, giving it to those who work it, destroying latifundism and procuring to reestablish, on the basis of the indigenous communities . . . the new agrarian and agricultural organism" (291). The seventh point reaffirms the centrality of the indigenous community and adds the need to bring "all the help of modern technology to the admirable Inca system" (291). The eighth point restates the importance of incorporating "scientific bases" in this "renovation of the system of production in land" (291). The twelfth, thirteenth, and fourteenth points all refer, in different ways, to the need to "abolish the power of the land holding class" (292). The fifteenth and final point takes up as the motto of the new political party Emiliano Zapata's slogan for the Mexican Revolution: "land and freedom."

43. Federico Finchelstein has described the APRA party as "a Peruvian nationalist protopopulist organization" (*From Fascism to Populism in History* 116).

44. Implicit in Guevara's text is an erotics of personalist politics—the relationship between "Fidel and the mass" is, for instance, described in orgasmic terms.

45. The accusations of fascism traveled down a two-way strada. Haya, for instance, wrote about Mariátegui in a letter to Eudocio Ravines: "I know that military fascism similar to that in Chile is being developed for Peru.

Mariátegui, like the Italian communists in 1921 is opening the doors for them. The Mussolini with epaulets of Peru (helped by the imperialists) will build Mariátegui a monument with one leg" (qtd. in Flores Galindo, "Un viejo debate" 98–99). (Haya is referring to the fact that Mariátegui had one leg amputated as result of the myelosis that ultimately killed him.)

46. Flores Galindo's "Un viejo debate: El poder" includes as an appendix the full text of the letters Haya sent to Ravines. Years later, after breaking with Communism, Ravines would become a CIA agent and an anti-communist agitator and pundit.

47. During discussions that led to the founding of the Socialist Party, it was decided that there would be a secret Marxist cell running it (Flores Galindo, *La agonía de Mariátegui* 33–34). However, as Flores Galindo notes: "The main problem with the model of a two-faced party is that it puts in question [its] internal democracy, because, if the majority ignores the existence of the cell, it means the majority ignores the direction the party is taking. . . . [D]epending on the perspective taken, it is, therefore, a refined or crass manipulation, that evidently contradicts the notion of politics as truth held by Mariátegui" (*La agonía de Mariátegui* 34). Given its secret nature, this cell would have difficulty maintaining control of a party run democratically. Although the notion of the secret cell could be seen as a way to appease the Comintern, there is no record of this proposal in any of Mariátegui's extant texts, whether public or private.

48. According to Che Guevara, "The Cuban Revolution contributed three fundamental lessons to the conduct of revolutionary movements in America. They are: 1. Popular forces can win a war against the army. 2. It is not necessary to wait until all the conditions for making revolution exist; the insurrection can create them. 3. In underdeveloped America the countryside is the basic area for armed fighting" (*Guerrilla Warfare* 1).

### Chapter 2

1. According to Cortázar, the panels were on "genocide and ethnocide in Latin America," "the political situation and the revolutionary struggles" in the region, "intellectuals and politics," "guerrilla narrative," "aboriginal cultures facing the (ideal) of consumer culture," and "the social and economic problems of our lands" ("La América Latina no oficial" 11).

2. Moira Cristiá has noted in an article detailing the effects and aftereffects of May 1968 on Argentine culture: "The main objectives [of Amérique Latine Non-officielle] was to break with the superficial and stereotyped

representation of Latin America, denounce imperialism, economic power, the oppressiveness of the system, and the use of torture in the region's countries."

3.  I have not been able to find any previous analysis dedicated specifically to the panel "The Intellectual and Politics," with the exception of Cortázar's "La América Latina no oficial" and his "Viaje alrededor de una mesa." Curiously, despite the cultural importance of Vargas Llosa and Cortázar, the writing on the Amérique Latine Non-officielle events has been almost exclusively concerned with the plastic arts exhibitions; see, for instance, the articles by Moira Cristiá and Isabel Plante. In fact, Plante, who never mentions the panels, spends some time trying to figure out what films were shown at the event, beyond *The Hour of the Furnaces*: "Possibly there were more films from Buenos Aires shown at Amérique Latine Non-Officielle. In a letter dated March 1970, Le Parc mentioned a number of films that Getino had recommended. He informed that, based on recommendations, they had selected the *Cineinformes* of the CGTA (General Federation of Argentine Workers), news reels filmed by the Cine Liberación group (Getino, Gerardo Vallejo and Nemesio Juárez) between 1968 and 1969, and *Argentina, mayo de 1969: los caminos de la liberación* [Argentina, May 1969: The Paths to Liberation], built up from a series of short films directed, written, and edited by Getino, Solanas, Szir, Nemesio Juárez, Enrique Juárez, Humberto Ríos, Jorge Martín, Eliseo Subiela, Rodolfo Kuhn and Jorge Cedrón" (80).

4.  After quoting Edgard Morin's statement that "the writer who writes a novel is a writer, but if she speaks about the use of torture in Algeria, she is an intellectual," Claudia Gilman notes: "This definition gives solidity to a displacement in terms from the category of writer to that of the intellectual; [this displacement] had a long tradition beginning with Zola, who became the prototype of the man of letters as prosecutor of his society toward the end of the 19th century, but it was never more fluid than in the Latin American literary field of the time. In the politicized literary horizon of the time, it was natural that both designations would circulate as synonyms" (69).

5.  As we will see below, Carlos Fuentes also participated in intellectual discussions, but this was not the case for García Márquez. While the author of *One Hundred Years of Solitude* nominally supported the Cuban Revolution and, in his own practice, became an example for many writers in Latin America and beyond, he was generally adverse to writing critical or political texts. However, despite publicly supporting the Cuban government, both García Márquez and Fuentes had become

somewhat distanced from the revolution and the political debates it generated.

6.  Ángel Rama has written about the Boom: "I have satirized the Boom . . . as the most exclusive group ever known in the cultural history of Latin America. It is a club that holds to the intangible principle of having only five seats and not one more in order to safeguard its elitist vocation. As in the Academies, four are assigned in perpetuity: those corresponding to Julio Cortázar, Carlos Fuentes, Mario Vargas Llosa and Gabriel García Márquez. The fifth is freely assigned. It has been granted to writers from Carpentier to Donoso, from Lezama Lima to Guimarães Rosa. To complete the picture, someone has instituted a second class title of 'consul before the Boom,' with which Salvador Garmendia has been distinguished on the flap of his last novel, *Los pies de barro*" ("El Boom en perspectiva"). The four "permanent members" of the club shared a commitment to what could be called the modernization of the Latin American novel, and achieved critical and commercial success in the 1960s; beyond this, it is difficult to find much in common between them. After all, Cortázar, born in 1914, was twenty-two years older than Vargas Llosa, so the Boom included writers from two distinct generations, at least chronologically. Moreover, Cortázar's surrealist-inflected novel *Hopscotch* (1963), set in Paris and Buenos Aires in the 1950s, shares little stylistically with the rural magical realism of García Márquez's *One Hundred Years in Solitude* (1967), and the two are distant from the searing realism of Vargas Llosa's *The Time of the Hero* (1963). If one were to take this modernizing thrust as the key to the Boom, older authors who shared in this trait, such as Carpentier or Lezama Lima, could be included. However, if achieving celebrity in the 1960s is the main criterion, then one could easily grant Manuel Puig or Guillermo Cabrera Infante the fifth floating seat. Beyond these two traits—commitment to one or another form of modernism and literary celebrity—support for the Cuban Revolution is the common link among these writers.

7.  Gilman notes, "One of the conceptual particularities of the time is that the formula progressive intellectual implied a redundancy. . . . In other words, what could not be considered, except as a social aberration or a thought experiment, was the notion that a reactionary intellectual deserved to be considered an intellectual" (57).

8.  This stress on the importance of the Cuban Revolution as central to bringing together the four main Boom writers should not be seen as synonymous with arguing that "the new Latin American novel is the ouvre of the Cuban revolution," a position criticized by Rafael Rojas in

the introduction to *La polis literaria*. In fact, all four writers had written important works before they met each other and would continue writing after they no longer held common political positions. The importance of the Cuban Revolution for the "new Latin American novel" is that it helped bring together writers, such as the four core Boom authors, who would otherwise have no doubt developed brilliant careers on their own.

9. Vargas Llosa had criticized the Cuban government's support for the Soviet Union's intervention in Czechoslovakia in 1968 in his article "Socialism and the Tanks," where he noted that "it is distressing to see Fidel reacting in the same conditioned and reflexive way as the mediocre leaders of the Latin American Communist parties who rushed to justify the Soviet intervention" (83). I have argued in *Mario Vargas Llosa: Public Intellectual in Neoliberal Latin America* that, despite its public statement of support for the Cuban Revolution, Vargas Llosa's reception speech for the Rómulo Gallegos Award—"Literature Is Fire"—can be seen as an implicit criticism of the growing repressiveness of the Cuban government.

10. The centrality of Cuba was brought to the awareness of the mostly apolitical Donoso by Carlos Fuentes, who, at least in the Chilean novelist's telling, was the main catalyst in the transformation of the Boom writers into a coherent literary group. Writing about his first meeting with Fuentes in 1962, Donoso reminisces: "The most important thing that Carlos Fuentes told me . . . was that after the Cuban Revolution he agreed only to talk of politics, never of literature and that now Latin America could only look toward Cuba" (48).

11. The "Padilla affair," which had been simmering since 1968, when Heberto Padilla's poetry collection *Fuera del juego* was banned, exploded in March 1971 when Padilla and his wife, Belkis Cuza Malé, were jailed. For a detailed narration of this event and its political and cultural contexts, see Gilman 209–18 and 235–63.

12. However, the Casa de las Américas group would capitulate as early as 1969. On the growing cultural rigidity of the Cuban Revolution, see Gilman, especially chapter 5, "Cuba, patria del antiintelectual latinoamericano" (189–231).

13. When Celia de la Serna, Che Guevara's mother, had to stay in Paris on her way back to Argentina from Cuba, she stayed in Vargas Llosa's apartment, exemplifying the novelist's closeness to the Cuban regime. (The roundabout route was due to the blockade suffered by the island.) On this episode, see Vargas Llosa's "The Death of Che," 296–97.

14. In the introduction to his *La polis literaria*, Rafael Rojas traces the beginnings of the disagreements between the Boom and the Cuban

revolution back to 1965. The reason for this early date, which refers to the establishment of the Cuban Communist Party as the only political party on the island, is that Rojas stresses the role of Cuban writers, such as Guillermo Cabrera Infante, in his definition of the Boom. Regardless of whatever reservations our four authors may have about the growing political rigidity of the Cuban Revolution, they expanded their collaboration with the revolution during these same years. As Rojas notes, Vargas Llosa joined the Comité de Colaboración (collaborative committee) of the Casa de las Américas in 1965. (Cortázar was already a member.)

15. According to van Delden and Grenier, "In the mid-1970s, Vargas Llosa declared for the first time that the Soviet Union and Cuba did not represent the socialist ideal in which he still believed. One had to wait a few more years (until 1979, according to Kristal) to see him disavow his socialist convictions" (197). On Vargas Llosa's break with the Cuban Revolution, also see my *Mario Vargas Llosa: Public Intellectual in Neoliberal Latin America* (5–6, 10–11, 32–36).

16. This passage is not found in the version of "The Trumpet of Deya" included in *Making Waves*, nor is it found in the original Spanish-language version published in *El País* on 28 July 1991, though it is included in the longer version published in 1993 by Vargas Llosa in *Vuelta* 25 and published in translation in *Review of Contemporary Fiction* in 1997.

17. In Spanish in Orloff.

18. Despite the fact that his next novel, *62: A Model Kit* (1968) will radicalize Cortázar's literary experimentations even further, the Argentine writer expressed his growing identification with the Cuban Revolution in "Meeting" (1964), a brief short story first published in *Verde Olivo*, the magazine of the Cuban revolutionary forces. Inspired by Ernesto "Che" Guevara's *Reminiscences of the Cuban Revolutionary War* (1963) and in response to what the Boom novelist considered to be its "literary poverty" (qtd. in Orloff 123), Cortázar tells the story of the landing of the Granma in 1956. Narrated by a Che Guevara–like character, it explicitly compares Luis—the military name used for the Fidel Castro character—with Mozart. In this manner, it folds politics into art and thus avoids dealing with the social and cultural contexts that made the Cuban Revolution possible. In an ironic twist, "after talking to Che Guevara about 'Reunión,' [Fernández] Retamar informed Cortázar that Guevara had not rated the story very highly, Cortázar was altogether quite disappointed (not to say vexed)." (Orloff 123n3). However, the story's confluence of politics with art seems to foreshadow the

connections Cortázar established between high art and revolution. That said, the vast majority of his stories continue to follow the ludic and metafictional patterns dominant in his writing.

19. In her reading of Castro's "Words to Intellectuals," Diana Sorensen notes: "The move toward the suppression of freedom of expression is a well-known chapter in the history of contemporary Cuba: as early as 1961 Fidel Castro's speech 'Palabra a los intelectuales' marked the limits of what was acceptable within the cultural field, dictating a singular and stable vision" (11). However, interpretations in the 1960s of Castro's words emphasized the manner in which the Cuban Revolution broke with the earlier Soviet imposition of socialist realism as the only acceptable literary and artistic mode.

20. Cortázar's next and final novel, *A Manual for Manuel* (1973), deals explicitly with radical politics.

21. Cortázar's text "Viaje alrededor de una mesa" frames his presentation at Amérique Latine Non-officielle with comments about the audience's anti-intellectual politics.

22. Two of Peru's most important guerrilla movements of the decade— the Ejército de Liberación Nacional, led by Héctor Béjar, and the Movimiento de Izquierda Revolucionaria, led by Luis Felipe de la Puente—were defeated in 1965. That year, Paul Escobar, a militant of the MIR and close friend of Vargas Llosa, was killed by the army. Vargas Llosa memorialized Escobar in his essay "In Normandy, Remembering Paul Escobar" and in passages of his novel *The Bad Girl.*

23. The articles were collected under the title *Literatura en la revolución y revolución en la literatura* and published in book form in 1970.

24. Cortázar is here echoing a famous moment in Tomás Gutiérrez Alea's film *Memories of Underdevelopment* (1968). In it, real-life playwright Jack Gelber addresses a round table that includes Edmundo Desnoes and Mario Tronti, asking, "Why is it that if the Cuban Revolution is a total revolution, they have to resort to an archaic form of discussion such as a round table?" (Gutiérrez Alea and Desnoes 77).

25. Writing about these innovative works of art, Cortázar argues: "Now, this work—and this is where the misunderstanding of many revolutionary readers and politicians resides—if it truly merits the title of creation, it adds new mental or sensorial conquests to the patrimony we leave to the new man, [if this is the case], it is always in discord with its time. This is the discord in which a Van Gogh, who never sold one of his paintings that today are worth millions, lived; this is the discord in which a Schoenberg, a James Joyce, or a Mayakovsky lived. The more

revolutionary a work, the more it is ahead of its time" ("Viaje alrededor de una mesa" 12).

26. In his *La vuelta al día en 80 mundos*, a collection of short essays, reviews, and other miscellanea, published the same year as the panel (1970), Cortázar explicitly distances Borges's writings from his political ideas by criticizing those who dismiss the author of *The Aleph* precisely from a "committed" perspective similar to that expressed by the attendees of "América Latina no oficial": "I once decided to waste a night at San Martín and Corrientes or in a café at Saint-German-des-Prés, and I spent my time listening to some Argentine writers and readers set sail on that [literary] current they consider 'committed' and that consists roughly in being 'authentic' (?), in facing reality (?) in eliminating all Borgesian Byzantinism (thus hypocritically solving their inferiority before Borges's best work by means of the usual fallacy of using his sorry political or social aberrations to diminish a work that has no connection with these)" (158). Cortázar expands on these ideas in his "Literatura en la revolución, revolución en la literatura," adding: "I consider myself committed to and face to face with reality, but at a level in which any judgment on the works of Borges requires Borgesian tools, in other words, the highest level of intelligence and the most implacable rigor" (46).

27. It is well-known that the third signer of the manifesto, Diego Rivera, had no significant participation in its composition (see Selz 457–58n1). By 1938, Trotsky, having been expelled from Turkey, France, and Norway, had found his final sanctuary in Mexico, where he would be assassinated on Stalin's order in 1949.

28. Where I have translated "page," Cortázar used the word *hoja*, which can mean both page and leaf.

29. "How close and bright would the future appear if two, three, many Vietnams flowered on the face of the globe" (Guevara, "Create Two, Three, Many Vietnams" 361).

30. Perhaps the most complete reading of the issues on stage in the debate between Cortázar and Arguedas is found in Mabel Moraña's "Territorialidad y forasterismo." As Moraña notes about the two writers: "Each one represented the well-known traits of their respective cultural areas: the Eurocentric cosmopolitanism, joyfully *light* . . . and the tormented and militant localism of the Peruvian" (148–49).

31. Vargas Llosa's concept of the "demons" would be fully fleshed out in his dissertation on Gabriel García Márquez: *García Márquez: Historia de un deicidio*, the founding critical study on the author of *One Hundred Years of Solitude*. There he writes: "*Why* a novelist writes is viscerally

imbricated with *what* she writes about: the 'demons' in her life are the subject matter of her work. The 'demons': events, persons, myths, whose presence or absence, whose life or death, lead her toward enmity with reality. They became imprinted in her memory and torment her spirit. They become the matter of her enterprise to rebuild reality. She will simultaneously attempt to recuperate and exorcise them, with words and fantasy, in the exercise of the vocation that was born and nourished with them. She will do so in fictions in which they, hidden or explicitly, omnipresent or secret, appear and reappear transformed into 'subject matter'" (183).

32. Vargas Llosa's frequent reference to Balzac as the example of a conservative who writes "critical realist" literature may be influenced by the example of Marx, who, according to Paul Lafargue, "admired Balzac so much that he wished to write a review of his great work *La Comedie Humaine* as soon as he had finished his book on economics. He considered Balzac not only as the historian of his time, but as the prophetic creator of characters which were still in the embryo in the days of Louis Philippe and did not fully develop until Napoleon III."

33. A significantly revised version of "Novela primitiva y novela de creación en América Latina" was translated into English and published as "The Latin American Novel Today" in the respected journal *Books Abroad* in 1970.

34. As should be obvious, Vargas Llosa's and the Boom's disparaging of their Latin American predecessors as "primitive" must be seen both as a case of Bloomian parricide and as a way of clearing the ground for the reception of the then-new Latin American novel without the preconceptions created by the earlier realist novels.

35. Vargas Llosa's treatment of José María Arguedas in both essays is of interest given the polemic between Arguedas and Cortázar that was taking place at the time. In "Novela primitiva y novela de creación en América Latina," after praising Guimarães Rosa's *The Devil to Pay in the Backlands*, Vargas Llosa writes about Arguedas's *Deep Rivers*: "Ambiguity (a distinctive human trait that the primitive novel ignored) also characterizes *Deep Rivers*. . . . Although, among the new writers, he is the one closest to the patterns of the primitive novel, Arguedas does not incur its most obvious defects because he does not attempt to photograph the indigenous world (which he knows in depth). Instead, he tries to place the reader within it" (32). There is, however, no mention of José María Arguedas in the revised version published in *Books Abroad*.

36. After the award was made public, Cuban novelist and diplomat Alejo Carpentier made known to Vargas Llosa the suggestion that Haydeé

Santamaría, the director of the principal Cuban cultural institution Casa de las Américas, had made that Vargas Llosa publicly donate the money to Che Guevara's guerrilla movement while privately being reimbursed by the Cuban government. Vargas Llosa's Rómulo Gallegos Award speech, "Literature Is Fire," expresses his nascent doubts regarding the Cuban Revolution (see my *Mario Vargas Llosa: Public Intellectual in Neoliberal Latin America* 47–50).

37. It should be clear, however, that while Vargas Llosa in 1970 provides a sui generis version of the new critical "intentional fallacy," it is less clear that he believes in the "affective fallacy," the notion that the interpretation of the text should disregard its emotional effects on the reader.

38. According to Raymond Leslie Williams, Fuentes "was among the very first foreign intellectuals to arrive in Cuba when the revolution triumphed: on January 2, 1959, Fuentes, Fernando Benitez and Manuel Becerra Acosta were on a Mexicana Airlines flight for Havana at the same time that Fidel Castro rode triumphantly in a jeep from Santiago to the Cuban capital. Fuentes, upon arriving, found a 'great jubilation' in Havana, as the populace celebrated the revolution. The three Mexicans experienced an intense week of the Cuban Revolution, watching the celebrations and festivities, meeting with Fidel Castro, and lending their support" (*The Writings of Carlos Fuentes* 28). Fuentes has also written about his personal relationship with the Cuban Revolution; see "Cuba's Paradise Lost."

39. According to van Delden: "Fuentes's relationship with the Cuban Revolution did not remain unaffected by the attack of the Cuban intellectuals. In a letter he wrote to Fernando Benitez in February 1967, Fuentes stated that he was prepared to go to Cuba 'to demonstrate my permanent solidarity with the Cuban Revolution,' but the trip was never made. In the 'Cronología personal' Fuentes wrote in 1995 . . . he describes the methods used by the Cuban intellectuals in their attack on Neruda and him as Stalinist, and states that from this moment on he did not return to Cuba. Yet the difference between Fuentes's two assessments (in 1967 and 1995) of the imbroglio with the Cubans reveals a significant shift in Fuentes's position. On both occasions. Fuentes emphatically deplores what he regards as the misguided response of the Cubans to the presence of Neruda and himself at the New York PEN meeting. In 1967, however, Fuentes's primary concern is to emphasize his solidarity with the Cuban Revolution. By 1995 the value of solidarity takes a back seat to the value of pluralism" (50).

40. According to García Márquez scholar Gene Bell-Villada, "A highly self-conscious and sophisticated artist and a master stylist, he seldom comments on purely literary matters and is supremely bored with aesthetics, criticism, or theory" (14). Likewise, as Gilman notes, "There were also cases of writers who did not occupy the position of intellectual, even if it seems questionable: it is the case of García Márquez throughout this period" (58).

41. We will analyze Vargas Llosa's versions of totality in the second section of this chapter.

42. Vargas Llosa and García Márquez first met at Caracas's Maiquetía Airport when they were there to attend the Rómulo Gallegos award ceremonies for Vargas Llosa. They had, however, corresponded earlier on literary and personal topics. On this first personal encounter of both future Nobel Prize winners and their activities during and after Rómulo Gallegos events, see Esteban and Gallegos's *De Gabo a Mario* 47–60.

43. Vargas Llosa's misrepresentation of Aureliano Buendía is surprising given that the Peruvian novelist is the author of *García Márquez: Historia de un deicidio* (1971), the first major study on García Márquez and his oeuvre, including *One Hundred Years of Solitude*.

44. There are, however, two unflattering references to anarchism. The first is by implication. Doctor Alirio Noguera, who plays a role in organizing the *liberal* resistance against the *conservador* government, is described as "a charlatan. Behind his innocent façade of a doctor without prestige there was hidden a terrorist" (*One Hundred Years of Solitude* 97). He developed a plot "in which in one master stroke covering the whole nation would liquidate the functionaries of the regime along with their respective families, especially the children, in order to exterminate Conservatism at its roots" (98–99). Later, Fernanda, who represents colonial values in the novel, describes her union activist brother-in-law José Arcadio II as an "anarchist in the family" (207), and later expresses the fear that her grandson Aureliano Babilonia "had inherited the anarchist ideas of Colonel Aureliano Buendía and told him to be quiet" (348). However, if Alirio Noguera is presented in a manner that repeats early twentieth-century stereotypes of the "anarchist" as a mass murderer without even using the word, Fernanda's pejorative use of the word *anarchist* reflects her own ultramontane ideology.

45. According to James Higgins, "While in strictly chronological terms the events of the novel roughly span the century from the years after Independence to around 1930, the early phase of Macondo's history evokes Latin America's colonial period, when communities lived isolated

from one another and the viceroyalties themselves had little contact with the distant metropolis" (70). Higgins's chronology is, however, problematized by the references in the novel to García Márquez himself and his bohemian writer friends, known collectively as the "Barranquilla group": "Aureliano [the last of the Buendía's] continued getting together in the afternoon with the four arguers, whose names were Álvaro, Germán, Alfonso, and Gabriel, the first and last friends that he ever had in his life" (388). As Higgins himself notes, García Márquez "was to render homage to this so-called Barranquilla Group by portraying them in the latter pages of *Cien años de soledad*" (64). This would place the ending of the novel in the 1950s. However, in addition to this "realistic" chronology—from the second third of the nineteenth century to the 1930s or mid-twentieth century—the novel also implies that the narrative takes place from the beginning of humanity to its end (at least in Macondo). From when "the world was so recent that many things lacked names, and in order to indicate them it was necessary to point" to when "Macondo was already a fearful whirlwind of dust and rubble being spun about by the wrath of the biblical hurricane" (García Márquez, *One Hundred Years of Solitude* 1, 416). What could be called the "magical reality effect" is to a great degree constructed from the simultaneous presence of divergent chronologies not only in their temporality—from the colonial foundation to the (near) present and, at the same time from the 1830s to the 1930s or 1950s—but also in their epistemological ground—myth and history.

46. "In this America of small revolutions, the same word, revolution, frequently lends itself to misunderstanding. We have to reclaim it rigorously and intransigently. We have to restore its strict and exact meaning. The Latin American Revolution will be nothing more and less than a stage, a phase of world revolution. It will simply and clearly be the socialist revolution. Add all the adjectives you want to this word according to a particular case: 'anti-imperialist,' 'agrarian,' 'national revolutionary.' Socialism supposes, precedes, and includes all of them" (Mariátegui, "Anniversary and Balance Sheet" 128).

47. Although one could easily establish points of contact between *liberales* and contemporary liberalism—whether in its US or European definitions—and between *conservadores* and contemporary conservatism, I have decided to keep the names of the nineteenth-century political tendencies in order to avoid confusion between these and current political movements.

48. There is debate among critics regarding which was the first novel of the Boom. Some, such as Carlos Granés and Juan José Armas, grant that

position to Vargas Llosa's *The Time of the Hero* (1963), a novel that as
the winner of the Seix Barral award received pan-Hispanic coverage
and distribution (Aguilar Sosa). One could also make a case for either
Fuentes's *The Death of Artemio Cruz* or his earlier *Where the Air Is Clear*
(1958). Vargas Llosa, to his credit, has argued that Fuentes's first novel
"announced the boom" (De Llano). The main argument against the
Peruvian Nobel Prize laureate's claim would be that *Where the Air Is
Clear* was published four years before the Boom could realistically be
seen as a group of writers and a collection of texts. After all, in 1962
and 1963 Fuentes, Vargas Llosa, and Cortázar all published their most
characteristic novels.

49. In *One Hundred Years of Solitude*, García Márquez modifies Colonel
Gavilán's character. In *The Death of Artemio Cruz*, Gavilán later becomes
apparently as much of an arriviste as Artemio Cruz, being among the
former followers of General Obregón who end up supporting President
Calles, who had had Obregón killed (Fuentes 124, 130). In *One
Hundred Years of Solitude*, Gavilán is a loyal union leader who is one of
the many disappeared by the government at the behest of the American
fruit company (300, 305).

50. Van Delden has noted the impact of the Cuban Revolution on Carlos
Fuentes: "In his political commentaries, Fuentes makes constant use
of unified categories—such as the notion of 'the people'—and appeals
repeatedly to a utopian vision of a disalienated society—for which Cuba
under the new revolutionary regime provides the model" (*Carlos Fuentes,
Mexico, and Modernity* 52).

51. Beckett's *Krapp's Last Tape*, a monologue built through the playing of
taped recordings, was first performed in 1958.

52. Many critics have noted that the novel seems to link Artemio with the
conquistadors and even the Aztecs. For instance, Robin Fiddian notes,
"In complicated ways, Cruz stands for all three terms in the equation
Spain + Anáhuac = Mexico. He is portrayed as a conquistador setting
foot on Mexico's Gulf Coast at Veracruz, like Cortés in a famous mural
painted by Diego Rivera. A New World Atlas, he carries on his shoulders
the whole of Mexican antiquity, including its landscapes, languages,
customs and civilisations" (130).

53. Fuentes's novel appears to be critical of the anarchists. The novel
notes about a friend of Lorenzo, Artemio's son: "Miguel criticized the
anarchists because, he said, they were defeatists" (*Death of Artemio Cruz*
229).

54. Van Delden has convincingly argued that Lorenzo's relationship with
the Spanish Republican partisan Dolores, which is frustrated because

of his death, constitutes an updated version of Sommer's national romance: "I think Sommer overstates the extent to which Fuentes in *Artemio Cruz* departs from his precursors, for the story of Lorenzo reveals how Fuentes continues to rely on romance as a way of imagining a political community. Thus, the encounter between Lorenzo and Dolores represents the rapprochement between Mexico and Spain—and so, in a broader sense, between Mexico and its Hispanic heritage—that resulted from the Mexican government's support for the Republic during the Spanish Civil War. The fact that the political community Fuentes imagines in *Artemio Cruz* with the help of Lorenzo and Dolores is not a *national* community does not diminish the novel's links with the tradition described by Sommer" (*Carlos Fuentes, Mexico and Modernity* 59).

55. Among many possible quotations that exemplify the Nietzschean basis of Sebastián's lessons, the following from Nietzche's *The Anti-Christ* is pertinent: "Let us not underestimate the fact that *we ourselves*, we free spirits already constitute a 'revaluation of all values,' a *living* declaration of war and victory over all old concepts of 'true' and 'untrue'" (11).

56. Although the role of Sebastián in Artemio Cruz's political and moral development has not received enough attention among scholars, the few who have studied it tend to agree with Roberto Cantú's description of his role: "Artemio moves from a pastoral existence in his native Cocuya, and from the idealism stemming from literacy and radicalism learned from don Sebastián in Mexico City, to his participation in the 1910 Mexican Revolution, followed by his progressive greed and corruption. In his rise and fall, Artemio mirrors the history of post-Revolutionary Mexico and its possibilities for immense fortunes made by a few" (11). What these readings do not consider is Nietzsche's well-known aversion to any and all revolutionary movements. For instance, in *The Anti-Christ* he denounces "the socialist rabble, the Chandala-apostles who undermine workers' instincts and pleasures, their feelings of modesty about their little existences,—who make them jealous, who teach them revenge" (60). Nietzsche is not only opposed to socialism but at any attempt at progressive social change: "Wrong never lies in unequal rights; it lies in the assertion of equal rights" (60).

57. Ironically, van Delden's stress on the need to keep the Cuban Revolution in mind as both the context for Fuentes's unsparing depiction of the Mexican Revolution and its aftermath, as well as the fulfillment of the promise of the Cuban Revolution, is in reaction to what he considers Martin's too-negative interpretation of *The Death of Artemio Cruz* (60).

58. In a presentation at the New School, Mariano Siskind provided an example of the kinds of readings that can be provided today to the ending of *One Hundred Years of Solitude*. After describing 1960s "Latin Americanist" readings of García Márquez's novel—represented above by Gerald Martin's reference to the Cuban Revolution as necessary to an understanding of the text—Siskind notes: "Instead, I would like to suggest a dystopian interpretation . . . with the potential to re-inscribe Gabriel García Márquez's novel as a global novel about the end of the world today, that speaks to our own experience of the end of the world, today, in Donald Trump's world of ecological catastrophes, refugee crises and the death of liberal democracy." He then adds: "Žižek famously wrote that it is easier for contemporary Western culture to imagine the end of the world than it is to imagine the end of capitalism. Read today, in the middle of our own perfect storm of ends of the world, I think the final pages of Gabriel García Márquez's novel can be read as one of Žižek's dystopian novels that announce the end of something that may be too magical and too alternatively modern to be identified with the logic of capital, but . . . it is not at all entirely strange with its history. The important difference with the Latin Americanist, post-Cuban interpretation is that we cannot see anything . . . after the destruction of Macondo and the Buendías, there's no room in our own context of reception to read in that apocalyptic wind the inauguration of a post-capitalist, self-reconciled world. All I can read in those final sentences is perhaps too literal but nevertheless insightful: there is no hereafter, the end is the end, and the end of the world is nothing but the end of the world, no 'second opportunity on earth'; and nothing more akin to our experience of end of times today, than Aureliano Babilonia reading about his own demise as it takes place in real time. Just like us reading today's paper."

59. According to Mark Anderson, "Vargas Llosa appears to have borrowed his terminology from Franco-Lithuanian novelist Romain Gary, who opposed the 'roman total' (total novel) to the 'roman totalitaire' (totalitarian novel). . . . Gary developed many of the key concepts that resurface in Vargas Llosa's reflections on the total novel, including: those concepts regarding the autonomy of art from ideological stances . . . and that the novelist 'plays God' within this fictional world" (202).

60. In his *García Márquez: Historia de un deicidio*, Vargas Llosa seems to stress the self-contained nature of *One Hundred Years of Solitude* as what defines it as a total novel: "It is a total novel in its subject matter to the degree that it describes a self-contained world, from its birth to its death, in all the orders that compose it—individual and collective,

legendary and historical, day to day, and mythic. And [it is a total novel] in its form, since its writing and structure, the way its subject matter is crystalized, have an exclusive nature, unrepeatable and self-sufficient" (479–80).

61. The "total" character of the best novels of the Boom is one of the reasons these writers were often seen as the central intellectuals of their time. As Nicholas Birns indicates, these texts included political, historical, and even philosophical reflection. Moreover, with the always-important exception of García Márquez, the Boom novelists continued their "total" intellectual activity outside their narrative by writing books of criticism, political commentary, and so on.

62. Although presented in positive terms, Marcos's evaluation of *One Hundred Years of Solitude* closely resembles Alberto Fuguet and Sergio Gómez's McOndian criticism of the García Márquez novel—and magical realism as a whole—because "to sell the continent as rural, when, in truth, it is urban . . . seems to us abhorrent, easy, and immoral" (18).

63. Taking the risk of making too much of what obviously was an improvised answer, it may be worth noting that core Boom author Cortázar is not mentioned in Marcos's list ("Subcomandante Marcos"). Even if Vargas Llosa includes *Hopscotch* in his list of paradigmatic total novels, the fact is that the world described by the Argentine novelist in *Hopscotch* is much less rooted in local Latin American experience. (As is well-known, the novel is set in Paris and in very specific and idiosyncratic locales in Buenos Aires—a tenement, a circus, and an insane asylum.) In this novel, Cortázar therefore does not share in Fuentes's, García Márquez's, and Vargas Llosa's attempts at presenting a cognitive map of significant geographical, historical, and intellectual regions of Latin America.

64. According to Sánchez López, Cabrera Infante was excluded from *Libre* at Cortázar's insistence. Cortázar's opposition to Cabrera Infante's participation was in response to negative public statements the Cuban author had made regarding the Argentine author's public comments on the "Padilla affair." On Cortázar's and Cabrera Infante's relationship at the time, see Sánchez López's *La emancipación engañosa*, 155, and "El proyecto literario y politico de la revista *Libre*," 31.

65. According to Gerald Martin: "On 12 February 1976 . . . he turned up at the premiere of a film version of *Survivors of the Andes*. As he arrived, Mario Vargas Llosa, in town for the event . . . was standing in the foyer. Gabo opened his arms and exclaimed, 'Brother!' Without a word Mario . . . floored him with one mighty blow to the face. With García Márquez semi-conscious on the ground, having struck his head as he fell,

Mario then shouted, depending on the source: 'That's for what you said to Patricia.' Or: 'That's for what you did to Patricia.' This was to become the most famous punch in the history of Latin America, still the subject of avid speculation to this day. There were many eyewitnesses and there are many versions not only of what actually happened but why" (*Gabriel García Márquez* 389).

66. Vargas Llosa's essays—most first published as part of the series of widely read biweekly journalistic essays disseminated under the general heading of "Piedra de toque" (Touchstone)—provide a clear record of his evolution. I have studied Vargas Llosa's political development and its impact in his literature in *Mario Vargas Llosa: Public Intellectual in Neoliberal Latin America*.

67. In Spanish the quotation from Cortazar's "Policrítica en la hora de los chacales" is as follows: "Tienes razón Fidel: sólo en la brega hay derecho al / Descontento, / Sólo de adentro ha de salir la crítica, la búsqueda de fórmulas / Mejores, / Sí, pero de adentro es tan afuera a veces, / Y si hoy me aparto para siempre del liberal a la violeta, de los / que firman los virtuosos textos" (34). Orloff, who has studied Cortázar's political evolution and activity, notes: "From the text it seems clear that Cortázar did not want to fall out with Castro or with Cuban readers. To that effect, he reduces the 'episode' to a 'crisis barata' [cheap crisis], ending the poem: 'Oye compadre, olvida tanta *crisis barata*. Empecemos de nuevo [ . . . ] / nunca estuve tan cerca / como ahora de lejos, contra viento y marea. El día nace'" (157n5). (Hey, buddy, forget so much cheap crisis / Let's start over [ . . . ] / I never was as close / as now, from afar, against wind and tide. The day is born). The poem achieved only in part the Argentine writer's goal of reconciling with the Cuban revolutionaries. As Orloff notes, "Cortázar became a figure of suspicion for many Cubans, especially in light of some of the articles that he wrote for the French press in defense of Padilla. In Padilla's own opinion, the suspicion that Cortázar now aroused in Cuba was the main reason why *Libro de Manuel* was never published or distributed in the island" (158).

68. In 1996, García Márquez spoke about his role as unofficial adviser to Fidel Castro: "I could not even tell you myself exactly how many prisoners and dissidents I have helped, completely anonymously, leave Cuba during the last twenty years. Many of them don't even know it and the ones who do are enough to keep my conscience at peace" (qtd. in Esteban and Panichelli 302–3).

69. Despite the fact that Vargas Llosa's own post-1960s novels seem to reflect the changes he himself describes, the Peruvian Nobelist has been somewhat critical of the evolution experienced by Latin American

narrative since the heyday of the Boom: "Another consequence of the evolution toward democracy is that Latin America's literature has progressively become depoliticized. Among young writers there is somewhat of a rejection toward the kind of literary commitment that used to be vindicated in our continent due to the repression and lack of freedom we experienced. It's one of the signs of the times. . . . It could be that another of the consequences of this depolitization is the mix of fantasy and autobiography in which the author becomes a character: autofiction" (qtd. in Rodríguez Marcos).

## *Chapter 3*

1. Writing in 1987 about Spanish American narrative in the twentieth century, Lucille Kerr notes: "From the early texts of Borges (perhaps the most European of the Spanish American writers, he is the writer whose eye has been fixed on European literature and philosophy for over fifty years now) to those of a novelist like Puig (perhaps one of the most 'popular' of Spanish American writer, he is the writer whose eye, fixed as it is on various forms of popular culture, is engaged in a unique way by Spanish American quotidian reality), the Spanish Americans have displayed a special interest in the problems of language and literature" (3). One could describe the type of narrative currently dominant in the region as fixing its eye on various forms of North American and European popular culture.

2. Chilean novelists Alberto Fuguet and Sergio Gómez note: "Latin America is irremediably MTV Latina, that hallucinating consensus, that flux that colonizes our conscience through cable" (16). Fuguet's work is an example of this influence. His breakthrough novel *Mala Onda* (1991) includes references to specific pop and rock songs such as Olivia Newton John's "Xanadu" and Queen's "Another One Bites the Dust," as well as to such diverse US and British musicians as Billy Joel, Jim Croce, Michelle Philips (of the Mamas and the Papas), Syd Barrett (of Pink Floyd), Anne Murray, and even Ray Conniff.

3. Barnet's poem would inspire the title and lyrics of a well-known song by Cuban troubadour Pablo Milanés, "Si el poeta eres tú" (The poet is you), first recorded in 1971 on an LP that also includes songs by Silvio Rodríguez and Noel Nicola. In the song, Milanés acknowledges the impact of Barnet's poem in the first line of the lyrics of the song: "As the poet said, the poet is you" (30).

4. As we saw in the previous section, *Libre* was a magazine created collaboratively by Vargas Llosa, Juan Goytisolo, Julio Cortázar, and many

of the major Hispanophone writers of the time in reaction to the Padilla affair and the general hardening of Cuban and, more generally, leftist culture. Despite the extraordinary quality of its collaborators, it only published four volumes during 1971 and 1972 before folding.

5. Crenzel notes about Argentina, "While human rights organizations place the total number of enforced disappearances at 30,000, the official count as of 2010 is 9,334 disappeared persons. . . . Another 12,890 people were jailed for political reasons, 2,286 were openly killed, and an estimated 250,000, in a population of 25 million, were forced into exile" (2). He adds: "In Chile, the victims were distributed differently. Following the coup, 2,000 people were sentenced to death by military courts and killed in extrajudicial executions or by application of the ley de fuga (fugitive law), another 1,200 were disappeared, 200,000 were forced into exile, 50,000 people were arrested and tortured, and 100,000 were fired from their jobs for political reasons" (2). Finally, "In Uruguay, an estimated 250,000 people were exiled, while 116 people were murdered, 172 were forcefully disappeared (the majority in Argentina), and 60,000 were arrested and jailed as long-term political prisoners" (2).

6. For a detailed study of Vargas Llosa's political evolution, see my *Mario Vargas Llosa: Public Intellectual in Neoliberal Latin America*, esp. 21–60; and the "Introduction" to *Vargas Llosa and Latin American Politics*, cowritten with Nicholas Birns.

7. In his memoir, *A Fish in the Water*, Vargas Llosa reminisces about his early collaborations with Hernando de Soto: "De Soto had organized in Lima, in 1979 and 1982, two international symposia to which he brought a roster of economists and thinkers—Hayek, Friedman, Jean-François Revel, and Hugh Thomas . . . I had collaborated with Hernando in staging these events, speaking at both, and helped him set up the Instituto Libertad y Democracia, closely followed his studies on the informal economy" (172).

8. In his "Elogio de la dama de hierro" (In praise of the Iron Lady), published in 1990, Vargas Llosa claims to feel for her "an admiration without reserves, an almost filial reverence, that I haven't felt for any other living politician, but which I've felt for many intellectual and artists (like Popper, Faulkner or Borges)" (12).

9. In *Temptation of the Word*, Kristal thanks "Mr. Vargas Llosa who graciously read a draft of this book" (xv). Even more relevant to our study, Kristal notes, Vargas Llosa's "most important correction involves *The Real Life of Alejandro Mayta*. I had the intuition that the novel had something to do with Joseph Conrad's depiction of the political fanatic

in . . . *The Secret Agent*. Mr. Vargas Llosa . . . suggested that I reread *Under Western Eyes*" (xv).

10. According to Rybalka: "This novel is thus at the same the quest for a character lost in the labyrinth of history and a quest for the meaning of time (seen as perpetual crisis); the closest equivalents I have found for it in terms of technique and content are the film *Citizen Kane* by Orson Welles and the novel *La Nuit du Décret* by Michel Del Castillo" (128)

11. O'Bryan-Knight also includes *Aunt Julia and the Scriptwriter* and *The Storyteller* among Vargas Llosa's "postmodern" novels. A similar point is made by M. Keith Booker in his suggestively titled *Vargas Llosa among the Postmodernists*: "If one adopts Brian McHale's suggestion that postmodernist fiction is principally concerned with the exploration of such ontological issues [i.e., the distinction between fiction and reality], then *Mayta* is a quintessentially post-modernist work" (101–2). However, Booker adds an important distinction: "On the other hand, the fact that the book is structured around the epistemological inquiries of the narrator into Mayta's past (inquiries that McHale would see as central to modernism) suggests that the distinction between epistemology and ontology by which McHale differentiates between modernism and postmodernism is unsteady at best" (102).

12. In his *Notes on the Death of a Culture*, Vargas Llosa criticizes Derrida, de Man, and other like-minded thinkers. According to the Peruvian novelist: "To break down some linguistic structure, whose assembly is seen, in the best of cases, as an intense formal nothingness, a verbose and narcissistic arbitrary work that teaches nothing about anything except itself, and which lacks any moral consequence, is to turn literary criticism into a gratuitous and solipsistic undertaking" (85). I have dealt at length with Vargas Llosa's opposition to postmodern literary and cultural theory in *Mario Vargas Llosa: Public Intellectual in Neoliberal Latin America* (93–108).

13. While Vallejos is described as being part of the military, he is a lieutenant in the Guardia Republicana, which guarded official buildings and prisons and provided border security. It was dissolved in 1988. Its functions are currently fulfilled by the Policía Nacional.

14. One cannot but be surprised by the absence of any reference to José Carlos Mariátegui, the iconic Peruvian Marxist of the 1920s, in the novel. On Mariátegui, see the first chapter of this study.

15. The information about Jacinto Rentería, Vicente Mayta, and Francisco Vallejos comes from Ángel Páez's "Vargas Llosa salvado por el periodismo."

16. I say "supposedly Maoist" since, as Iván Degregori argues: "But at the same time, within that great We some are more equal than others. The cosmocrat is one whose ego is exalted through a personality cult of unprecedented precocity in the history of the communist movement. Let us consider some examples. In the 'Bases for Discussion' elaborated for the First Congress and published in *El Diario* in 1988, the chapters are not presented as the decisions of a collective—whether the Central Committee or the Politburo—in keeping with Leninist tradition or the more general practice of political parties, but as the 'teachings of President Gonzalo.' Strangest of all, since the early 1980s militants had to sign a 'letter of submission,' not to the party or to the 'revolutionary line' but to President Gonzalo and his thought" (88).

17. There were, however, harbingers of what was to come. Journalist Ana Núñez reminisces: "One of the most 'memorable' blackouts . . . was on 3 December, 1982. [Shining Path leader] Abimael Guzmán Reinoso's birthday was used by the Shining Path as an excuse to plunge Lima and Callao for three hours into chaos and terror. The Shining Path blew up electrical towers in San Juan de Miraflores, Ñaña and Morón, and to top off its feat it used bonfires to form the shape of the hammer and sickle on the San Cristobal hill [overlooking downtown Lima]." Steve Stern notes: "Shining Path's expansion, which emphasized rural populations in accord with Maoist strategy of war and revolution, did not remain confined to the highlands. Eventually, the encirclement and strangulation of Lima would have to follow. In 1989, Shining Path declared it had reached 'strategic equilibrium.' By 1990–92, the war reached directly into metropolitan Lima, through a combined campaign of penetration of shantytown communities, including assassination of grassroots leaders, and select bombings in prosperous districts to inspire terror" (5).

18. For instance, according to Javier Navascués, "The portrayal bursts abruptly into the story and it couldn't be more negative: at the hands of Vargas Llosa, the historical figure of the Nicaraguan poet, politician, and priest becomes that of an insincere and histrionic caricature" (162).

19. Even such a precise and lucid critic as Deborah Cohn ascribes the violence portrayed in *The Real Life of Alejandro Mayta* to the Shining Path throughout her otherwise excellent "The Political Novels," her contribution to *The Cambridge Companion to Mario Vargas Llosa*. Take, for instance, the following passage: "The supposed narrative present in the novel, where the novelist interviews informants, is 1983. He conducts his research in a context of a nation devastated by Sendero

[Shining Path] violence and on the verge of being invaded by military forces from the USA, the Soviet Union, Cuba and elsewhere" (89).

20. While I have singled out Cornejo's interpretation, he is far from the only negative critic of *The Real Life of Alejandro Mayta*. The novel has been criticized for expressing in a naked form the Peruvian novelist's *liberal* or neoliberal ideology, perhaps for the first time in his writings; for reflecting an orientalist view of the Peruvian indigenous population; and even for expressing the homophobia that underlies his apparently liberal tolerance. Thus Iván Silen sees Vargas Llosa's *liberal* ideology as blinding him to perspectives and actions that a character like Mayta would have realistically held and performed. Jorge J. Barrueto has stressed the manner in which the novel continues colonial modes of seeing the local indigenous population. Paul Allatson has argued that *The Real Life of Alejandro Mayta* shows the homophobia that marks the limits of Vargas Llosa's liberal positions.

21. Mario Benedetti famously stated: "Fortunately, Vargas Llosa's work is clearly situated to the left of its author" (9). Benedetti made that statement in 1984, a few months before the publication of *The Real Life of Alejandro Mayta*, so when he refers to Vargas Llosa's "seven novels" (9), one may assume that he's including *The Cubs*, a short novella or long short story, in the group. However, he could have had access to *The Real Life of Alejandro Mayta*, which, by other accounts, would actually be Vargas Llosa's seventh novel.

22. However, a similar polysemy is evidenced by the critical response to *The War of the End of the World* (1983), Vargas Llosa's previous novel. Thus, as mentioned in this chapter, Antonio Cornejo Polar sees in the novel an example of the intellectual and moral bankruptcy of liberal thought: "*The War of the End of the World* proposed an interpretation of history as the painful and grotesque sequence of almost always bloody mistakes" ("La historia como apocalipsis" 363). Writing about the utopian potential found in the shantytowns of the global south, Slavoj Žižek proposes, "Arguably, the greatest literary monument to such a utopia comes from an unexpected source: Mario Vargas Llosa's *The War of the End of the World*" ("From Catastrophic to Revolutionary Utopia" 254). More recently, Rafael Rojas, comparing it to other contemporary novels about dictators, writes, "Curiously, among all those historical novels about Latin American authoritarianism during the Cold War, Vargas Llosa's was the one that most clearly reflected the ideological perspective of s democratic socialism defended by almost all of the Boom writers" (*La polis literaria*, ch. 6).

23. Historian Antonio Zapata noted that "within the Latin American region as a totality, Peru stands out as one of the countries most fully aligned with the right" (ch. 4).

24. Vargas Llosa's highlighting of the discrimination of gays by the Latin American and International Left coincided chronologically with the public showings of Néstor Almendros and Orlando Jiménez Leal's documentary on the persecution of queer Cubans, *Improper Conduct* (1984). One can argue, therefore, that 1984 marked a turning point regarding international awareness of official Cuban discrimination against its gay community.

25. The Spanish original says: "una pequeña vanguardia bien armada y equipada, con apoyo urbano e ideas claras sobre la meta estratégica y los pasos tácticos, podía ser el foco del que la revolución irradiaría hacia el resto del país, la yesca y el pedernal que desatarían el incendio revolucionario." The MacAdam English translation says: "a small, well-armed, well-equipped vanguard, with urban support and clear ideas about their strategic goals. Their accomplishments would be the focal point from which the revolution would radiate outward toward the rest of the nation—the tinder and steel that would spark the revolutionary blaze" (83–84). The English version mistranslates *pedernal*—flint—as steel. Even more importantly, it eliminates the actual physical and geographical aspect of Guevara's foco by breaking the sentence into two and adding a new subject: "their accomplishments."

26. Here is the Spanish original: "Si el foco hubiera durado, las cosas hubieran podido pasar según el cálculo de Mayta." The English translation again elides Vargas Llosa's explicit reference to Guevara's *foco*: "If the first action had lasted longer, things might have turned out the way Mayta planned" (169).

27. The importance of this speech as an expression of his political ideas is evidenced by Vargas Llosa using it as the basis for a handful of presentations over the years, including at the Lindau Nobel Laureate Meeting of 2014, where it is retitled "Confessions of a Latin American Liberal."

28. Efraín Kristal has noted the structural similarities between Vargas Llosa and de Soto's ideas and those of Mariátegui (see *Temptation of the Word*, 112). One obvious way in which Vargas Llosa and de Soto continue, renew, and invert Mariátegui's criticism of the republic's inability to break free from colonial structures is through their use of the term *mercantilism*, generally associated with the economic structures of absolute monarchies, to describe "a bureaucratized and law-ridden state that regards the redistribution of wealth as more important than the

production of wealth. And 'redistribution' . . . means the concession of monopolies or favored status to a small elite that depends on the state and on which the state is itself dependent" (Vargas Llosa, "Foreword" xiv).

29. In his essays, Vargas Llosa has noted the role of violence in the constitution not only of the Peruvian nation but of all nations. Moreover, in an essay that expands his distinctions between positive and negative fictions analyzed above, he notes: "I have nothing against fictions, I dedicate my life to writing them and I am convinced that existence would be intolerable without them for most mortals. But there are benign and malign fictions, those that enrich human experience and those that impoverish it and are a source of violence. For the blood that it has caused to be spilled throughout history, for the way in which it has contributed to stoke up prejudices, racism, xenophobia, lack of communication between peoples and cultures, for the alibis that it has provided for authoritarianism, totalitarianism, colonialism, religious and ethnic genocide, the nation seems to me to be a pristine example of a malign fantasy" ("Nation, Fictions" 300).

30. While, as we have seen, Vargas Llosa has profound disdain for postmodern theory, he makes a partial exception for Foucault. In his *Notes on the Death of a Culture*, there are several references to Foucault, the most telling being the following: "For all the sophisms and exaggerations that one can accuse him of, for example his theories about the 'structures of power' implicit in all language that always enact words and ideas that favour hegemonic social groups, Foucault has contributed to allowing certain marginal and eccentric manifestations (of sexuality, social repression and madness) to be openly acknowledged in the cultural sphere" (84). In fact, one could see the Peruvian novelist's too-brief analysis of the disciplinary function of the Inquisition as a kind of *Peruvianization* and miniaturization of Foucault's analysis of the prison and its modular role in modern society. Furthermore, Vargas Llosa finds some sort of ideological community with Foucault, unlike other French theorists, despite his criticisms (see *Notes on the Death of a Culture* 79). I have dealt with Vargas Llosa's opinion on Foucault more in depth in *Mario Vargas Llosa: Public Intellectual in Neoliberal Latin America* (95–96).

31. The positive reception of de Soto's *The Other Path* was not limited to Peru or South America. For instance, Perennial's 1990 English translation of the book includes praise from across the US political spectrum, including former presidents George H. W. Bush and Richard Nixon, supposedly progressive former senator Bill Bradley, former Carter

advisor Zbigniew Brzezinski, and conservative theologian Michael Novak, who sees theological implications to de Soto's study: "The big argument among Latin America's Catholics today may be symbolized thus: Gustavo [Gutiérrez: *The Theology of Liberation*] vs. Hernando [de Soto: *The Other Path*]" (ii). De Soto's fans also include Ronald Reagan and Bill Clinton, who called him "the world's greatest living economist" (qtd. in "Can This Man End World Poverty?")

32. As should be obvious from its original title—*El otro sendero. La revolución informal* (The other path. The informal revolution)—de Soto's study presents itself as an alternative to that other revolution, the one then being waged by the Shining Path. Implicit in the title is the idea that the reader has to choose between two alternatives: the populist neoliberal revolution represented by *The Other Path* or the violent revolution practiced by the Shining Path.

33. The first edition in English of *The Other Path* lists as its sole author Hernando de Soto on the cover, though it adds "in collaboration with the Instituto Libertad y Democracia" on its title page. In 2012 Mario Ghibellini and Enrique Ghersi won a suit to be listed as coauthors of the text and to receive their corresponding royalties. (Both had been listed as coauthors in the original Spanish language edition of 1986.) See "Hernando de Soto y Editorial Norma son multados por omitir a coautores."

34. According to Puig in "A Last Interview with Manuel Puig": "The structure of the novel was all set. I was here in New York around the end of '73, when I'd left Argentina, and I was gathering all the materials for the novel. . . . I'd done a certain amount of research" (572).

35. Federico Finchelstein has noted that both Isabel Perón's regime and the military dictatorship that deposed her were based on a widespread *nacionalismo*, understood as a fusion of conservative Catholicism and fascism. The Argentine historian ominously notes: "The trajectory of the fascist idea in Argentina is a central explanation of these links that transcended administrations and civilian and military leaders" (*Ideological Origins of the Dirty War*" 115). In "A Last Interview with Manuel Puig," the Argentine novelist noted that in order to write the novel, he interviewed political prisoners that had been freed by Héctor Cámpora, the placeholder president, who ran for office to circumvent the military veto against Juan Domingo Perón. Cámpora, who was in power only from 25 May to 12 July 1973, called for new elections in which Perón won.

36. In fact, one can easily argue that Vargas Llosa would become the region's most visible and widely read public intellectual in the decades following

the Padilla affair. Wilfrido H. Corral sympathetically notes Vargas Llosa's role in Hispanic cultural debates: "In particular since the Dreyfus Affair, novelists have rarely been absent from these intellectual skirmishes. Few Latin American writers have been as committed to them—in their essays, novels, reviews, journalistic texts and other writings—as Mario Vargas Llosa. Nevertheless, these categories are paltry when it comes to defining an intellectual's course. This ubiquitous author has also become, in the last and present centuries, the conductor of an international nongovernmental campaign in defense of freedom in literature and the ideas that nurture freedom in society" ("Vargas Llosa and the History of Ideas" 189).

37. According to José Miguel Oviedo, "It is of significance that after the international success of his most famous novel, *Kiss of the Spider Woman* . . . the text became a movie in 1985 . . . and then a Broadway musical; in this way the cycle of multiple appropriations common to popular culture was closed" (348–49). Although not part of popular culture per se, the one medium into which the novel has not been adapted is opera. There was, however, a frustrated attempt by German composer Hans Werner Henze (see Levine 345).

38. Despite its later commercial and critical success, the production of the film of *Kiss of the Spider Woman* was troubled, characterized by strife between the director, writers, and actors over the control of the production and its final form. However, "[producer David] Weisman encouraged his [Puig's] input, and the two even composed the lyrics of an absurd cabaret song, performed by [Sonia] Braga. Manuel's influence on the script was also felt in autobiographical nuances not explicit in the novel" (Levine 339). Regarding the musical, his participation was much more limited; however, he also met with the writer, composer, and producer (Levine 359–69).

39. According to Néstor Perlongher: "In August of 1971, a group of intellectuals inspired by the Gay Power Americano gave birth to the FLH [Frente de Liberación Homosexual] of Argentina" (qtd. in Encarnación 88).

40. According to Valeria Manzano, "the FLH participated in Peronist rallies and sent letters to representatives in Congress to state that in 'the struggle for liberation' they participated by 'dismantling bourgeois morality based on machismo and the ensuing domination of women and rejection of homosexuals'" (204). Puig, however, distanced himself shortly after helping found the Frente, so he did not actually take part in these political activities.

41. Among the novels that Balderston and Maristany classify as belonging to this "post-Stonewall gay literature" are Sylvia Molloy's *En breve cárcel* (1981), Luis Zapata's *Adonis García: A Picaresque Novel* (1979), and Reinaldo Arenas's *Before Night Falls* (1992) (209–10).

42. While more colorful than the norm, Roberto Bolaño's evaluation of Isabel Allende is not far from the mainstream: "I think that she is a bad writer, plain and simple. To call her a writer is to do her too much credit. I don't even think Isabel Allende is a writer, she's an *escribidora* [scribbler]" (qtd. by Maristain ch. 6).

43. One must, however, assume that someone must be currently working on adding to the "MLA Teaching Series" Bolaño's *2666* and *The Savage Detectives*.

44. Finchelstein has pointed that the *nacionalismo* (a sui generis fusion of fascism and conservative Catholicism) that first took power in 1930 with General José Félix Uriburu became the shared ideology of all dictatorial regimes that followed, as well as the populism of Juan Domingo Perón, though with important differences. This Argentine fascism was characterized by the demonization of psychoanalysis. This led, as a response, to liberal Argentines identifying psychoanalysis as the progressive discourse par excellence. As Finchelstein notes, "Thanks to nacionalismo's radical criticism, psychoanalysis became an identity of the liberal Argentina defeated by the military and Peronism" (*Transatlantic Fascism* 176).

45. During the Dirty War of the 1970s, the Argentine military saw its victims as the "radical other." Writing about the internment camps maintained by the military, Finchelstein notes: "Racism was a critical component of the camps. . . . Racism was also linked to a sexualized image of the enemy; the enemy was generally defined as sexually heterodox, whether as heterodox women and/or prostitutes or homosexual men" (*Ideological Origins of the Dirty War* 135).

46. Levine writes about Puig when he was still trying to break into film: "He would soon begin the 'failed screenplay' that became his own autobiography of childhood, *Betrayed by Rita Hayworth*" (121).

47. The screenplay for Cromwell's *The Enchanted Cottage* was written by DeWitt Bodeen, the screenwriter of *Cat People*. The first book-length study dedicated to Val Lewton—*Val Lewton: The Reality of Terror*, by Joel Siegel—was published in 1972. In 1974, the BFI put out a short forty-page book on John Cromwell—*John Cromwell* by Brenda Davies.

48. Puig's dismissal of Wyler's *The Best Years of Our Lives* and, for that matter, his preference for Garnett's *Seven Sinners* are not widely shared. Steven Spielberg claims in the documentary series *Five Came Back*, "I watch *The*

*Best Years of Our Lives* at least once a year. I don't think a year's gone by over the last thirty years that I haven't watched that film once a year, and try to bring people to see it for the first time, so I can relive it through their eyes" ("The Price of Victory"). Roger Ebert, who included the film in his *Great Movies III*, unwittingly contradicts Puig: "Seen more than six decades later, it feels surprisingly modern: lean, direct, honest about issues that Hollywood then studiously avoided. After the war years of patriotism and heroism in the movies, this was a sobering look at the problems veterans faced when they returned home" (68).

49. Nicholas Birns describes de Man and, through him, deconstructive revaluation of allegory in the following terms: "Allegory became revalued in the aftermath of the deconstructive turn because, by reaching back towards reference, it acknowledges its own failure" (*Theory after Theory* 97).

50. Puig writes on *Seven Sinners*: "*Seven Sinners* laid no claim to reflect real life. It was an unbiased look at power and established values, a very light-weight allegory on this theme" ("Cinema and the Novel" 399).

51. Throughout the novel, Valentín is critical of Molina's defense and identification with traditional gender roles. For instance, when Molina complains "what's the world coming to with all your politicians," Valentín replies: "Don't talk like a nineteenth-century housewife, because this isn't the nineteenth century . . . and you're not a house wife" (78). In "A Last Interview," Puig describes Molina as being one of the traditional homosexuals who have "accepted the models of behavior from the '40s— you know: the subdued woman and the dashing male—and they have, of course, identified with the subdued though heroic woman, and they don't want to change that fantasy—or they can't" (572).

52. Robin Wood has warned against interpreting *Cat People* or *I Walked with a Zombie*, the other Lewton/Tourneur collaboration "included" in *Kiss of the Spider Woman*, as an allegory: "*Cat People* and *I Walked with a Zombie* both suggest, and in a more conscious and sophisticated way than is the case in the majority of horror films, that the myths they draw on are capable of psychological interpretation; neither is reducible to clear-cut psychological allegory. They work by means of poetic suggestiveness rather than of clearly definable 'meaning' and any attempt to 'explain' them beyond a certain point can only do them harm" (258–59). However, Wood then basically proposes Valentín's interpretation, even if he claims it to be too obvious to merit discussion: "The sexual overtones of *Cat People* are clear enough: Irena is afraid that her 'cat' nature will be released if she is sexually aroused, and it eventually *is* released by sexual jealousy" (259). Where Puig and Wood disagree is that the former sees

the allegorical form as associated with the kind of narrative synthesis he sees as intrinsic to the best filmmaking, while Wood sees it as a reduction of a visual medium to its literary scaffolding: "Rather than attempt an allegorical interpretation (which would, inevitably, become an interpretation of the *script*), I want to examine some of the films' poetic detail, or poetic *movement*, to show something of their richness of suggestion" (259).

53. Writing about Plato's *Phaedrus* as a foundational text on desire, Judith Butler notes: "Plato will claim that he will speak briefly and in a figure, and what he offers us is an allegory that he never transcribes into more conventional philosophical argumentation. If allegory is in its most general formulation a way of giving a narrative form to something which cannot be directly narrativized, then what does it mean that desire is approached through allegory? Is it that desire cannot make itself plain through a more direct linguistic representation? What is elusive about this referent?" (370).

54. One of the dialogues between Molina and Valentín raises the issues of "softness"—that is, of giving in to one's feelings:
    —And what's so bad about being soft like a woman? Why is it men or whoever, some poor bastard, some queen, can't be sensitive, too, if he's got a mind to?
    —I don't know, but sometimes that kind of behavior can get in a man's way.
    —When? When it comes to torturing?
    —No, when it comes to being finished with the torturers. (29)

55. Both *Cat People* and *Kiss of the Spider Woman* have been described as criticisms of psychoanalysis. Writing about the two Lewton/Tourneur films incorporated into the novel, Chris Fujiwara notes: "Both *Cat People* and *I Walked with a Zombie* touch on the inadequacy of Western medicine (if we stretch the term to include the kind of psychoanalysis practiced by Dr. Judd)" (165). Likewise, according to Colás, "these notes do anything but praise the relevance of psychoanalytic theory, which is found wanting in its understanding of homosexuality" (90). However, as we will see in the main text, Puig, rather than criticizing psychoanalysis, is actually attempting to develop a more complete and complex understanding of homosexuality based precisely on Freudian ideas.

56. Following Donald J. West in his *Homosexuality: Its Nature and Causes* (1955, rev. 1968), Puig rejects hormonal imbalances, intersexuality, and heredity as causes (*Kiss of the Spider Woman* 59–65nn).

57. In his "A Last Interview," after mentioning that only *Betrayed by Rita Hayworth* and *Heartbreak Tango* were available in Argentina, Puig notes:

"I'm not distributed in Cuba either. So Argentina on the Right and Cuba on the Left: they both have something to object to in my books. In Cuba none of my books could appear. Extra officially I was told my work was too concerned with eroticism. Even worse, *Kiss of the Spider Woman* is concerned with homoeroticism, and that Castro certainly doesn't like. The harassment of homosexuals in Cuba is well known, and, I hate to say that, because there are aspects of the Cuban revolution I respect and admire" (575).

58. In the notes Puig argues: "It is in different terms that Theodore Roszak comments upon the sexual liberation movement in his work entitled *The Making of a Counter Culture*. There, he expresses the concept that the kind of woman who is most in need of liberation, and desperately so, is the 'woman' which every man keeps locked inside the dungeons of his own psyche. Roszak points out that this and no other is the form of repression that needs to be eliminated next, and the same with respect to the man bottled up inside of every woman" (196n).

59. An example of the congruence between Puig's ideas and the more radical versions of the so-called sexual revolution of the 1960s and early 1970s can be found in Julian Bourg's summary of the articles by the Front Homosexual D'action Revolutionaire (The Homosexual Front of Revolutionary Action) published in the left-wing "newspaper" *Ce que nous voulons: Tout!* (What we want: Everything) on 23 April 1971:

> The front page of the newspaper captured aspects of the agenda, as well as some of the dilemmas, of gay and feminist activists working together: Yes, our bodies belong to us.
> —free abortion and contraception
> —right to homosexuality and all sexualities
> —right of minors to the freedom of desire and to its accomplishment
> These exigencies raise questions about the limit points of life: about incest, rape, euthanasia, and suicide. . . . They have their extensions: refusal to submit one's body to the census, to pollution, to daily rhythms, to work accidents. . . . They exceed themselves: the free disposition of my body cannot exercise itself against those of others. This freedom only really exists in the blossoming [*l'épanouissement*] of all. They designate the ends of the revolution: the perfection of happiness. (183)

60. I am fully aware that mine is a minority reading. In fact, while some critics admit some doubts about Molina's politicization, these are almost always marginalized even when they are stated. For instance, Lucille Kerr in her authoritative *Suspended Fictions* admits, "It could be argued that

the discourse on sexuality, or the defense of homosexuality, wins out over, perhaps even suppresses in some way, the political discourse by the end of the novel" (187). However, she begins the chapter on *Kiss of the Spider Woman* by providing a summary of the novel's plot that concludes by noting, "By the end of their time together it appears each manages to seduce the other to his own way of seeing and doing this, that each manages to get the other to play a role to which he initially seems totally opposed" (184).

61. The novel includes a report on Valentín by the Ministry of the Interior: "Arrested October 16, 1972, along Route 5, outside Barrancas, National Guard troops having surrounded group of activists involved in promoting disturbances with strikers at two automotive assembly plants. . . . Took part in hunger strike protesting death of political prisoner Juan Vicente Aparicio while undergoing police interrogation. . . . Conduct reprehensible, rebellious, reputed instigator of above hunger strike as well as other incidents supposedly protesting lack of hygienic conditions in Pavilion and violation of personal correspondence" (148–49). Given the source for the "document," one can only see his "promoting disturbances" and "conduct reprehensible" as actually meaning the opposite of what is explicitly being stated.

62. According to one of the "reports to the warden" included in the novel, Valentín was arrested 16 October 1972, and transferred on 4 April 1975 into the cell with Molina (148–49).

63. Complaining against his fate as a prisoner, Valentín states: "I've always acted with generosity, I've never exploited anyone . . . and I fought, from the moment I possessed a little understanding of things . . . fought against the exploitation of my fellow man" (178). The novel makes clear that Valentín attempts to live up to this description.

64. These are the lyrics of Mario Clavel's "La carta" as translated in the English version of *Kiss of the Spider Woman*: " 'Dearest . . . I am wanting you once more now, night . . . brings a silence that helps me talk to you, and I wonder . . . could you be remembering too, sad dreams . . . of this strange love affair. My dear . . . although life may never let us meet again, and we—because of fate—must always live apart . . . I swear, this heart of mine will be always yours . . . my thoughts, my whole life, forever yours . . . just as this pain . . . belongs . . . to you. . . . 'Pain' or 'hurt,' I don't remember which. It's one or the other." (137)

65. If the revolutionaries of the 1960s aimed to implement socialism by violent means and Allende's Unidad Popular believed it was possible to implement a maximalist revolution by democratic means, after 1989 new radical political movements all work within the political horizon

of liberal democracy. This is also the case with the Zapatista movement that rose up in arms in 1994. At first the Zapatistas seemed to follow older guerrilla politics by presenting as its first "order" the military takeover of the country and the substitution of the existing government by a new more democratic one set up by the rebels: "Advance to the capital of the country, overcoming the Mexican federal army, protecting in our advance the civilian population and permitting the people in the liberated area the right to freely and democratically elect their own administrative authorities" (Zapatista National Liberation Army 313). The name that the movement took—Ejército Zapatista de Liberación Nacional (Zapatista National Liberation Army), which echoes the name of earlier guerrilla movements—seems to stress the need for the violent takeover of the state in order to achieve liberation, even if this term is not explained. Despite this rhetorical nod to earlier definitions of revolution as the necessary product of violence, the Zapatista document does not mention socialism or communism. As John Beverley notes, "The Zapatistas, while they were willing to challenge the state militarily, refused, unlike guerrilla movements of the 1960s and 1970s, to bid for state power, claiming that the space of their intervention was Mexican 'civil society' and that they would rule by obeying" (ch. 7). One must note that this refusal included the rejection of any and all electoral participation or, for that matter, giving support to the mainstream left in Mexican elections. Evaluating the effects of their political abstentionism in 2011, Beverley argues that "the Zapatistas' calculation that sitting out the election would strengthen the case for a radical alternative to the status quo turned against them . . . their influence and authority have certainly been contained" (ch. 7). By 2019, Zapatismo, which once inspired many to change the world without taking power, has faded almost completely from public influence, with only a partial exception in its home base in Chiapas. Thus, despite the radical connotations of their action and discourse, the Zapatistas and their spokesperson, Subcomandante Marcos, the postmodern revolutionary, shared the ethos of their time.

### *Chapter 4*

1. The economists who advised the Chilean military government as it founded the first radical free-market economy were first known as either "Chicago Boys," in reference to their academic alma mater, or "monetarists," in reference to their mentor Milton Friedman's ideas about the centrality of monetary emission—that is, the number of bills and

coins put into circulation by the nation's central bank—in determining inflation, growth, and so on. However, as other versions of radical free-market policies emanating from other universities and even disagreeing with Friedman's basic ideas started to exert influence on policy in Chile and in other countries, these names stopped being fully applicable. These assorted free-market proposals became known as neoliberalism.

2. In a review in *Babelia*, the cultural supplement of *El País*, Spanish novelist Francisco Solano criticized the awarding of the Alfaguara Prize to *In the Distance with You* because it represented the commercialization of the award: "The novel *Contigo en la distancia*, written by Carla Guelfenbein (Santiago de Chile, 1959), received the XVII Alfaguara Prize, which is no small achievement if one considers the monetary amount of the award and the award's original vocation to unify Spanish-speaking writers from both sides of the Atlantic. The amount of the Prize has been consistent throughout the years, but not the vocation that rapidly changed into a concern with economic rewards over literary considerations. One cannot identify equal economic rewards to all the winning works, but an overview of the winning works not only undermines literary considerations, but also actually contradicts them. Following this tendency, therefore, this novel stays in the tranquil waters on which such accommodating fiction sails, unwilling to offend the spirit of commerce."

3. In an interview with Gabriela Wiener, herself a poet, journalist, and Peruvian novelist, Guelfenbein states: "I believe, without any compunction, that my writing is women's writing. On the contrary, I feel that is one of my traits, it's the way I express my interior world, what I am, and I think this is honest" ("Las escritoras seguimos siendo víctimas del prejuicio")

4. The Rómulo Gallegos Award was originally given to the best novel published within a five-year period—the rule in play when Vargas Llosa's *The Green House* and García Márquez's *One Hundred Years of Solitude* won the award in 1967 and 1972, respectively. Starting in 1989, the award was given biannually for the best novel published within a two-year period.

5. Chris Andrews, the translator of many of Bolaño's short novels and later an interpreter of Bolaño's works, argues regarding the critical success of Bolaño's longer novels: "A 'great' book is often a big book: one whose text is long, whose story is extensive in space and time, and that can give an impression of exhaustiveness. *2666* satisfies these conditions" (24). And: "Logically enough, 'greatness' correlates with size, but it also seems, still, to correlate with epic themes, in the Homeric sense: war

and adventurous voyaging, both of which figure strongly in Bolaño's novels. . . . I am not suggesting that these themes were chosen in a bid for glory. . . . I am noting that Bolaño's themes, especially in the two long novels, tally with an ancient and gendered conception of what makes for great literature" (24–25).

6. The unsigned *N+1* article "On Bolaño" attempts to answer the question. According to its author or authors, the reasons for the Chilean novelist's success in Latin America was Bolaño's "anti-eloquence": "An idiom encrusted with poeticisms needs a solvent bath" (11). The Chilean novelist's success in the United States is explained in the same terms as the success of Sebald, the other author recently canonized in the country: "Neither fiction writer writes as if he believes in fiction" (11). I consider both reasons to be flawed.

7. Noted Salvadoran novelist Horacio Castellanos Moya refers to Pollack's essay and concurs: "What isn't the fault of the author is that American readers, with *The Savage Detectives*, want to confirm their worst paternalistic prejudices about Latin America, as Pollack's text says, like the superiority of the Protestant work ethic or the dichotomy according to which North Americans see themselves as workers, mature, responsible, and honest, while they see their neighbors to the South as lazy, adolescent, reckless, and delinquent. Pollack says that from this point of view *The Savage Detectives* is 'a very comfortable choice for US readers, offering both the pleasures of the savage and the superiority of the civilized.' And I repeat: nobody knows for whom it works. Or as the poet Roque Dalton wrote: 'Anyone can make the books of the young Marx into a light eggplant puree. What is difficult is to conserve them as they are, that is to say, as an alarming ants' nest.'"

8. For Rancière, this "ethical turn" originates in the waning belief in revolution linked to the fall of the Soviet bloc. Even if arguably more an exemplar of this change than its actual origin, Jacques Derrida's own version of the ethical turn has been influential. As Nicholas Birns notes, "Derrida's work on forgiveness is grounded in history, in particular the two historical legacies the postmodern West has found the most troubling to overcome: the Holocaust and racism" (*Theory After Theory* 117). One must note that Bolaño apparently had little interest in Derrida's thought. For instance, there is no mention of the French philosopher in Bolaño's *Between Parentheses*.

9. According to Bruno Bosteels: "Ethics, then, no longer founds the internal consistency of a political process within a specific situation but instead becomes a new external point of authority from which all

     militant processes can be found guilty of dogmatism, authoritarianism, or blind utopianism" (309).

10. "The evident inability of the Soviet Union to develop into a more open and democratic society and its repression of the reform movement in Czechoslovakia in 1968 destroyed hope among still-idealistic socialists that 'socialism with a human face' was possible within the Soviet sphere" (Cook 7). According to Julian Bourg: "After 1968 a serious reconsideration of this inheritance [i.e., revolution] took place. . . . France simply de-Marxified in new ways, the Cold War ending in Paris before the Berlin Wall fell. Remarkably, radical politics had provided some of the most important resources for overcoming radical politics: Marxism was present at its own funeral. The end of the politics of the living revolution, which was concretely embodied in French Marxism, coincided with the return of political ethics" (9).

11. Ignacio Bajter has identified the character of Auxilio Lacouture as a fictionalization of the real-life Uruguayan poet Alcira Soust Scaffo. On Soust's life and her relationship with Bolaño, see Bajter.

12. This is the standard figure for the number of dead at Tlatelolco. For instance, see Coerver, Pasztor, and Buffington, where "300 to 400" dead is mentioned on five separate occasions (33, 144, 151, 300, 501).

13. Tlatelolco is mentioned several times in Bolaño's *Amulet*. For example: "I can't remember all the places we went together: La Villa, Coyoacán, Tlatelolco (that time I didn't go, it was just him and Elena)" (55). A more significant instance may be when Belano and his friends are described as "a generation sprung from the open wound of Tlatelolco, like ants or cicadas or pus, although they couldn't have been there or taken part in the demonstrations of '68; these were kids who, in September '68, when I was shut up in the bathroom, were still in junior high school" (77). The novel continues, "It's over now, the riot police have left the university, the students have died at Tlatelolco, the university has opened again" (77). In a characteristic gesture, the second mention of Tlatelolco presents Belano, implicitly Bolaño himself, as a product of the massacre, while admitting the obvious fact that he was not present at the event.

14. Raúl Rodríguez Freire has noted about *Amulet*: "This novel . . . has its 'antecedents' in the children's crusade that took place during the twelfth century of the Common Era. This legend narrates the story of thousands of children from France and Germany that decided to rescue the Holy Sepulchre" (35). Rodríguez points out that Borges saw in the story of the Pied Piper of Hamelin an "echo" of the children's crusade (35).

15. Perhaps the best example of this ideological turnabout is provided by well-known New School economist Robert Heilbroner. Once one of the best-known US radicals, he famously begins his article "The Triumph of Capitalism," significantly published in January 1989, by stating: "The Soviet Union, China and Eastern Europe have given us the clearest possible proof that capitalism organizes the material affairs of humankind more satisfactorily than socialism: that however inequitably or irresponsibly the marketplace may distribute goods, it does so better than the queues of a planned economy. . . . [T]he great question now seems how rapid will be the transformation of socialism into capitalism, and not the other way around, as things looked only half a century ago" (98).

16. According to Jon Lee Anderson, "For better or for worse, Ernesto had chosen Guatemala's leftist revolution as the first political cause he openly identified with. Despite its many flaws and defects, he told his family, Guatemala was the country in which one could breathe the 'most democratic air' in Latin America" (123). Anderson also describes the plight of the revolutionaries who, when they first landed in Cuba, had been attacked by Batista's military force: "Che had been lucky. His neck wound was only superficial. Although some of his comrades escaped with their lives, over the coming days Batista's troops summarily executed many of the men they captured, including the wounded and even some of those who had surrendered. The survivors tried desperately to gain refuge in the mountains and, somehow, to find one another. Of the eighty-two men who came ashore from the Granma, only twenty-two ultimately regrouped in the sierra" (207).

17. While Bolaño in his Rómulo Gallegos speech attacks the Left, he is fully aware that the main perpetrator of human rights violations in Chile was the Pinochet government. As he notes in "A Modest Proposal": "Sometimes, when I'm in the mood to think pointless thoughts, I ask myself whether we were always like this. I don't know. The left committed verbal crimes in Chile (a specialty of the Latin American left), it committed moral crimes, and it probably killed people. But it didn't put live rats in any girl's vagina. It didn't have the time to create its own evil, it didn't have the time to create its own labor camps. Is it possible that it would have, if given the time? Of course it's possible. Nothing in our country's history allows us to imagine a more optimistic alternate history. But the truth is that in Chile the concentration camps weren't the work of the left, and neither were the firing squads, torture, the disappeared, repression. All of this was accomplished by the right. All

of this was the work of the government that took power after the coup" (90).

18. Bolaño is not alone in believing the necessarily catastrophic consequences of any attempt at radical social change. We have already seen how Vargas Llosa's *The Real Life of Alejandro Mayta* presents the protagonist's failed—and minuscule—attempt to start a guerrilla movement as leading to a political apocalypse.

19. Nazism is also presented as the origin of contemporary horrors in Bolaño's *By Night in Chile*. The novel includes passages set in Paris during the Nazi occupation with real-life writers Salvador Reyes and Ernst Jünger as protagonists (25–39), and it also presents an allegorical dream of falcons that seems to represent this migration of fascism from Europe to Chile and Latin America: "I cried. I had disturbing dreams. I saw women tearing their clothes. I saw Fr. Antonio, the priest from Burgos, who, as he lay dying, opened one eye and said: It's wrong, my friend, it's wrong. I saw a flock of falcons, thousands of falcons flying high over the Atlantic Ocean, headed for America. Sometimes the sun went black in my dreams" (79). *Nazi Literature in the Americas*, which includes an earlier, briefer version of the story that Bolaño will develop in *Distant Star*, invents a genealogy for hemispheric fascism rooted in that of Europe. Likewise, *2666* is partially set during World War II itself. Hans Reiter, also known under the pen name of Benno von Archimboldi, the novelist whose work obsesses the critics in "The Part about the Critics" and whose story is told in "The Part of Archimboldi," fights in the World War for the German army.

20. Finchelstein argues: "I actually think that in Bolaño's work the ethico-political appears as a displacement of the political, but it does so in a way that presents the literary act, and especially the literary inquiry into the limits and potentialities of fascism, as a kind of vicarious political participation against it. In other words, writing on fascism appears as the best political response to it. It is the actual, official politics, the politics of power as degraded by politicians of right and left that are problematic for Bolaño, not politics as such. Bolaño is not antipolitical but he sees formal politics as neglecting the real danger which is a dormant sort of fascism that for him never ceased to exist" ("On Fascism, History, and Evil" 24). Finchelstein's description of Bolaño's politics, predicated on "writing" as the best response to potential fascism is, at least to my mind, fully consistent with the ethical turn.

21. Bolaño is not alone in considering power as linked to criminality. According to Jacques Derrida, "all three of them, the animal, the criminal, and the sovereign, are outside the law, at a distance from or

above the laws: criminal, outcast, and sovereign strangely resemble each other while seeming to be situated at the antipodes, at each other's antipodes" (39).

22. Rancière's criticism of Giorgio Agamben's ideas is, with caveats already mentioned, applicable to Bolaño's novels: "His analysis, however, sums up well what I call the 'ethical tum.' The state of exception is a state that erases the difference between henchmen and victims, including even that between the extreme crimes of the Nazi State and the ordinary everyday life of our democracies" ("Ethical Turn" 192).

23. It is not an accident that the review by José-Carlos Mainer of Vargas Llosa's *The Discreet Hero* in *El País* was titled "Cuando se arregló el Perú" (When Peru was patched up). The review's title is a play on and answer to a famous question asked in Vargas Llosa's 1969 masterpiece *Conversation in the Cathedral*: "At what precise moment had Peru fucked itself up?" (3). As Mainer notes: "If in the unforgettable beginning of *Conversation in the Cathedral* we never find out how Peru had fucked itself up, in the pages of *The Discreet Hero*, we find out how it began to fix itself. . . . The high bourgeoisie of Peru is able to take advantage of its work throughout the years and the emergent autotchtonous entrepreneurial middle class continues in its effort to modernize the country. . . . Despite all problems, everything has become better than it once was." As should be obvious, Mainer shares Vargas Llosa's political beliefs.

24. Aviva Chomsky, quoting Julie Marie Bunck, notes: "The UMAP were created in 1965 to 'rehabilitate' men who were considered unfit for military service. 'Between 1965 and 1967 the UMAP became a catch-all for delinquents who had been denounced by their neighbors or the CDRs. These military units took in any person who failed to conduct himself in accordance with the official definition of proper behavior. The UMAP housed persons rounded up as vagrants, counterrevolutionaries, and so-called deviants: homosexuals, juvenile delinquents, and religious followers, including Catholics, Baptists, and Jehovah's Witnesses'" (121). Chomsky adds: "Both nationally and internationally, people—including many supporters of the Revolution—protested the UMAP, and they were terminated between 1967 and 1969. Many of the protests were based not on a positive view of gay rights, but rather against the cruelty and brutality of the camps" (121).

25. I have modified the translation. The original word translated as "indefinitely" is "indéfiniment." A better translation would be "without end." The original passage is as follows: "Mais ce n'est plus pour préserver la promesse d'émancipation. C'est au contraire pour attester

indéfiniment de l'aliénation immémoriale qui fait de toute promesse d'émancipation un mensonge réalisable seulement sous la forme du crime infini, crime infini auquel l'art répond par une 'résistance' qui n'est que le travail infini du deuil" (Rancière, "Le tournant éthique").

26. Aztec sacrifices are mentioned in several passages of *2666*, such as the following: "When the fat old Indian woman served them the posole, Epifanio sat looking at the earthenware dish as if he'd seen someone else's face reflected in its surface. Do you know where posole comes from, Lalito? he asked. No idea, said Lalo Cura. It's from the middle of the country, not the north. It's a Mexico City specialty. The Aztecs invented it, he said. The Aztecs? well, it's good, said Lalo Cura. Did you eat posole in Villaviciosa? asked Epifanio. Lalo Cura thought about it, as if Villaviciosa were very far away, and then he said no, in fact he hadn't, although now it seemed strange to him that he hadn't tried it before he came to live in Santa Teresa. Maybe I did try it and now I don't remember, he said. Well, this posole isn't quite the same as the original posole, said Epifanio. It's missing an ingredient. What ingredient is that? asked Lalo Cura. Human flesh, said Epifanio. Don't fuck with me, said Lalo Cura. It's true, the Aztecs cooked posole with pieces of human flesh, said Epifanio" (472–73).

27. The one exception to this is, of course, Venezuela, which under the presidency of Nicolás Maduro (2013– ) has degenerated into repression and political and economic chaos. One must also note that the rise of hard-Right elected governments in Latin America, such as Jair Bolsonaro's in Brazil, opens the disturbing possibility of repressive "democratic" regimes, or even of elected fascism.

28. In *In the Distance with You*, Vera Sigall—the writer whose mysterious life and death serve as a catalyst for the reflections, memories, and investigation of Daniel (Vera's neighbor), Emilia (a young French woman writing her dissertation on her novels), and Horacio (poet and former lover)—is described as having been jailed, like Guelfenbein's mother, at Tres Alamos:

> Emilia looked over the pages for a few minutes. Then she said, "Vera was there. In that prison camp."
>
> "Not possible."
>
> "It's on the first page: 'Tania Calderón, Cecilia Usón, and Vera Sigall were arrested in a police raid.'" (Guelfenbein 291)

29. For instance, *La mujer de mi vida* (2005) is set in both Chile and London and has as its main characters Antonio, a Chilean student, activist, and later pundit; Clara, a Chilean dancer; and Theo, a British student, later turned war journalist, fluent in Spanish.

30. The main exception are the "critics" in Bolaño's *2666*.

31. One of the most virulent critics of Guelfenbein's work is the respected Chilean academic and book reviewer Patricia Espinosa, who writes about the Alfaguara Award–winning *In the Distance with You*: "Once more the author exhibits in this volume what is her specialty: a sentimental story about frivolous characters that belong to the elites, who exhibit without any modesty their upper-class habits. Guelfenbein considers that elegance is a value in itself; that is why her characters are beautiful, live in luxurious houses, and dedicate their time to gossiping and reflecting on their banal lives" (Review of *Contigo en la distancia*). Likewise, she criticizes *Nadar desnudas* as a "fourth rate feuilleton" and argues that "the incontinence of its sentimentalism reduces to the minimum the tragic character of the events" (Review of *Nadar desnudas*). While Espinosa is more trenchant than most, many other critics have also complained of Guelfenbein's appeal to sentimentality. For instance, Francisco Solano, in a mixed review published in *Babelia*, the cultural supplement of *El País*, complains of Guelfenbein's "bourgeois sentimentalism," and Adrian Turpin, in an otherwise positive review in *The Financial Times*, claims that *The Rest Is Silence* "sometimes teeters on the sentimental."

32. According to Ariel Dorfman, "very few of the eight billion people alive today could remember or be able to identify what happened in Chile" ("The Last September 11" 1). This forgetting may also apply to Chile and its writers. As Patricio Guzmán noted in 2002: "There is no great literature on repression. In Chile great writers have not spoken out with the exception of Ariel Dorfman. Movie directors turn away from the topic. Most artists feel it is a tired theme. They want to move on, to write about or cover other things. I think we'll have to wait for those who are 15 now to address this past" (qtd. in Riding). However, this "forgetting" may be far from accidental. Avelar argues, "Growing commodification negates memory because new commodities must always replace previous commodities. . . . The free market established by Latin American dictatorships must, therefore, impose forgetting not only because it needs to erase the reminiscence of its barbaric origins but also because it is proper to the market to live in a perpetual present" (2).

33. Guelfenbein's exact wording is "Historia, con mayúsculas" (134)—"History in capital letters." (Trautenberg 134).

34. According to Claudia Gilman, "An unexpected event decided a change in direction that perhaps was already taking place within the revolutionary process: the growing closeness with the USSR scandalously announced— in the eyes of many—by Cuba's support to the Warsaw Pact's troops invasion of Czechoslovakia, during the night of August 20 to August 21.

In this manner, the process of constructing socialism independently from the USSR was violently interrupted" (208–9).

35. However, perhaps an older Alexander Dubček would have agreed with Fuentes's equating of postsocialist Czechoslovakia and the Prague Spring. In 1990, he supposedly said about Margaret Thatcher, one of the architects of our neoliberal world: "For us, she is not the Iron Lady. She is the kind, dear Mrs. Thatcher" (qtd. in Dale 122).

36. Cortázar also used the interview with *Life* as a way of attacking Peruvian *indigenista* writer José María Arguedas, who had criticized the Argentine writer's stress on the need to live abroad in order to write about Latin America: "Talking of labels José María Arguedas has given us a whole chemist's shop of them in a recent article published in the Peruvian magazine *Amaru*. Obviously preferring resentment to intelligence, something always deplorable . . . neither Arguedas nor anyone else will get very far by means of these regional complexes" ("Julio Cortázar" 299). I have dealt with the debate between Cortázar and Arguedas earlier in this book and in *The Spaces of Latin American Literature* (100–101).

37. Simon Collier and William F. Sater, among many others, describe "the Nixon administration, already nervously (and rather ridiculously) contemplating a 'second Cuba' after the election of Allende" (329).

38. Despite its pseudofeminist name, Poder Femenino would later support the military coup.

39. Among the regimes that have experienced "pots and pans protests" are Venezuela (throughout the Chávez regime continuing into the Maduro presidency), Québec (2012, against restrictions to the right to assembly), and Spain (2003, against participation in the Iraq War).

40. Although, Žižek does not compare 9/11/73 with 9/11/01, and he writes with greater theoretical sophistication, "Welcome to the Desert of the Real," his well-known essay on the attack on the Twin Towers, makes points similar to Dorfman's. In his conclusion, the Slovenian philosopher notes: "Either America will persist in, strengthen even, the attitude, 'Why should this happen to us? Things like this don't happen here!'— leading to more aggression toward the threatening Outside, in short: to a paranoiac acting out—or America will finally risk stepping through the fantasmatic screen separating it from the Outside World, accepting its arrival into the Real world, making the long-overdue move from 'Things like this should not happen here!' to 'Things like this should not happen anywhere!' America's 'holiday from history' was a fake: America's peace was bought by the catastrophes going on elsewhere. Therein resides the true lesson of the bombing" (*Welcome to the Desert of the Real*, 389).

41. According to Shenon, "The leaders of the independent commission investigating the Sept. 11 terrorist attacks agreed Sunday that evidence gathered by their panel showed the attacks could probably have been prevented." However, the victims themselves had no way of knowing they were in danger.

42. The novel describes the failed coup: "A military regiment commanded by a certain Colonel Souper attempted a coup. They arrived at a place with tanks and trucks full of soldiers. In an exchange of fire that lasted for more than two hours, twenty-two people died" (Guelfenbein, *Nadar desnudas* 143).

43. " 'They attacked him last night when he left a meeting in the house of a comrade. They beat him with clubs inside a station wagon and then left him in front of the house,' Sophie stops. Morgana hears her weep" (Guelfenbein, *Nadar desnudas* 104).

44. In fact, the novel also describes Diego and Morgana's fear of the coup: "How many times did they mention the military coup, discussed it and feared it? Until it slowly established a place in their consciences. But it was not enough for them to believe that it would take place, because within the space of the possible there was still a corner of the impossible, and they were there, in that small fragment where dreams live, where nothing or no one could touch them" (Guelfenbein, *Nadar desnudas* 159–60).

45. The conversation between Carlos Yushimito and Santiago Roncagliolo, two of the best-regarded contemporary Peruvian writers, can show how today's intellectuals no longer consider revolutionary and even reformist politics as relevant to their work. Comparing themselves to Vargas Llosa and Fuentes, Roncagliolo states, "Theirs was a generation fascinated by power. Our generation, on the other hand, is much less trusting of power. I for one feel like all the things I've believed in have collapsed one after the other: the socialism of my parents' generation, 90s capitalism, even the libertarian ideal of democracy. I've seen how, in a democracy, the rich can behave like dictators—even censoring information or books. . . . But I think it's precisely that lack of certainty that makes me a storyteller. My stories show a world without truth, where the line between good and evil has become very blurred." While adding that "the market is a force as real as a dictator of a banana republic," Yushimito concludes: "the biggest divide between us and the writers you name is that, for all of them, the line between a writer's political or social commitment and his writing, is much vaguer. . . . I would say that, now, those of us writers who share a similar sensibility (a disillusioned one, if you like, but here again there are many degrees of disillusionment) have

a better sense of what we can and can't do within literature and outside it. However you look at it, we don't have the same ambition to wield authority outside of the text."

# Works Cited

Adorno, Theodor. "Cultural Criticism and Society." In *Prisms*, 17–34. MIT Press, 1983.

Aguilar Sosa, Yanet. "¿Cuál es la novela del 'Boom' latinoamericano?" *El Universal*, 26 December 2012. *archivo.eluniversal.com.mx/cultura/70668.html*.

Ahmad, Aijaz. *In Theory: Classes, Nations, Literatures*. Verso, 1994.

Allatson, Paul. "Mario Vargas Llosa, the Fabulist of Queer Cleansing." In *Vargas Llosa and Latin American Politics*, edited by Juan E. De Castro and Nicholas Birns, 85–102. Palgrave Macmillan, 2010.

Allen, Esther, editor and translator. *José Martí: Selected Writings*. Penguin, 2002.

Anderson, Jon Lee. *Che Guevara: A Revolutionary Life*. Grove, 2010.

Anderson, Mark. "Dissonant Worlds: Mario Vargas Llosa and the Aesthetics of the Total Novel." In *Critical Insights: Mario Vargas Llosa*, edited by Juan E. De Castro, 201–18. Salem, 2014.

Andrews, Chris. *Roberto Bolaño's Fiction: An Expanding Universe*. Columbia University Press, 2014.

Anonymous. "Bajo la bandera de Lenin. Instrucciones sobre la jornada de las tres LLL." *Socialismo y Participaciòn* 11 (1980): 25–33.

Avelar, Idelber. *The Untimely Present: Postdictatorial Latin American Fiction and the Task of Mourning*. Duke University Press, 1999.

Bajter, Ignacio. "Poeta, vagabunda y bellamente desolada." *La Lupa*, 9 January 2009, 1–3.

Balderston, Daniel, and José Maristany. "The Lesbian and Gay Novel in Latin America." In *The Cambridge Companion to the Latin American Novel*, edited by Efraín Kristal, 200–216. Cambridge University Press, 2005.

Barnet, Miguel. "Poema." *Tricontinental Magazine* 81–83 (1982): 29.

Barrueto, Jorge J. "Discovering the 'Bizarre': The Peruvian Indian, Travel Writing and Temporal Distancing in Vargas Llosa's *Historia de Mayta*."

*Jouvert: A Journal of Postcolonial Studies* 7 no. 2 (2003). *legacy.chass.ncsu .edu/jouvert/v7i2/con72.htm.*

Bazin, André. "Adaptation, or the Cinema as Digest." In *Film Adaptation*, edited by James Naremore, 19–27. Rutgers University Press, 2000.

Bell-Villada, Gene. "Introduction." In *Gabriel García Márquez's* One Hundred Years of Solitude*: A Casebook*, edited by Gene Bell-Villada, 3–16. Oxford University Press, 2002.

Benedetti, Mario. "Ni corruptos ni contentos." *El País*, 9 April 1984, 9–10.

Bensaid, Daniel. "Esa gran fatiga." Le Site Daniel Bensaid, 1984. *danielbensaid.org/Esa-gran-fatiga?lang=fr.*

Beverley, John. *Latin Americanism after 9/11.* Duke University Press, 2011. Kindle.

Birns, Nicholas. *Contemporary Australian Literature: A World Not Yet Dead.* Sydney University Press, 2015.

———. *Theory after Theory: An Intellectual History of Literary Theory from 1950 to the Early 21st Century.* Broadview, 2010.

Bolaño, Roberto. *2666: A Novel.* Translated by Natasha Winner. Farrar, Straus and Giroux, 2008.

———. *Amulet.* Translated by Chris Andrews. New Directions, 2006.

———. *Amuleto.* Anagrama, 1999.

———. *By Night in Chile.* Translated by Chris Andrews. New Directions, 2003.

———. "Caracas Address." In *Between Parentheses: Essays, Articles, and Speeches, 1998–2003*, edited by Ignacio Echevarría, translated by Natasha Wimmer, 28–37. New Directions, 2011.

———. *Distant Star.* Translated by Chris Andrews. New Directions, 2004.

———. "The Last Interview." Interview by Mónica Maristain. In *Roberto Bolaño: The Last Interview and Other Conversations*, translated by Sybil Perez, 93–123. Melville House, 2009.

———. "A Modest Proposal." In *Between Parentheses: Essays, Articles, and Speeches, 1998–2003*, edited by Ignacio Echevarría, translated by Natasha Wimmer, 87–91. New Directions, 2011.

———. "Positions Are Positions and Sex Is Sex." Interview by Eliseo Alvarez. In *Roberto Bolaño: The Last Interview and Other Conversations*, translated by Sybil Perez, 69–92. Melville House, 2009.

———. "Two Novels by Vargas Llosa." In *Between Parentheses: Essays, Articles, and Speeches, 1998–2003*, edited by Ignacio Echevarría, translated by Natasha Wimmer, 319–24. New Directions, 2011.

Bolívar, Simón. "Letter to Colonel Patrick Campbell, British Chargé d'Affaires: Plague America with Miseries." In *El Libertador: Writings of Simón Bolívar*, edited by David Bushnell, translated by Frederick H. Fornoff, 172–73. Oxford University Press, 2003.

Booker, M. Keith. *Vargas Llosa among the Postmodernists*. University of Florida Press, 1994.

Bosteels, Bruno. *Marx and Freud in Latin America: Politics, Psychoanalysis and Religion in a Time of Terror*. Verso, 2009.

Bourg, Julian. *From Revolution to Ethics: May 1968 and Contemporary French Thought*. McGill-Queen's University Press, 2007.

Boyers, Robert. *The Dictator's Dictation: The Politics of Novels and Novelists*. Columbia University Press, 2005.

Breton, André, and Leon Trotsky. "Manifesto: Towards Revolutionary Art." In *Theories of Modern Art: A Source Book by Artists and Critics*, edited by Herschel Browning Chipp, Peter Selz, and Joshua C. Taylor, translated by Dwight MacDonald, 483–86. University of California Press, 1968.

Browitt, Jeff. "From Parable to Pedagogy: Mario Vargas Llosa's War on Fanaticism." In *Critical Insights: Mario Vargas Llosa*, edited by Juan E. De Castro, 93–101. Salem, 2014.

Butler, Judith. "Desire." In *Critical Terms for Literary Study*, 2nd edition, edited by Frank Lentricchia and Thomas McLaughlin, 369–86. University of Chicago Press, 1995.

"Can This Man End World Poverty?" *Irish Times*, 12 November 2007. *www.irishtimes.com/business/can-this-man-end-world-poverty-1.981458*.

Cantú, Roberto. "Introduction." In *The Reptant Eagle: Essays on Carlos Fuentes and the Art of the Novel*, edited by Roberto Cantú, 1–23. Cambridge Scholars, 2015.

Castellanos Moya, Horacio. "Bolaño Inc." *Guernica: A Magazine of Global Arts and Politics*, 1 November 2009. *www.guernicamag.com/bolano_inc*.

Castro, Fidel. "History Will Absolve Me." *Fidel Castro Reader*, edited by David Deutschmann and Deborah Shnookal, 45–105. Ocean Press, 2008.

———. "Mexican Magazine Has Exclusive with Fidel" (Translation of an interview conducted by Mario Menéndez Rodríguez in *Sucesos* No. 1738, Mexico City, 10 September 1966, 11–58). Latin American Network Information Center, Castro Speech Data Base. *lanic.utexas.edu/project/castro/db/1966/19660910.html*.

————. "The Second Declaration of Havana" (Havana, 4 February 1962). In *Fidel Castro Reader*, edited by David Deutschmann and Deborah Shnookal, 241–67. Ocean Press, 2008.

————. "Speech by Cuban Prime Minister Maj Fidel Castro Ruz Closing the National Congress on Education and Culture" (1 May 1971). Latin American Network Information Center, Castro Speech Data Base. *lanic.utexas.edu/project/castro/db/1971/19710501.html.*

————. "Words to Intellectuals: Havana, June 30, 1961." In *Fidel Castro Reader*, edited by David Deutschmann and Deborah Shnookal, 213–39. Ocean Press, 2008

Castro, Fidel, and Ignacio Ramonet. *Fidel Castro: My Life, a Spoken Autobiography*, translated by Andrew Hurley. Scribner, 2009.

Cayabyab, Marc Jayson. "Vargas Llosa on Defeating Dictators and Literature." Lifestyle.INQ, 9 November 2016. *lifestyle.inquirer .net/243291/vargas-llosa-on-defeating-dictators-with-literature.*

Chang Rodríguez, Eugenio. *Pensamiento y acción en González Prada, Mariátegui y Haya de la Torre*. PUCP, 2012.

Chomsky, Aviva. *A History of the Cuban Revolution*. 2nd edition. Wiley, 2015.

Coerver, Don M., Suzanne M. Pasztor, and Robert M. Buffington. *Mexico: An Encyclopedia of Contemporary Culture and History*. ABC-Clio, 2004.

Cohn, Deborah. "The Political Novels: *The Real Life of Alejandro Mayta* and *Lituma en los Andes*." In *The Cambridge Companion to Mario Vargas Llosa*, edited by Efraín Kristal and John King, 88–101. Cambridge University Press, 2012.

Colás, Santiago. *Postmodernity in Latin America: The Argentine Paradigm*. Duke University Press, 1994.

Collier, Simon, and William F. Sater. *A History of Chile, 1808–2002*. 2nd edition. Cambridge University Press, 2004.

Conway, Christopher. "The Limits of Analogy: José Martí and the Haymarket Martyrs." *A Contracorriente* 2 (2004): 33–56

Cook, Bernard A. "Introduction." In *Europe Since 1945: An Encyclopedia*, edited by Bernard A. Cook, vii–viii. Routledge, 2013.

Cornejo Polar, Antonio. "La historia como apocalipsis (sobre *Historia de Mayta* de Vargas Llosa." In *Crítica de la razón heterogénea. Textos esenciales*, vol. 2, edited by José Antonio Mazzotti, 363–81. Fondo Editorial de la Asamblea Nacional de Rectores, 2013.

————. *Writing in the Air: Heterogeneity and the Persistence of Oral Tradition in Andean Literatures.* Translated by Lynda J. Jentsch. Duke University Press, 2013.

Corral, Wilfrido H. *Bolaño traducido: Nueva literatura mundial.* Escalera, 2011.

————. "General Introduction." In *The Contemporary Spanish-American Novel: Bolaño and After*, 1–17. Bloomsbury, 2013.

————. "Vargas Llosa and the History of Ideas: Avatars of a Dictionary." In *Vargas Llosa and Latin American Politics*, edited by Juan E. De Castro and Nicholas Birns, 189–211. Palgrave Macmillan, 2010.

Cortázar, Julio. "Acerca de la situación del intelectual latinoamericano." *Último Round*, vol. 2, 265–80. Siglo XXI, 1989.

————. "La América Latina no oficial." *Revista Triunfo*, 25 July 1970, 10–13.

————. *Hopscotch.* Translated by Gregory Rabassa. Pantheon Books, 1987.

————. "Julio Cortázar." Interview by Rita Guibert. In *Seven Voices: Seven Latin American Writers Talk to Rita Guibert*, by Rita Guibert, translated by Francis Partridge, 277–302. Alfred A. Knopf, 1973.

————. "Literatura en la revolución, revolución en la literatura: Algunos malentendidos a liquidar." In *Literatura en la revolución y revolución en la literatura*, edited by Oscar Collazos, Julio Cortázar, and Mario Vargas Llosa, 38–77. Fondo de Cultura Económico, 1971.

————. "Meeting." Translated by Suzanne Jill Levine. In *The Spanish American Short Story: A Critical Anthology*, edited by Seymour Menton, 423–37. University of California Press, 1980.

————. "Policrítica a la hora de los chacales." *Cuadernos de Marcha* 49 (1971): 33–36.

————. "Viaje alrededor de una mesa." *Revista Triunfo*, 1 August 1970, 10–14.

————. *La vuelta al día en 80 mundos.* Vol. 1. Siglo XXI, 1970.

Crenzel, Emilio. "Introduction: Present Pasts: Memory(ies) of State Terrorisms in the Southern Cone of Latin America." In *The Memory of State Terrorism in the Southern Cone: Argentina, Chile, and Uruguay*, edited by Francesca Lessa and Vincent Druliolle, 1–13. Palgrave, 2011.

Cristiá, Moira. "Reflejos imaginarios entre Francia y Argentina. Circulación de personas, ideas e imágenes alrededor de mayo del 68." *Afuera: Estudios de crítica cultural* 6, no. 10 (2011).

Dale, Ian, editor. *As I Said to Denis: The Margaret Thatcher Book of Quotations.* By Margaret Thatcher and Ian Dale. Robson Books, 1997

Davis, Kimberly Chabot. "Audience, Sentimental Postmodernism, and *Kiss of the Spider Woman.*" *CLCWeb: Comparative Literature and Culture* 10, no. 3 (2008). doi.org/10.7771/1481-4374.1376.

De Castro, Juan E. *Mario Vargas Llosa: Public Intellectual in Neoliberal Latin America.* University of Arizona Press, 2011.

———. *The Spaces of Latin American Literature: Tradition, Globalization, and Cultural Production.* Palgrave Macmillan, 2008.

De Castro, Juan E., and Nicholas Birns. "Introduction." In *Vargas Llosa and Latin American Politics,* edited by Juan E. De Castro and Nicholas Birns, 1–18. Palgrave Macmillan, 2010.

De Costa, Elena. "Workshop." In *Concise Encyclopedia of Latin American Literature,* edited by Verity Smith, 632–34. Routledge, 2000.

Degregori, Carlos Iván. *How Difficult It Is to Be God: Shining Path's Politics of War in Peru, 1980–1999.* Edited by Steve J. Stern, translated by Nancy Applebaum, Joanna Drzewieniecki, Héctor Flores, Eric Hershberg, Judy Rein, Steve J. Stern, and Kimberly Theidon. University of Wisconsin Press, 2012.

De Llano, Pablo. "Don Mario y la dictadura perfecta." *El País,* 22 November 2012 *.cultura.elpais.com/cultura/2012/11/22/ actualidad/1353565080_234215.html.*

Del Prado, Jorge. "Mariátegui, marxista-leninista." In *Mariátegui y los orígenes del marxismo latinoamericano,* edited by José Aricó, 71–90. Cuadernos Pasado y Presente, 1980.

De Man, Paul. "Literary History and Literary Modernity." *Daedalus* 99, no. 2 (Spring 1970): 384–404.

Derrida, Jacques. *The Beast and the Sovereign.* Edited by Geoffrey Bennington and Peggy Kamuf. Translated by Geoffrey Bennington. University of Chicago Press, 2009.

Devés Valdés, Eduardo. *El pensamiento latinoamericano en el siglo XX. Entre la modernización y la identidad.* Biblos, 2004.

Donoso, José. *The Boom in Spanish American Literature.* Translated by Gregory Kolovakos. Columbia University Press, 1977.

Dorfman, Ariel. "Epitaph for Another September 11." *Nation,* September 2011, 17–18.

———. "The Last September 11." In *Chile: The Other September 11; An Anthology of Reflections on the 1973 Coup*, 2nd edition, edited by Pilar Aguilera and Ricardo Fredes, 1–4. Ocean, 2006.

Ebert, Roger. "*The Best Years of Our Lives.*" In *The Great Movies III*, 68–71. University of Chicago Press, 2010.

Encarnación, Omar Guillermo. *Out in the Periphery: Latin America's Gay Rights Revolution*. Oxford University Press, 2016.

Espinosa, Patricia. Review of *Contigo en la distancia*, 19 June 2015. *letras. mysite.com/pesp100716.html.*

———. Review of *Nadar desnudas. Las últimas noticias*, 31 August 2012. *letras.mysite.com/pes010912.html.*

"Esquema del plan de México." In *Apuntes para una interpretación marxista de historia social del Perú*, vol. 2, by Ricardo Martínez de la Torre, 290–93. Empresa Editora Peruana, 1948.

Esteban, Ángel, and Ana Gallego Cuñas. *De Gabo a Mario. La estirpe del boom*. Espasa Calpe, 2009.

Esteban, Ángel, and Stephanie Panichelli. *Fidel and Gabo: A Portrait of the Legendary Friendship between Fidel Castro and Gabriel García Márquez*. Pegasus Books, 2009.

Farndale, Nigel. "Dinner with Margaret Thatcher: The Story of a Secret Supper." *Guardian*, 7 December 2013. *www.theguardian.com/ theobserver/2013/dec/07/dinner-with-margaret-thatcher-literary.*

Fernández Retamar, Roberto. "These Are the Times We Have to Live In: An Interview with Roberto Fernández Retamar." Interview by Goffredo Diana and John Beverley. *Critical Inquiry* 21, no. 2 (1995): 411–33.

Fiddian, Robin. "Carlos Fuentes: *La muerte de Artemio Cruz.*" In *Carlos Fuentes'* The Death of Artemio Cruz: *Bloom's Modern Critical Interpretatations*, edited by Harold Bloom, 115–34. Chelsea House, 2006.

Finchelstein, Federico. *From Fascism to Populism in History*. University of California Press, 2017.

———. *The Ideological Origins of the Dirty War*. Oxford University Press, 2014.

———. "On Fascism, History, and Evil in Roberto Bolaño." In *Roberto Bolaño as World Literature*, edited by Nicholas Birns and Juan E. De Castro, 23–39. Bloomsbury, 2017.

———. *Transatlantic Fascism: Ideology, Violence, and the Sacred in Argentina and Italy, 1919–1945*. Duke University Press, 2010.

Fiori, José Luis. *O poder global e a nova geopolítica das nações*. Boitempo Editorial, 2007.

Flores Galindo, Alberto. *La agonía de Mariátegui. La polémica con la Komintern*. Desco, 1980.

———. "Un viejo debate: El poder." In *Tiempo de plagas*, 57–106. El caballo rojo, 1988.

Foner, Philip, editor. *Inside the Monster: Writings on the United States and American Imperialism*. Translated by Elinor Randall, Luis A Baralt, Juan de Onís, and Roslyn Held. Monthly Review Press, 1975.

———. "Introduction." In *When Karl Marx Died: Comments in 1883*, edited by Philip S. Foner, 61–66. International Publishers, 1973.

Fornet, Ambrosio. "El quinquenio gris: Revisitando el término." *Revista Casa de las Américas* 246 (2007): 3–16.

Foucault, Michel. "Nietzsche, Genealogy, History." In *The Foucault Reader*, edited and translated by Paul Rabinow, 76–100. Pantheon Books, 1984.

Fountain, Anne. *José Martí, the United States, and Race*. University Press of Florida, 2014.

Franco, Jean. "Questions for Roberto Bolaño." *Journal of Latin American Cultural Studies* 18, nos. 2–3 (2009): 207–17.

———. *Spanish American Literature since Independence*. Ernest Benn Limited, 1973.

Fuentes, Carlos. "Cuba's Paradise Lost: Fed Up with Fidel Castro? Join the Club." *LA Times*, 20 April 2003. *articles.latimes.com/2003/apr/20 /opinion/op-fuentes20*.

———. *The Death of Artemio Cruz*, translated by Alfred Mac Adam. Farrar, Straus and Giroux, 1991.

———. *La nueva novela hispanoamericana*. J. Mortiz, 1969

———. "68: modelo para armar." *Página 12 Radar*, 27 November 2005. *www.pagina12.com.ar/diario/suplementos/radar/9-2651-2005-11-28 .html*.

———. *This I Believe: An A to Z of a Life*. Random House, 2005.

Fuguet, Alberto, and Sergio Gómez. "Presentación del país McOndo." In *McOndo*, edited by Alberto Fuguet and Sergio Gómez, 9–18. Grijalbo/ Mondadory, 1996.

Fujiwara, Chris. *Jacques Tourneur: The Cinema of Nightfall*. McFarland, 1998.

Garcés, Joan. *Allende y la experiencia chilena. Las armas de la política*. Siglo XXI, 2013.

García Márquez, Gabriel. *One Hundred Years of Solitude*, translated by Gregory Rabassa. Harper Perennial, 2006.

García Márquez, Gabriel, and Mario Vargas Llosa. *Diálogo sobre la novela latinoamericana*. Horizonte, 1988.

Gilman, Claudia. *Entre la pluma y el fusil. Debates y dilemas del escritor revolucionario en América Latina*. Siglo XXI, 2003.

Gott, Richard. *Cuba: A New History*. Yale University Press, 2005.

Green, Duncan, and Sue Branford. *Faces of Latin America*. 4th edition. Monthly Review Press, 2013.

Guelfenbein, Carla. "La dictadura chilena fue un accidente impensable." *La Prensa*, 28 November 2012. *www.prensa.com/cultura/Carla-Guelfenbein -dictadura-accidente-impensable_0_3535896418.html*.

———. "Las escritoras seguimos siendo víctimas del prejuicio." Interview by Gabriela Wiener. *La República*, 12 April 2015. *larepublica .pe/archivo/869244-carla-guelfenbein-dobry-las-escritoras-seguimos-siendo -victimas-del-prejuicio*.

———. *In the Distance with You*. Translated by John Cullen. Other Press, 2018.

———. *La mujer de mi vida*. Alfaguara, 2005.

———. *Nadar desnudas*. Alfaguara, 2013.

Guevara, Ernesto "Che." "Create Two, Three, Many Vietnams: Message to the Tricontinental." In *Che Guevara Reader: Writings on Politics and Revolution*, edited by David Deutschmann, 350–62. Ocean, 2003.

———. *Guerrilla Warfare*. Translated by J. P. Morray. BN, 2012.

———. "Socialism and Man in Cuba." In *Che Guevara Reader: Writings on Politics and Revolution*, edited by David Deutschmann, 212–28. Ocean, 2003.

Gutiérrez Alea, Tomás, and Edmundo Desnoes. "The Continuity Script." In *Memories of Underdevelopment*, edited by Michael Chanan, 31–110. Rutgers University Press, 1990.

Gyurko, Lanin. "*La muerte de Artemio Cruz* and *Citizen Kane*." In *Carlos Fuentes: A Critical View*, edited by Robert Brody and Charles Rossman, 64–94. University of Texas Press, 1982.

Harvey, David. *A Brief History of Neoliberalism*. Oxford University Press, 2005.

Haya de la Torre, Víctor Raúl. "What is A.P.R.A.?" *Labour Monthly* 8, no. 12 (1926): 756–59.

Heilbroner, Robert. "The Triumph of Capitalism." *New Yorker*, 23 January 1989, 98–109.

"Hernando de Soto y Editorial Norma son multados por omitir coautores." *La Republica*, 31 January 2013. *larepublica.pe/economia/607733-hernando -de-soto-y-editorial-norma-son-multados-por-omitir-a-coautores.*

Higgins, James. "Gabriel García Márquez: *Cien años de soledad.*" In *Gabriel García Márquez's* One Hundred Years of Solitude, *new edition,* edited by Harold Bloom, 63–80. Infobase, 2009.

Hoyt, Katherine. *The Many Faces of Sandinista Democracy.* Ohio University Press, 1997.

Iber, Patrick. *Neither Peace nor Freedom: The Cultural Cold War in Latin America.* Harvard University Press, 2015.

Jameson, Fredric. *Postmodernism, or, The Cultural Logic of Late Capitalism.* Duke University Press, 1991.

Jrade, Cathy L. *Modernismo, Modernity and the Development of Spanish American Literature.* University of Texas Press, 1998.

Kerr, Lucille. *Suspended Fictions: Reading Novels by Manuel Puig.* University of Illinois Press, 1987.

Kirk, John. "From 'Inadaptado Sublime' to 'Líder Revolucionario': Some Further Thoughts on the Presentation of José Martí." *Latin American Research Review* 15, no. 3 (1980): 127–47.

Klarén, Peter. *Modernization, Dislocation and Aprismo: Origins of the Peruvian Aprista Party, 1870–1932.* University of Texas Press, 1973.

Krauze, Enrique. *Redeemers: Ideas and Power in Latin America.* Random House, 2011.

Kristal, Efraín. "La política y la crítica literaria. El caso Vargas Llosa." *Perspectivas* 4, no. 2 (2001): 339–51.

———. *The Temptation of the Word: The Novels of Mario Vargas Llosa.* Vanderbilt University Press, 1999.

Lafargue, Paul. "Reminiscences of Marx" (September 1890). Marxists Internet Archive. *www.marxists.org/archive/lafargue/1890/xx/marx.htm.*

Larsen, Neil. *Determinations: Essays on Theory, Narrative, and Nation in the Americas.* Verso, 2001.

Lazo, Raimundo, editor. *José Martí. Sus mejores páginas.* Editorial Porrúa, 1978.

Lenin, Vladimir Ilyich Ulyanov. *What Is to Be Done? (1902).* Marxists Internet Archive. *www.marxists.org/archive/lenin/works/download/what-itd .pdf.*

Levine, Suzanne Jill. *Manuel Puig and the Spider Woman: His Life and Fictions.* Farrar, Straus and Giroux, 2000.

Lomas, Laura. *Translating Empire: José Martí, Migrant Latino Subjects, and American Modernities*. Duke University Press, 2008.

López, Alfred J. *José Martí and the Future of Cuban Nationalisms*. University of Florida Press, 2006.

López-Calvo, Ignacio. "Introduction." In *Roberto Bolaño, A Less Distant Star: Critical Essays*, edited by Ignacio López-Calvo, 1–14. Palgrave Macmillan, 2015.

Mainer, Juan-Carlos. "Cuándo se arregló el Perú." *El País*, 6 September 2013. *cultura.elpais.com/cultura/2013/09/04/actualidad/1378294928_994745.html*.

Manrique, Nelson. *"¡Usted fue aprista!" Bases para una historia crítica del APRA*. Fondo Editorial Universidad Católica del Perú, 2009.

Manzano, Valeria. *The Age of Youth in Argentina: Culture, Politics and Sexuality from Perón to Videla*. University of North Carolina Press, 2014.

Mariátegui, José Carlos. "Anniversary and Balance Sheet." In *José Carlos Mariátegui: An Anthology*, translated and edited by Harry E. Vanden and Marc Becker, 127–31. Monthly Review Press, 2011.

———. "Henri de Man and the Crisis of Marxism." In *José Carlos Mariátegui: An Anthology*, translated and edited by Harry E. Vanden and Marc Becker, 189–90. Monthly Review Press, 2011.

———. *José Carlos Mariátegui. Correspondencia, 1915–1930*. Edited by Antonio Melis. 2 volumes. Editora Amauta, 1994.

———. "Manifesto of the General Confederation of Peruvian Workers to the Peruvian Working Class." In *José Carlos Mariátegui: An Anthology*, translated and edited by Harry E. Vanden and Marc Becker, 345–55. Monthly Review Press, 2011.

———. "The Process of Contemporary French Literature." In *José Carlos Mariátegui: An Anthology*, translated and edited by Harry Vanden and Marc Becker, 179–80. Monthly Review Press, 2011.

———. "Programmatic Principles of the Socialist Party." In *José Carlos Mariátegui: An Anthology*, translated and edited by Harry Vanden and Marc Becker, 237–42. Monthly Review Press, 2011.

———. *Seven Interpretive Essays on Peruvian Reality*. Translated by Marjorie Urquidi. University of Texas Press, 1988.

———. "The Unity of Indo-Hispanic America." In *José Carlos Mariátegui: An Anthology*, translated and edited by Harry Vanden and Marc Becker, 445–49. Monthly Review Press, 2011.

Marinello, Juan. "Martí y Lenin." *Katatay: Revista crítica de literatura latinoamericana* 7, no. 9 (2011): 120–23.

Maristain, Mónica. *Bolaño: A Biography in Conversations*. Translated by Kit Maude. Melville House, 2014. Kindle.

Martí, José. "[Cartas de Martí] Nueva York, 29 de marzo de 1883." In *En los Estados Unidos: Periodismo de 1881 a 1892*, edited by Roberto Fernández Retamar and Pedro Pablo Rodríguez, 237–47. ALLCA XX/ Archivos, 2003.

———. "Correspondencia." In *En los Estados Unidos: Periodismo de 1881 a 1892*, edited by Roberto Fernández Retamar and Pedro Pablo Rodríguez, 1157–65. ALLCA XX/Archivos, 2003.

———. "Our America." In *José Martí: Selected Writings*, translated by Esther Allen, 288–96. Penguin, 2002.

———. "Tributes to Karl Marx Who Has Died: Selections." In *José Martí: Selected Writings*, translated by Esther Allen, 130–39. Penguin, 2002.

Martin, Gerald. *Gabriel García Márquez: A Life*. Bloomsbury, 2008.

———. *Journeys through the Labyrinth: Latin American Fiction in the Twentieth Century*. Verso, 1989.

Marx, Karl, and Frederick Engels. *The Communist Manifesto: A Modern Edition*. Verso, 1998.

Massari, Roberto. *Che Guevara. Grandeza y riezgo de la utopía*. Tlaxlaparta, 1992.

Melis, Antonio, editor. *José Carlos Mariátegui. Correspondencia, 1915– 1930*. 2 volumes. Editora Amauta, 1994.

———. "Mariátegui, el primer marxista de América." In *Mariátegui y los orígenes del marxismo latinoamericano*, edited by José Aricó, 201–25. Cuadernos Pasado y Presente, 1980.

Mella, Julio Antonio. "Glosas al pensamiento de José Martí." In *Como un leño encendido. Selección de textos*, edited by Juan Carlos Zamora, 30–37. Ruth Casa Editorial, 2008.

Milanés, Pablo. "Si el poeta eres tú." In *Cuba va*, with Silvio Rodríguez and Noel Nicola. AUI-A/M 1, 1971

"Minutes of the Second Congress of the Communist International: Seventh Section, July 30 [1919]." Marxists Internet Archive. *www.marxists.org/ history/international/comintern/2nd-congress/ch07.htm#v1-p260*.

Morán, Francisco. 2014 *Martí, la justicia infinita. Notas sobre ética y otredad en la escritura martiana (1875–1894)*. Verbum, 2014.

Moraña, Mabel. "Territorialidad y forasterismo: La polémica Arguedas/ Cortázar revisitada." In *La escritura del límite*, 143–58. Iberoamericana, 2010.

Mudde, Cas, and Cristobal Rovira Kaltwasser. *Populism: A Very Short Introduction*. Oxford University Press, 2017.

Navascués, Javier. "Revolución, cristianismo y literatura en América Latina." *Anuario de la Historia de la Iglesia* 11 (2002): 155–63.

Nietzsche, Friedrich. *The Anti-Christ*. In The Anti-Christ, Ecce Homo, Twilight of the Idols, *and Other Writings*, edited by Aaron Ridley and Judith Norman, translated by Judith Norman, 1–68. Cambridge University Press, 2005.

Novak, Michael. "Illusions and Realities—Latin America's Poor: Entrepreneurs, Not Proletarians." *Crisis Magazine*, 1 July 1987. *www.crisismagazine.com/1987/illusions-and-realities-latin-americas -poor-entrepreneurs-not-proletarians*.

Núñez, Ana. "Lima, ciudad en penumbra. Una larga noche . . . " *La República*, 16 August 2003. *larepublica.pe/archivo/345649-lima-ciudad -en-penumbra-una-larga-noche*.

O'Bryan-Knight, Jean. " 'Let's Make Owners and Entrepreneurs': Glimpses of Free Marketeers in Vargas Llosa's Novels." In *Vargas Llosa and Latin American Politics*, edited by Juan E. De Castro and Nicholas Birns, 29–68. Palgrave Macmillan, 2010.

———. *The Story of the Storyteller:* La tía Julia y el escribidor, Historia de Mayta, *and* El hablador *by Mario Vargas Llosa*. Rodopi, 1995.

"On Bolaño." *N+1*, no. 7 (Fall 2008): 10–19.

Orloff, Carolina. *The Representation of the Political in Selected Writings of Julio Cortázar*. Támesis, 2013.

Oviedo, José Miguel. *Historia de la literatura hispanoamericana: De Borges al presente*. Vol. 4. Alianza Editorial, 2001.

Padura, Leonardo. *Yo quisiera ser Paul Auster. Ensayos selectos*. Verbum, 2015.

Paez, Ángel. "Vargas Llosa salvado por el periodismo." *La República*, 4 November 2010. *blogs.larepublica.pe/asuntosinternos/2010/11/04/vargas -llosa-salvado-por-el-poeriodismo*.

Palacios Rodríguez, Raúl. *Historia de la República del Perú [1933–2000]*, edited by Héctor López Martínez. El Comercio, 2000.

Paz, Octavio. "Revolt, Revolution, Rebellion." In *Alternating Current*, translated by Helen Lane, 139–44. Arcade Publishing, 1990.

———. *Sor Juana, or, The Traps of Faith*. Translated by Margaret Sayers Pedersen. Harvard University Press, 1988.

Pinto Albiol, Ángel César. "Contraréplica al Dr. Julio Le Riverend." In *El pensamiento filosófico de Martí y la revolución cubana y otros ensayos*, 24–64. Editorial Jaidy, 1946.

Plante, Isabel. "Amérique Latine Non Officielle o París como lugar para exhibir contrainformación." *A Contracorriente* 10, no. 2 (2013): 58–84.

Plotkin, Mariano Ben. *Freud in the Pampas: The Emergence and Development of Psychoanalytic Culture in Argentina*. Stanford University Press, 2001.

Pollack, Sarah. "Latin America Translated (Again): Roberto Bolaño's *The Savage Detectives* in the United States." *Comparative Literature* 61, no. 3 (2009): 346–65.

Poniatowska, Elena. *La noche de Tlatelolco: Testimonios de historia oral*. Era, 1998.

"The Price of Victory." Season 1, episode 3 of *Five Came Back*. Directed by Laurent Bouzereau. Netflix, 2017.

Puig, Manuel. "Cinema and the Novel." Translated by Nick Caistor. In *The Oxford Book of Latin American Essays*, edited by Ilan Stavans, 395–400. Oxford University Press, 1997.

———. *Kiss of the Spider Woman*. Translated by Thomas Colchie. Vintage, 1980.

———. "A Last Interview with Manuel Puig." Interview by Ronald Christ. *World Literature Today* 65, no. 4 (Autumn 1991): 571–78.

Rama, Ángel. "El Boom en perspectiva." In *La novela en América Latina: Panoramas 1920–1980*. Santiago: Ediciones Alberto Hurtado, 2013. Kindle.

———. "Diez problemas para el novelista latinoamericano." In *La novela en América Latina: Panoramas 1920–1980*. Santiago: Ediciones Alberto Hurtado, 2013. Kindle.

———. "Literature and Exile." Translated by Pamela Pye. *Review* 15, no. 30 (1981): 10–13.

Ramírez, Sergio. "El evangelio según Cortázar." *Revista de la Universidad de México* 1 (2004): 25–29.

Rancière, Jacques. "The Ethical Turn of Aesthetics and Politics." In *Dissensus*, edited and translated by Steven Corcoran, 184–202. Continuum, 2010.

———. "Le tournant éthique de l'esthétique et de la politique." Caute@l'autre, April 14, 2009. *www.caute.lautre.net/spip.php?article1673*.

Rangel, Carlos. *The Latin Americans: Their Love-Hate Relationship with the United States.* Routledge, 2017.

Riding, Alan. "Telling Chile's Story, Even If Chile Has Little Interest." *New York Times*, 3 October 2002. *www.nytimes.com/2002/10/03/arts/ telling-chiles-story-even-if-chile-has-little-interest.html.*

Ripoll, Carlos. "The Falsification of José Martí in Cuba." *Cuban Studies* 24 (1994): 3–38.

Rodríguez Freire, Raúl. "La traición de la izquierda en *Amuleto* de Bolaño." *Guaraguao: Revista de Cultura Latinoamericana* 15, no. 37 (2011): 33–45.

Rodríguez Marcos, Javier. "Una literatura despolitizada." *El País*, 3 December 2016. *elpais.com/cultura/2016/11/24/babelia/1480014723 _069953.html.*

Rojas, Rafael. *José Martí: La invención de Cuba.* Colibrí, 2000.

———. *La polis literaria. El Boom, la revolución y otras polémicas de la Guerra Fría.* Taurus, 2018. Kindle.

Rybalka, Michael. "Mario Vargas Llosa from a French Perspective." *Latin American Literary Review* 15, no. 29 (January–June 1987): 121–31.

Sánchez López, Leopoldo. *La emancipación engañosa. Una crónica transatlántica del Boom (1963–1972).* Universidad de Alicante, 2009.

———. "El proyecto literario y político de la revista *Libre*." *Iberoamericana* 5, no. 17 (2005): 29–39.

Santí, Enrico Mario. "José Martí and the Cuban Revolution." *Cuban Studies* 16 (1986): 139–50.

Saumell-Muñoz, Rafael. "Castro as Martí's Reader in Chief." In *Re-reading José Martí One Hundred Years Later (1853–1895)*, edited by Julio Rodríguez-Luis, 97–114. State University of New York Press, 1999.

Schmitz, David. F. *Thank God They're on Our Side: The United States and Right-Wing Dictatorships, 1921–1965.* University of North Carolina Press, 1999.

Selz, Peter Howard. "Arts and Politics: The Artist and the Social Order: Introduction." In *Theories of Modern Art: A Source Book by Artists and Critics*, edited by Herschel Browning Chipp, Peter Selz, and Joshua C. Taylor, 456–61. University of California Press, 1968.

Shenon, Philip. "Leaders of 9/11 Panel Say Attacks Were Probably Preventable." *New York Times*, 5 April 2004. *www.nytimes.com/2004/ 04/05/us/leaders-of-9-11-panel-say-attacks-were-probably-preventable.html.*

Shnookal, Deborah, and Mirta Muñiz, editors. *The José Martí Reader: Writings on the Americas*. Ocean Books, 2007.

Silen, Ivan. "El AntiMayta." *Revista de critica literaria latinoamericana* 12, no. 24 (1986): 269–75.

Siskind, Mariano. "Globalization and Apocalypse, Or, In What Sense *One Hundred Years of Solitude* Was (and Continues to Be) a Global Novel." Lecture at The New School, New York City, October 19, 2017.

Solano, Francisco. "Música de bolero." Review of *Contigo en la distancia*. Babelia, 16 June 2015. *elpais.com/cultura/2015/06/10/babelia/1433947776_149627.html*.

Solimano, Andrés. *Chile and the Neoliberal Trap: The Post-Pinochet Era*. Oxford University Press, 2012.

Sommer, Doris. *Foundational Fictions: The National Romances of Latin America*. University of California Press, 1991.

Sorel, Georges. *Reflections on Violence*. Translated by T. E. Hulme and J. Roth. Dover, 2005.

Sorensen, Diana. *A Turbulent Decade Remembered: Scenes from the Latin American Sixties*. Stanford University Press, 2007.

Soto, Francisco. " 'The Dream of Paradise': Homosexuality and Lesbianism in Contemporary Cuban-American Literature." In *Cuba: Idea of a Nation Displaced*, edited by Andrea O'Reilly Herrera, 285–300. State University of New York Press, 2007.

Stern, Steve. "Introduction. Beyond Orientalism in Twentieth Century Peru: Carlos Iván Degregori and the Shining Path War." In *How Difficult It Is to Be God: Shining Path's Politics of War in Peru, 1980–1999*, by Iván Degregori, 3–17. University of Wisconsin Press, 2012.

"Subcomandante Marcos: The Punch Card and the Hourglass." Interview by Gabriel García Márquez and Roberto Pombo. *New Left Review* 9 (May–June 2001): 69–79.

Suárez Fernández, Luis, Demetrio Ramos Pérez, José Luis Comellas, and José Andrés Gallego. *Reformismo y progreso en América (1840–1905)*. Vol. 15 of Historia general de España y América. Ediciones Rialp, 1989.

Taibo, Paco Ignacio, II. *68*. Translated by Donald Nicholson Smith. Seven Stories Press, 2004.

Tarcus, Horacio. *Marx en la Argentina. Sus primeros lectores obreros, intelectuales y científicos*. Siglo XXI, 2013.

Trautenberg, Ezekiel Edward. "Los cruces globales de Carla Guelfenbein: Una entrevista sobre su novela *Nadar desnudas*, la literatura chilena y el alcance global de su obra." Interview with Carla Guelfenbein. *Mester* 42, no. 1 (2013): 131–41.

Turpin, Adrian. Review of *The Rest Is Silence*. *Financial Times*, 6 May 2011. *www.ft.com/content/b5b1578c-7ce7-11e0-a7c7-00144feabdc0*.

van Delden, Maarten. *Carlos Fuentes, Mexico and Modernity*. Vanderbilt University Press, 1999.

———. "José Martí: The End of a Myth." *Literal: Latin American Voices* 10 (2008): 31–33.

van Delden, Maarten, and Ivon Grenier. *Gunshots at the Fiesta: Literature and Politics in Latin America*. Vanderbilt University Press, 2009.

Vanden, Harry, and Marc Becker, editors and translators. *José Carlos Mariátegui: An Anthology*. Monthly Review Press, 2011.

Varela, Beatriz. "Ethnic Nicknames of Spanish Origin in American English." In *Spanish Loanwords in the English Language: A Tendency towards Hegemony Reversal*, edited by Félix Rodríguez González, 139–58. Mouton de Gruyter, 1996.

"Vargas Llosa: 'México es la dictadura perfecta,'" *El País*, 1 September 1990. *elpais.com/diario/1990/09/01/cultura/652140001_850215.html*.

Vargas Llosa, Mario. "Albert Camus and the Morality of Limits." In *Making Waves: Essays*, translated and edited by John King, 107–16. Penguin, 1998.

———. "Confessions of a Latin American Liberal." Lindau Nobel Laureate Meetings, 10 September 2014. *www.lindau-nobel.org/mario -vargas-llosa-confessions-of-a-latin-american-liberal*.

———. "Confessions of a Liberal." American Enterprise Institute Annual Dinner, Irving Kristol Lecture, 2 March 2005. *www.aei.org/publication/ confessions-of-a-liberal*.

———. *Conversation in the Cathedral*. Translated by Gregory Rabassa. Harper Collins, 1975.

———. "The Death of Che." In *Making Waves: Essays*, translated and edited by John King, 294–98. Penguin, 1998.

———. "Elogio de la Dama de Hierro." In *Desafíos a la libertad*, 11–15. Madrid: Aguilar, 1994.

———. "El escritor y la política." *Triunfo* 25, no. 421 (27 June 1970): 34–35.

———. *A Fish in the Water: A Memoir*. Translated by Helen Lane. Farrar, Straus and Giroux, 1994.

———. "Foreword." In *The Other Path: The Invisible Revolution in the Third World*, by Hernando de Soto in collaboration with the Instituto

Libertad y Democracia, translated by June Abbott, xi–xx. Perennial Library, 1990.

———. "Four Centuries of *Don Quixote*." In *Wellsprings*, 13–25. Harvard University Press, 2008.

———. *García Márquez: Historia de un deicidio*. In *Mario Vargas Llosa. Obras Completas*, edited by Mario Vargas Llosa and Antoní Munné, 109–698. Círculo de Lectores/Galaxia Gutemberg, 2006.

———. "In a Normandy Village, Remembering Paul Escobar." In *Making Waves: Essays*, translated and edited by John King, 25–27. Penguin, 1998.

———. "The Latin American Novel Today." *Books Abroad* 44, no. 1 (1970): 7–16.

———. "Literature Is Fire." In *Making Waves: Essays*, edited and translated by John King, 70–74. Penguin: 1998.

———. "Luzbel, Europa y otras conspiraciones." In *Literatura en la revolución y revolución en la literatura*, edited by Oscar Collazos, Julio Cortázar, and Mario Vargas Llosa, 78–93. Mexico: City Siglo XXI, 1970.

———. "Nations, Fictions." In *Making Waves: Essays*, edited and translated by John King, 299–304. Penguin, 1998.

———. *Notes on the Death of Culture: Essays on Spectacle and Culture*. Edited and translated by John King. Farrar, Straus, and Giroux, 2012.

———. "Novela primitiva y novela de creación en América Latina." *Revista de la universidad de México* 7 (1969): 29–35.

———. "Prólogo." In *Historia de Mayta*, 9–10. Punto de Lectura, 2008.

———. *The Real Life of Alejandro Mayta*. Translated by Alfred MacAdam. Farrar, Straus and Giroux, 1986.

———. "Sartre, Fierabrás and Utopia." In *Making Waves: Essays*, translated and edited by John King, 127–30. Penguin, 1998.

———. "Socialism and the Tanks." In *Making Waves: Essays*, translated and edited by John King, 79–82. Penguin, 1998.

———. "Transforming a Lie into Truth: A Metaphor of the Novelist's Task." *National Review*, 15 October 1990, 68–70.

———. "The Trumpet of Deyá." Translated by Dane Johnson. *Review of Contemporary Fiction* 17, no. 1 (1997): 25–34.

———. "Una mujer contra el mundo." *El País*, 30 December 2007. *elpais.com/diario/2007/12/30/opinion/1198969213_850215.html*.

"A Vigorous and Fruitful Thinker (*New York Sun*, March 16, 1883)." In *When Karl Marx Died: Comments in 1883*, edited by Philip S. Foner, 66–68. International Publishers, 1973.

Vila-Matas, Enrique. "Un plato fuerte de la China destruida." In *Bolaño salvaje*, edited by Edmundo Paz Soldán and Gustavo Faverón Patriau, 45–52. Candaya, 2008.

Williams, Raymond. *Keywords: A Vocabulary of Culture and Society.* Revised edition. Oxford University Press, 1983.

————. *Marxism and Literature.* Oxford University Press, 1977.

Williams, Raymond Leslie. *Mario Vargas Llosa.* Ungar, 1986.

————. *The Writings of Carlos Fuentes.* University of Texas Press, 1996.

Winn, Peter. *A Revolução Chilena.* Translated by Magda Lopes. Editora Unesp, 2010

Wood, Robin. "The Shadow World of Jacques Tourneur: *Cat People* and *I Walked with a Zombie*." In *Personal Views: Explorations in Film*, revised edition, 253–72. Wayne State University Press, 2006.

Wright, Thomas C. *Latin America in the Era of the Cuban Revolution.* Greenwood, 2001.

Yushimito, Carlos, and Santiago Roncaligolo. "Carlos Yushimito and Santiago Roncagliolo in Conversation." Translated by Ollie Brock. *Granta: The Magazine of New Writing*, 3 December 2010. granta.com/in-conversation-yushimito-roncagliolo.

Zapata, Antonio. *Pensando a la derecha.* Planeta, 2016. Kindle.

Zapatista National Liberation Army. "Declaration from the Lacandon Jungle." In *The Postmodernism Debate in Latin America*, edited by John Beverley, José Oviedo, and Michael Aronna, 311–13. Duke University Press, 1995.

Žižek, Slavoj. "From Revolutionary to Catastrophic Utopia." In *Thinking Utopia: Steps into Other Worlds*, edited by Jörn Rüsen, Michael Fehr, and Thomas W. Rieger, 247–62. Berham Books, 2005.

————. *Welcome to the Desert of the Real: Five Essays on September 11 and Related Days.* Verso, 2002.

# Index

CPSIA information can be obtained
at www.ICGtesting.com
Printed in the USA
LVHW011426070120
642777LV00003B/251/P